WHITE MINDS

WHITE MINDS

Everyday Performance, Violence and Resistance

Guilaine Kinouani

First published in Great Britain in 2023 by

Policy Press, an imprint of
Bristol University Press
University of Bristol
1–9 Old Park Hill
Bristol
BS2 8BB
UK
t: +44 (0)117 374 6645
e: bup-info@bristol.ac.uk

Details of international sales and distribution partners are available at
policy.bristoluniversitypress.co.uk

British Library Cataloguing in Publication Data
A catalogue record for this book is available from the British Library

ISBN 978-1-4473-5746-9 paperback
ISBN 978-1-4473-5747-6 ePub
ISBN 978-1-4473-5748-3 ePdf

Cover design: Nicky Borowiec
Front cover image: AdobeStock/raland
Bristol University Press and Policy Press use environmentally responsible
print partners.
Printed and bound in Great Britain by CPI Group (UK) Ltd, Croydon, CR0 4YY

FSC
www.fsc.org
MIX
Paper | Supporting
responsible forestry
FSC® C013604

For those who are not afraid to think, even when thinking challenges what they think of themselves.

Contents

Acknowledgements   x
Preface   xii
Note on language   xix

Introduction   1

1   Whiteness, time and space   16

2   White gazes   36

3   White envy   52

4   White sadism   68

5   White trauma   85

6   White dissociation   101

7   White shame   114

8   White ambivalence   128

9   White complicity   149

Whiteness and resistance: by way of conclusion   162

References   166
Index   180

Acknowledgements

I wrote the bulk of *White Minds* during one of the toughest periods of my life, and it is absolutely certain that I could not have started, let alone taken the book to the finish line, without the help of so many. Firstly, I am indebted to Bristol University's Policy Press and to Paul Stephens in particular. While many editors would have run miles from my messy writing and even messier thinking, Paul held strong, believing something worthwhile would eventually emerge. I can only hope his efforts and patience were worth this book. A note of gratitude too to the anonymous peer reviewers who have shown the book extraordinary support. I want to thank Dr Joanna Wilde for 'pressing the start button' on the book with the confidence I did not quite have myself at the beginning of this project. I am incredibly grateful to peers and colleagues at Birkbeck College, University of London, to those in the Department of Psychosocial Studies and particularly to Professor Jo Winning for welcoming me warmly, nurturing many of the radical ideas the book presents and for pushing my thinking forward. A special thank you also to Professor Stephen Frosh, for going above and beyond in terms of supervisory support, for his thoughtful and constructive feedback on the last drafts of the manuscript and, critically, for introducing psychosocial studies to me. All my gratitude to the Institute of Group Analysis and all those who have sustained my arduous home-making there, particularly to Dr Earl Hopper, Valentina Krajnovic, Dick Blackwell, Dr Farhad Dalal, John Schlapobersky, Monica Doran and Beverley Stobo, without their trust, confidence and reflections over the years, I would not be playing with the ideas that I am playing with here. To Professors Alana Lentin, Gordon Lewis and to Alya Al-Sultani and Dr Karim Wafa Al-Hussaini thank you for helping me formulate some of my thoughts on racialisation and stratification. I thank those who have responded to the call for contributions, both those whose stories I was able to include and those whose I could not, you made the book concepts come to life in my head and on 'paper'. I send my thanks to Charlotte Maxwell, for helping to keep me organised reference-wise, no small feat. To the individuals and institutions who have again and again exposed me to the brutality of whiteness and the uglier side of humanity; the violence you dished on my body made my mind sharper and my activism more determined. Thank you always and forever to Race Reflections' members and clients, particularly those who gifted me with candid conversations on race. To all anti-racists across the racial spectrum and across the globe, to the social transgressors, the disrupters and the white minds who continue to struggle through often in the shadows, despite being repeatedly 'ambushed' by whiteness, to those who hold onto hope, in the moments the rest of us falter, I send my appreciation and solidarity. To my family, and to my blood and struggle sisters, I send my love, in particular to my 'yayas' Clara and Ursula for making space for me to regress to my stroppy teen self when writing and life get tough, for accepting me as I am and parading me like a well-groomed and clever little dog, as only older sisters can do. To Malia, Yael and Hayan, I know writing this book has meant me being less available, more tired and less fun a mother, I hope you'll forgive me and that perhaps you too, one day, might find some of the ideas in the book of some use. Thank you for loving me anyway. Finally, to you maman, there is no greater pain for me as a writer than writing words you no longer understand, thank you for smiling and clapping all the same.

Preface

Smelly, leaky parcels. Neighbours repeatedly disposing of their rubbish on my doorstep. This is what first comes to mind when I think of my earliest encounter with whiteness in the UK. It was only weeks after I arrived in England and moved into a northwest London flat. I was in my early 20s and did not really know anyone aside from my husband-to-be. It was me who had to deal with the nausea-inducing, overflowing bags of waste, which often required cleaning the entire entrance to our flat, usually when I was on my way out to university, because I left later in the morning. This went on intermittently for weeks until I decided that I had had enough.

So, one morning, I finally opened these now familiar, smelly, leaky parcels. I kneeled outside in the cold and rummaged through several bin bags, in search of clues as to the identity of their owner. I dug and dug in the rubbish. And, eventually, I found full names and an address. The perpetrators had helpfully not attempted to cover up their tracks. I went to knock on the door of the newly identified neighbours. The address was home to a woman and her adult son. Both were people racialised as white and markedly older than me. The son was at least double my age. I had seen them around. They rarely left their flat and I assumed that they were unemployed. As I faced the woman with the indignant confidence of someone who had just survived the most undignified of ordeals, I explained that bin bags had been appearing outside of my front door for a while. Then, I showed her the proof of address and identity I had managed to gather. Finally, I announced that I would be keeping these documents so that in the event of any further incidents, I would simply go straight to the police. The white woman started begging and crying. It was clear she knew exactly what had been going on. She claimed that her son, who was nowhere to be seen, was 'doing it' and pleaded for me not to report him to the police. I never did. The bin bags stopped appearing in front of our door from that day on.

This relatively common, albeit disturbing, anecdote contains layers and layers of symbolism. It exposes the complexity of everyday interracial relations as penetrated by socio-political materialities and historical realities. It is significant that it was two older, working-class, albeit unemployed, white people who chose to harass a young working/studying black couple on their way to making a better life for themselves. A couple who were not only the only black couple on the small estate but who also happened to be migrants. Migrants unashamedly treated as rubbish collectors. And me, as an imaginary maid or cleaner, one might say. A racialised and gendered role often socially expected of those deemed inferior and thus who exist to be forever of service to whiteness; both materially and psychically. We metaphorically became the repository of the white subject's disowned rubbish. The displacement and misplacement of bins perhaps too speak of anxieties related to scarcity and competition. Of how class oppression can so easily find an outlet for its material resentment and this so-called 'economic anxiety' in racial oppression and xenophobia.

To deal with the hateful campaign, I had to get my hands dirty, as we often have to do when confronting whiteness. I got my hands dirty going through a mess which did not belong to me. A white mess, which I symbolically handed back. The story ends with a white woman crying these tears white women often cry when held to account for racism – an introduction to a phenomenon I would go on to encounter again and again over the years to come.

What we also therefore have is a much older white woman who, in the comfort of her own home, stood by the racist abuse of a white man, as I, a young black woman, barely out of my teens, in a country I did not know, was attempting to make a home, in part because of the racism I had experienced in my homeland. A woman who was, at best, an accomplice or an accessory to hatred but who through her crying positioned herself as the vulnerable and fragile party. Although these white tears may or may not have been performative or may or may not have been guilt- or shame-filled, they revealed an elusive shift in power in that brief, surreal moment. A shift brought by the direct confrontation of white violence, a violence I was, it seems, not expected to confront directly. Hence, perhaps, the lack of attempt to hide its source. And so, rather than the injured party, I was transformed into the injuring and feared party, a racialised role-reversal steeped in colonial history.

This experience illustrates why I often say that I did not choose to study whiteness; it chose me. My encounters with white violence created in me the need rather than the want to understand and thus theorise its workings. Theorising whiteness has therefore always been about surviving whiteness. Surviving until I could attempt to thrive while living, while black. I am not the only one who has found themselves in this predicament. I believe most, if not all, marginalised scholars who commit to understanding and dismantling structures of domination have in some way been marked in their flesh. The late bell hooks reminded us of this reality when she famously wrote that she started to engage with the world of ideas because she was hurting in the world [1]. Theorising the social structures which were inflicting pain made overcoming that pain possible. Or, at least made living with it bearable.

For the last 15 years or so, I have observed, conversed and trained on all matters related to whiteness, centring its impact on individuals, groups, social structures, institutions and society. Primarily, I have worked with those at the receiving end of white violence who, like hooks, were seeking healing and understanding. In parallel, I have supported white individuals, groups and organisations wanting to develop their anti-racism practice. Those seeking to 'do the right thing' or to 'do the work', as we say, were rarely aware of their own healing needs or conscious that they, too, were hurting. My first book, *Living while black* [2], exposes the consequences of living under the weight of white supremacy, its deriving psychological functioning and trauma for bodies racialised as black. It is a book dedicated to the impact of existing within the timeless bubble that is whiteness and weathering its everyday and often invisibilised, yet cumulatively debilitating, injustices. *White minds*, as the title indicates, focuses on some of the psychosocial processes that keep that bubble intact.

By way of social location, I would say that I am a child of inner-city France. I therefore write from a displaced position in England. I now live as a migrant woman on this island. My parents were both born colonial subjects in the Congo. A bloodied part of Africa that is shadowed by whiteness and its heartlessness. This history lives in the archive that is my body and I, to some degree, continue to live that history. Although it was in France that I discovered the naked and unapologetic brutality of racism, it is England that has taught me the most about the complexities and veils whiteness adorns itself with. Those of us with a heavy history of racial violence and who are connected to a part of the world with an even more brutal colonial history are often gagged when we attempt to speak. What we have to say, need to say, can be hard to hear, to contain, to contemplate and to process. Our memories and experiences deeply disturb. And because they so disturb, we are expected, ordered, to forget and 'move on'. Engaging with our thinking requires a kind of radical openness that those racialised as white struggle to embody despite fashionable neoliberal and naive evocations of debate in the 'free marketplace of ideas'. Invocations of the importance of debate take place in the midst of suffocation. The conversations on whiteness that we initiate are typically shut down psychologically and they are shut down structurally. Forced into social and psychic oblivion. Confined to that fantasy land we call the 'past'. But remembering is resisting.

And so, we speak anyway. And when we bring that so-called 'past' into the present, we can so easily become the object of hostility, 'projective violence',[1] the scapegoat, or, in group-analytic terms, the location of disturbance,[2] a site onto which leaky, smelly rubbish may be dumped. We are therefore left vulnerable to being pathologised and othered by all sorts of projections of dysfunction and deficiency. To become here too the receptacle of what is not ours. Like many, I have experienced these psychic assaults. Often, I have felt them in my body, sometimes to the point of nausea or dizziness.

For a long time I did not have the language and linguistic tools to name what I saw unfolding in white spaces, nor the conceptual frames to translate what I felt so deeply and viscerally into words. Although there is nothing more complex than verbalising that which involves the non-verbal, as Mbembe notes, there was a particular form of injustice at play in this complex exercise in translation for women [3]. This form of injustice has been given a name; Fricker terms it 'hermeneutic injustice', a consequence of marginalised groups' exclusion from the creation of interpretative resources, the cause of oppression and often the effect of further subjugation, since it causes marginalised speakers or knowers to struggle to make their experience intelligible to themselves and to others. This in turn disadvantages them in their capacity to contribute to collective hermeneutical resources that would aid the understanding of what we struggle to make intelligible [4]. And so *White minds* is an exercise in translation. I hope that, by translating and conceptualising what is often felt in the body, I can contribute something to this ongoing epistemic lacuna. Most of what I know about whiteness is borne out of my own reflections, although I have been nurtured and supported by communities of radical scholars and activists, mostly outside of academia. I am particularly thankful to social media, its democratisation of knowledge and its bringing together of a community of liberated thinkers, for the support I sustained there across geopolitical borders, when very few stood by my ideas.

Although I primarily centre the lived and the body, the scholarly foundations of *White minds* are multiple. My first degree was in cultural, societal and language studies, while psychology is what I spent most of my years in academia studying. About seven years to be precise. Professionally, I still identify as a psychologist, even though the discipline has been largely inhospitable to my thinking and frankly to my body. I consider this self-definition and disciplinary claim an act of resistance. Psychology, which is often the first in line to critique adjacent disciplines for their institutionalised violence, most notably psychiatry, still dissociates from its own. Its whiteness, its colonial history and its ongoing complicity in systems of racial injustice are often no-go territories for conscious black minds.

I wrote this book after some introductory studies in psychoanalysis and the completion of group-analytic training, which took, more or less, a further seven years. I am currently engaged in a PhD in psychosocial studies, a discipline which has offered me a home to think. I hope it will take me less than seven years to complete. Fragments of my developing thesis, and a few theorisations I started to develop elsewhere, have made their way into this book. These fields of knowledge production, united through my commitment to social and racial justice, reveal the multidisciplinary genealogy of the conceptualisations that are to follow. I do not believe in the sanctity of ideas, and I use and play with them unapologetically. Each discipline has a contribution to make. Each, too, has its own tensions when it comes to ethnocentrism and Eurocentrism, thus, whiteness. Additionally, we must contend with important limitations when it comes to theorising the workings of racialised power in society from scholarly spaces dedicated to the study of disturbed minds and so-called 'psychiatric cases'. By and large, analytic scholarship originates from clinical work and caution must therefore be exercised when transferring this thinking outside the clinic [5].

Indeed, when reflections on race have been integrated within analytic formulations, the intent has rarely been to dismantle white supremacy. In fact, rarely did the founding heads of the disciplines I was educated in concern themselves with the question of race and certainly not with that of whiteness. And more to the point here, the disciplines we utilise to enlighten whiteness could themselves be accused of finding their foundation within colonial and imperial logics. Lorde's words of caution about using the master's tools to dismantle the master's house resonate at this juncture [6]. This warning, however, as I read it, is to question the uses, misuses and the functions of particular tools and, more importantly, is about reclaiming those that have been discarded, marginalised and derided to support our liberatory project. There is a long tradition of collecting ideas and actions, as Hill Collins says, which have been 'thrown away' within black feminist thought [7].

The master's tools, we may argue, were never the master's tools. No tool has ever exclusively been his alone and no tool has been exclusively the province of the oppressed. Many of these tools we take to belong to the master, for example, 'rationality', were in fact appropriated, hoarded and often corrupted to serve particular racialised politics, all centred on the accumulation and distribution of capital. Similarly, ways of being in the world that we now associate with subjugated subjectivities or identities, for example, interconnection, have existed and continue to exist within Western thinking, thus, within whiteness, however deprecated or repressed these processes may have needed to be, to further wider extractive projects. More than that, as Gilroy unequivocally demonstrates, focusing on blackness, figurations of immutable, absolute ethnic 'differences' awash within racial discourses cannot be theoretically sustained given that processes of 'creolisation, métissage, mestizaje and hybridity' are necessarily engaged in the socio-cultural, historical and political phenomena of different regions [8].

Colonial formations and their associated territorial mentality, which sustain necropolitical world (dis)orders and exist within most scholarly disciplines, are consequently reified in the social world by the essentialising of such 'differences' [9]. Binary constructions are largely illusory splits, which, on the whole, sustain myths of purity, individualism and border logics. There are babies we must try to safeguard from these apparently colonial waters. These belong to us all and often find their genesis outside the West. Plenty of babies are still to be born at the meeting of these 'disciplines'. It is at their intersections, I suggest, that we find the most fruitful and innovative conceptual building blocks for the present undertaking. We will attempt to develop and employ them freely. Where we can, playfully.

I have reflected on who *White minds* might be for and for whom it may be game. I have attempted to write an engaging and challenging book, which may be accessible to those located outside of the academic terrain. At least, as accessible as I could make the complex scholarship which underscores it. I do not make distinctions along racial lines in the expected readership of the book. However, I do address the reader racialised as white directly, since we are dealing mainly with their functioning, both lay people and 'specialists'. Necessarily, readers will use the text as they need to, though my wish would be that this usage goes beyond the theoretical for the reader racialised as white. I know the ideas I propose would have spared me so many headaches and heartaches when I needed to protect my head and my heart from the violence of whiteness. I hope those racialised as others find the book a helpful conceptual resource.

White scholars and 'experts' on race, colonialism and decolonial thought abound. In my experience they are no less oblivious than the less formally educated or so-called lay white person when it comes to recognising the racialised dynamics that are recurrently laid bare, often right under their noses, in the domain of the mundane and the everyday. Most struggle as a result, like the common mortal, to disrupt them. Put differently, they struggle to embody and live their theories. Hence, the historical resonance of the quotidian inexorably falls into white abysses. Repetitions are mostly not seen and, where they are seen, quickly unseen in the midst of social discourses and invocations of this imperative to 'move on'. My hope is that the book goes some way to help them engage in self-reflection so they may address that white elephant in the room and within themselves, which, in fact, freezes time and movement.

For black and brown bodies, this stuckness in time and space, as we will see, is deeply felt. It makes breathing laborious, as Fanon has so powerfully articulated throughout his oeuvre [10, 11, 12]. I have felt these invisible hands on my mouth too. Sometimes they have merged into institutionalised tools of gagging. The pressure to keep silent, which is externally imposed and socially sanctioned, eventually becomes internalised by most of us. In truth, my body and my mind have at times been affected by my wish to speak as I have tried to navigate this terrain, mainly because I dared to describe the terrain I was navigating. As a result, I learnt to speak differently. As I say in *Living while black*, there are various ways to resist. I chose to disrupt through my activism, through my thinking and, of course, through my writing, since writing is speaking more freely. This book is the product of this labour of therefore not only finding words but also finding air. Between gagging someone and suffocating someone there is only a thin line.

This attempt at making sense of the often senselessness of whiteness by articulating so much of the deeply embodied, as Fanon may say, by giving shape to our corporeal realities, is also an attempt at preserving the integrity of the body. Although *White minds* speaks to my intellectual defiance – the act of me speaking anyway – it emerges first and foremost from my need to simply breathe. To breathe freely. And to breathe easy. The most basic of human needs. If thinking is in some ways breathing, then my capacity to think is my capacity to remain connected to life forces. Looking consciously into the 'darkness' of whiteness is the only way of not becoming absorbed and disappeared by it. I hope we find the courage to dismantle white structures that exist externally and internally. I hope we can find it within ourselves to confront whiteness so we may make space for something radically new in the world, first by imagining these new world orders within the spaces of our minds.

Notes

[1] Projective violence here is used in the analytic/Freudian sense to refer to the process by which the (white) subject disowns and discharges aggressive wishes onto those who name whiteness. The object often feels the silent and unconscious hostility which is usually denied.

[2] The group analytic concept of location of disturbance which is further elaborated on in Chapter 7 speaks of the displacement of group pathology and dysfunction onto individuals who are essentially selected to perform scapegoating functions.

Note on language

Seeking unproblematic terms to describe problematic and fictitious categorisations is naïve. But more than naïve, it reinscribes in our collective mind the fantasy of race, thus reproducing the very existence of the structure we wish to dismantle. And yet we do need a common language to conceptualise and to engage in liberatory conversations. This is a paradox which has long been noted. Language necessarily changes and evolves and what is considered acceptable today may not have been just a few years ago, and may not be again in the future. Still, a number of linguistic terms are available to capture or approximate racial phenomena and so-called racial differences today.

In *White Minds*, I try to repeatedly return to descriptions that include racialisation – for example, 'people racialised as white' refers to people of European descent, 'people racialised as black' refers to people of African descent (I include here those groups who were displaced from the African continent through the transatlantic slave trade) and 'people racialised as brown' who for the purpose of this book includes people of Asian, Middle Eastern, Indigenous and North African descent who are not racialised as black or white.

This is not a perfect system. I wish to remind the reader that racial categorisations based on perceived skin colour or melanin-related differentiations and associated morphological attributes are largely arbitrary. They speak of complex processes by which social actors are hierarchised and stratified based on a combination of myths, symbols and fantasies. Nonetheless, for accessibility reasons, I also use phraseologies which have become more common in everyday parlance, such as black/white/brown people or people of colour (which here refer to brown and black people) or, more rarely, I say whites. These descriptors have their own genealogy and limitations which continue to be subject to heated debates and controversies. Although these discussions are largely outside the scope of this book, I elaborate on aspects of the problematics of these categories in Chapter 1.

Introduction

'When I first started my job, my manager told me in one of our first meetings that her family owned plantations in Kenya. For context, she is white South African and I am black British. I questioned why she felt the need to tell me this and felt very uncomfortable. Particularly as, after she told me this, she stared at me, awaiting a reaction. I just responded by saying "OK" and moved the conversation on. Subsequently I had numerous problems in my relationship with this manager, she would switch between appearing overly anxious/frightened in my presence to being very abrupt with me. She would frequently say things to me that were very clear dog whistles such as saying I was aggressive and needed to watch my tone and then would later deny having said these things when I reported them. I requested another manager but was denied and it got to the point where I refused to meet with her unless it was recorded.

Eventually I left the job, and I raised a formal complaint regarding her behaviour, namely gaslighting – the fact she would constantly say things to me and advise me to do things and then completely deny ever doing it which contributed to great difficulty in me doing my job. There were also several other issues in the department. When I went to the hearing for my complaint, the chairperson – a white male – confessed he had not read my complaint in full and so I had to explain again in detail the nature of my complaint and the racialised nature of it. I waited weeks for the outcome. The outcome of the complaint was that there was no evidence to support my claims even though I provided video footage as evidence. The thing that struck me the most was that he commented in a lot of detail about how polite my manager had been in communicating and how she appeared very good at listening and responding to me. This was not the complaint I had raised – it was about gaslighting and there was no evidence that he had paid any attention to what she had actually been saying in the videos and only the fact that she seemed nice as she was saying it.' (Samantha, black woman, 30s, UK)

I have chosen to start *White minds* with a story. First, this is to help contextualise the reflections and interrogations that are to follow and, second, to put the everyday performances of whiteness straight under the spotlight, under our analytic and critical gaze. The story is that of Samantha, a black British woman of African (Kenyan) descent in her 30s. It was generously offered to me during the call for experiential contributions to the book.

Samantha's story presents a poignant encounter with some of the key dynamics and processes that underlie whiteness – denial, displaced aggression, structural complicity and white dissociation amidst black pain. This is the theoretical context to the chapters the book aims to explore. It gets us started when it comes to thinking about the myriad ways racialised relationships are governed by the 'past'. And how that 'past' can engender to race-based relational fractures in the present, to fear – often on both sides of the power divide – but also to shame, associated *mea culpas*, dysfunction, provocations, incomprehension and, again and again, power plays. Often the kind of power plays, as we will see, that set unreachable 'evidence' thresholds and ensure whiteness fails to confront its very own existence in the same way the category of the 'past' continues to be used to avoid confronting the present. And the modern politics, some might say, of the plantation.

Little has changed when it comes to racial injustice and inequality. My work has demonstrated this to me. The contemplation of this reality calls for some deep and uncomfortable reflection. The contemplation of this reality requires us to be prepared to engage with the complex phenomenon of race differently. This means apprehending and interrogating race inequality well beyond the cognitive shortcuts or heuristics, which so many continue to insist are the main cause for the existence of racial disparities within institutions and within society at large. Many of us have been engaged in this endeavour. My approach to anti-racism combines my experience of the world; how I apprehend racial dynamics in my relational and structural encounters with whiteness and what I have learnt as a scholar. Ironically, I have been exclusively taught by university professors racialised as white. My understanding of the world colours the kind of psychology that I do and my understanding of whiteness as a multi-layered psychosocial phenomenon. It also shapes the kinds of questions I would like readers to ask themselves when considering Samantha's experience. Questions well beyond matters of personal bias but also not quite graspable within institutional discrimination frameworks. I would therefore invite your curiosity into more profound epistemic, perhaps even metaphysical, interrogations.

Why would a manager racialised as white voluntarily 'disclose' her violent colonial history to Samantha, a woman racialised as black and the descendant of colonial subjects? What functions might this serve psychologically, relationally and structurally for whiteness? What might the relevance be of the manager's positionality as a white South African woman? How may South Africa's history of apartheid and associated colonial atrocities have intruded into the relationship between the two women and in the functioning of the organisation? Why was gaslighting so central to Samantha's grievance and distress and what does this tell us about subjugation, about knowing and about racialised epistemic exchanges? Beyond the individual social actors involved, what needs might the conflict fulfil for the entire institution? Might these fraught encounters reveal something important about the macro context and the political situation of the nation?

These questions challenge much of what I was taught about the world by psychology. They also arguably go beyond traditional sociological conceptualisations. Yet exploring these questions is to start to confront the deep, sinister and thorny waters of whiteness. Troubled waters that do not like to be troubled. Naming whiteness and rendering it strange and simultaneously absurd and intelligible is central to decolonial, liberatory and racially transgressive work [1]. It is consequently fundamental to *White minds*. And so, in the book you are about to read, I have chosen to start each chapter with 'white' to remind us of the task at hand and of the need to continue to name and disrupt whiteness. This deliberate and possibly discomforting linguistic device is employed to sustain our focus on the phenomenon under exploration. Through this device, I also hope to desensitise those needing to be desensitised to the visibilising of whiteness.

I propose, in the pages that follow, that ingrained 'internal' dysfunctions are required to sustain the 'external' structure of whiteness so that we cannot fully grasp whiteness without understanding how groups racialised as white have had to operate psychologically and psychically to sustain that structure. In turn, the structure of whiteness now reproduces particular dysfunctional modes of being and acting in and on the world. And dysfunctional ways of relating to the black and brown subject. The case is not that the defences, dysfunctions and processes of interest here are exclusive to white psyches or even to Western societies, rather, that they have been and continue to be mobilised in the interest of maintaining the fortress of whiteness. We could argue that psychic and social structures are one and the same, and in places we do. However, to delineate entry points for resistance and better understand the everyday, micro performances of whiteness, we consider white minds, both from the inside out and the outside in.

White minds aims to render mergings more easily discernible, and hence, I hope, more easily subverted. To do so, we need to explore the relationship of whiteness with time and with space, how it moves, how it shifts and how it continues to be performed on a day-to-day basis so as to support resistance. Particularly, resistance by those who are racialised as white who want to understand their complicity within this pathogenic and traumatogenic structure they were born into – which shapes us all – so as to attempt to reclaim their humanity. However, there is no revolutionary objective in *White minds*. Contemporarily, we see vehement opposition to that understanding and particular hostility towards thinking that centres the structural. In this both new and old age of anti-intellectualism, critical theories generally, and Critical Race Theory in particular (or least some

3

fantasy of what it constitutes), are under sustained attack by structures of power.

But there is nothing opaque, incomprehensible or even remotely illogical in Critical Race Theory. The framework, put simply, seeks to make visible the ways in which race as a social construction has acquired permanence by becoming embedded into the structures of society. It is this embeddedness that protects the racialised social (dis)order it posits. Thus, beyond more blatant expressions which tend to attract mass attention, collective outrage and opposition, Critical Race Theorists see racism as ordinary, rather than as aberrational. As 'normal science'. As the default way society does business, hence, race inequality become objectivised and naturalised. Because the racialised social (dis)order Critical Race Theory posits serves the material interests of white groups overall, there is little to no incentive to dismantle it. An important concept in the framework, which is of particular interest in *White minds*, is that of 'interest-convergence'. The notion that racial progress is only achieved when the self-interests of white groups are perceived to be aligned with the racial claims of groups of colour. This claim takes us to the heart of the need for the white subject to understand the damage they themselves sustain as a result of whiteness.

Popular opposition and resistance to Critical Race Theory is therefore, in the main, strategic propaganda. Defensive and disparaging politically sanctioned gestures. We could even argue that the framework currently serves as a theoretical scapegoat, a political football, onto which racialised anxieties related to social change and loud black voices, such as those of the Black Lives Matter movement, can be projected. A symptom of imperial nostalgia, one might argue, which has led to the sort of hysterical demonisation, 'absurdisation' and, in places, censorship, evocative of Red Scares and of those imagined to be enemies of the state. That millions reject Critical Race Theory based on the demagoguery of those with vested interests in propagating neoliberal myths of meritocracy (thus colourblindness) and 'individual responsibility', which frequently do not even serve the interests of those who adhere to them, should remind us of the limitations of 'education' systems. Their 'failure' to instil independent thinking is central to their function as hegemonic apparatuses and, as such, is really not a failure. This is something Critical Race Theory is ideally placed to theorise.

Critical Race Theory does offer important insights into the structural life of racism and the temporality of white supremacy. However, here we are primarily concerned with the afterlife of colonialism and imperialism since this history 'represents a store of unlikely connections and complex interpretative resources. The imperial and colonial 'past' continues to shape political life in the overdeveloped-but-no longer-imperial countries' [2, p 13]. Because examining the legacies of histories marked by colonial and imperial trauma sits largely outside of its scope, the framework is limited in its capacity to precisely theorise at the intersection of history, social and psychic structures.

Further, and more crucially, this gap easily allows social actors to locate racialised and social pathology outside of themselves. As existing 'out there' in some external, structural, macro reality, independent from social actors as individuals and as groups. 'Racism without racists' is a product of that school of thought. A proposition, we may argue, which is sustained by the fundamental modernist splits *White minds* attempts to resist.

Yet it is undeniable that social actors of today continue to edifice the structures of the 'past' through performances and repeated actions. In the same way, Foucault's 'technologies of power' invite us to see power as what we *do* to dominate others, that is to say, how power is repeatedly exercised through strategies, tactics and manoeuvres, ultimately techniques [3]. Yancy argues that these repetitions give the illusion of permanence [4]. White groups cannot therefore wash their hands and claim that racialised asymmetries and injustices, which find their roots in the 'there and then', exist outside of their doing, will or functioning, as individuals and as groups, in the 'here and now'. The proposition put forth is that structures do represent a collective mind, will and contract that unites all social actors [5]. And that the distinction between subjects and the structures they inhabit is largely illusory. This is why psychosocial and group-analytic thinking is central to *White minds*. The psychosocial, as a field of enquiry, disrupts and challenges the separation of the supposedly 'internal' psyche and the supposedly 'external' society. Proposing instead, more precisely, that '[p]sychological issues and subjective experiences cannot be abstracted from societal, cultural, and historical contexts; nor can they be deterministically reduced to the social. Similarly, social and cultural worlds are shaped by psychological processes and intersubjective relations' [6]. Psychosocial scholarship, as a consequence, aligns with group analysis. For our purpose, we may define group analysis as a theoretical and clinical method focused on understanding the psyche and human functioning as socially and historically located multi-personal and transpersonal phenomena. Group analysis is similarly premised on the fact that 'we cannot isolate biological, social, cultural and economic factors, except by special abstraction. Mental life is the expression of all these forces, both looked at horizontally, as it were, in the strictly present reality and vertically, in relation to past inheritance' (Foulkes, 1990, p 252 [7]).

Both group analysis and psychosocial inquiry, it follows, force us to rethink the theoretical and unsustainable splits between the mind and the structure, the 'past' and present, the individual and the group, the victim and the perpetrator, the mad and the sane, and many other binary propositions widely promulgated under dominant Western thought. Doing so will help to bring into our collective consciousness some of the more complex and averted – perhaps precisely averted because complex – ongoing psychological, relational and group phenomena involved in the structure of whiteness, while interrogating their temporality. Whiteness harms both people of colour and white groups in multiple and intersecting ways that engage every single level of human functioning and every level of communication. Maintaining white innocence in the face of this collective and shared suffering requires the use of complex psychological and psychic strategies, defences and manoeuvrings which go well beyond the simplistic premises that underscore the equality, diversity and inclusion industrial complex, a complex which, as we'll posit later in the book, largely maintains social disturbances.

Despite this, by and large, psychology as a discipline has been absent from conceptualisations of whiteness as a structure. This is so despite the long-documented stark race inequalities within the mental health system, which include, we could summarise, the descendants of the enslaved and colonised being consistently assessed as madder than white groups, and treated as threats requiring control, restraint and the deprivation of freedom. Outside of the clinic, psychology's main offering when it comes to tackling race equality has been centred on issues of unconscious bias contributing heavily to the extraction of the micro from the meso and the macro; reducing complex unconscious dynamics and societal processes to the cognitive, to the domain of personality and arguably to the neurobiological. This exclusive focus on the micro has, no doubt, done more harm than good when it comes to racial injustice and has placed unconscious bias training firmly within the grip of the neoliberal project. So, while I do not seek to deny the implication of implicit (or explicit) biases or even biological processes – which I will briefly touch upon – in the maintenance of racial inequality and injustice, believing they are the most effective factors implicated in the maintenance of the status quo is at best naive and at worst an act of complicity in white supremacy, as we will argue in the final chapter.

When the discipline has sought to tackle the harm of racism head on, it has focused on the psychological impact on people of colour [8, 9, 10, 11]. It is however the case that this excess of psychological 'problems' within groups racialised as black and brown is formulated and assessed with epistemic and ontological frameworks anchored in the medical model and its silent modernistic and adjacent neoliberal values which are largely blind to social forces, history and resulting group functioning. More importantly, in and of itself, locating psychopathology or disturbance within the black subject (and the brown subject, though to lesser extent) is a form of racialised symbolic and psychic violence which repeats colonial formations. Discourses of black dysfunction, black deficiency, black inferiority, all while rarely, if ever, shifting the location of disturbance or the analytic gaze onto whiteness. In other words, we may argue, the ongoing social archetypes of blackness as madness or irrationality, blackness as primitivity, blackness as dangerousness, clearly evidence the presence of colonial logics and coloniality within mental health systems of 'care'. They sustain suffocating anti-black and necropolitical world orders outside the clinic.

Beyond traditional formulations of madness, and the locating of pathology in the other, in those who appear to be suffering, the invitation here is to engage in alternative ways of conceptualising sanity and considering psychic disturbances. Mbembe asks if, in our post-Fanonian age, we can, as implored by the revolutionary himself, recognise the signs of madness in the way that we relate to each other [12]. In the way that our societies, institutions and communities operate. In the ways, therefore, I would go further, that white subjects who continue to be formed as the healthy norm when it comes to psychological functioning may as a group be deeply disturbed if not psychologically harmed and damaged by the violence of whiteness. This provocation necessitates the kind of shift in the analytic gaze that Morrison invited us to adopt. It requires a fundamental shift in the direction of power [13].

As Morrison had already posited some 30 years ago, comparatively, little attention has been paid to the psychological world of those racialised as white. Before her Fanon had already called us to investigate the 'sickness' colonialism inflicts on colonial powers; his call has in the main not been responded to [14]. This absence means important gaps exist in our understanding of the intersubjective dimension of the phenomena which keeps the system going.

Our understanding of whiteness, and of the specific mechanisms and techniques which allow it to be articulated and rearticulated, produced and reproduced, created and reinvented, is still, at best, fragmented. When whiteness is considered to be an issue that only impacts those racialised as black or brown, systems of segregation, ghettoisation or colonialism are replicated [15].

The reflections and theorisations that follow are borne out of a commitment to seeing the workings of whiteness as a psychosocially and historically located phenomenon. But also as a phenomenon that is both located in time and in space as much as it defies time and space locations. Thus, the historicising of the psychic functioning underlying whiteness which is core to the present text is required to grasping the reality of white supremacy, and just simply grasping reality. But similarly, understanding the present sheds light on the 'past'. Both understanding the 'past' and the present helps us shape the future. The psychological and psychic context that leads to the constant recreation of history and, with that, the creation of new 'victims' and new 'perpetrators', which are, nonetheless, of course, also old victims and old perpetrators, and both victims and perpetrators.

The book and the ideas it makes the reader privy to, I have no doubt, will activate strong emotions. Important affective and embodied insights into what it feels like for those of us stuck in whiteness, a bubble some of you may be free escape from. Or at least the conscious awareness of it. Feeling strongly for or against something is independent from the truth or reality of that something. And feeling attacked does not imply that persecutory intentions underpin this book. White groups, it has been said, often confuse discomfort with danger [16].

I am writing the pages of this book uncensored. My aim is not to soothe. The book is not written to appease the white reader. It is not written to convince. It is not written to plead or to please. Nor is my aim to make those racialised as white feel uncomfortable for the sake of making them feel uncomfortable or for some other form of gratification that might arise from such discomfort.

The confrontation of white supremacy by those who most benefit from it is painful. Resistance to anti-racism is often based on that affective reality. Put differently, the distress of racism distresses the white subject. The distress that white subjects cause distress the white subject. If institutions and individuals cannot tolerate the distress occasioned by contemplating whiteness, and are so distressed that they simply refuse to engage with reality or disengage when confronted with that reality, we have a serious problem and, indeed, we do have a serious problem. As James Baldwin puts it, 'not everything that is faced can be changed. But nothing can be changed until it is faced' [17].

Much in 'our' society forces us, black social actors, to comfort and coddle those in position of power. To breastfeed those who do us harm. To console them and protect their sensibilities so as to ensure they are not too troubled when we speak of the troubles, if not violence, they enact and/or benefit from interpersonally, structurally and geopolitically. This will not be happening here. I refuse to collude with such infantilisation. And I continue to have faith in white groups' capacity to connect to their own humanity in the way that I hold so sacred. As sacred as those whose lives are first in line to be sacrificed. Baldwin's words foreground the importance of a form of epistemic courage, the courage to know and to face reality, if we stand any chance of changing that reality.

Until this is achieved, I do not believe we stand any chance of groups racialised as white being able to connect to ours. To that end, it is imperative that readers racialised as white collectively learn to tolerate race-based discomfort and challenges to their sense of self, without engaging in retaliation, psychic collapse or intellectual short-circuits. I continue to believe this is one of the most transformative and socially transgressive skills any white person seeking to dismantle whiteness can develop. Without learning to bear the 'internal' disturbances caused by the structural disturbances of whiteness and consequently managing associated emotions and fantasies, structures of power cannot be disrupted. And without such disruption the status quo is bound to remain in place. As I have already hinted at, and will continue to see later in the book, groups racialised as white have a tendency to project that which disturbs them onto certain bodies. They accuse black others of that which they are guilty themselves. This is a power move that is also deeply anchored in colonial functioning.

Should you dare to engage with this book, remember that disrupting your equilibrium is not the aim of *White minds*. I accept, however, that it may well be an inevitable by-product. This disruption is not only legitimate, but also necessary and ethical to dethroning white-centeredness. It is necessary to free the white subject from the 'bad faith' that haunts their lives [18]. So, although, disturbance is an expected response to being dethroned, my aim always, first and foremost, is my own liberation and resistance. My second aim is the liberation and resistance of those whose bodies look like mine. Third, I hope to support those in dominant positions – as far as racialisation – who want to work towards their own liberation.

We have inherited much of the social world and the structures it is built upon. The pre-existence of whiteness as a structure does limit our agentic power and means that we are constituted as racialised subjects before we are even capable of understanding our own subjectivity or processes of racialisation. Part of the collective dysfunction is to fall into extremes. Thus, we either believe that we have complete power over the world or that we have none whatsoever. White and dominant groups more generally tend to overestimate their power. The subjugated other has bought into this narcissistic lie, giving away so much of their own power in the process and becoming complicit in the machinery that is white supremacy. The ultimate power, I often argue, is the power to convince others they are powerless. Like most of my intellectual foremothers, I have never believed that we are powerless. Perhaps this book also strives in some small way to rebalance the distribution of power and powerlessness. It is a minuscule offering to the world I was born into. This book is for those who still believe in liberation and that a fairer world can be built.

Epistemic reflections

Similarly to the overwhelming majority of psychologists trained in empiricism, I was educated to accept many problematic concepts borrowed uncritically from the natural sciences. Ideas such as neutrality and objectivity are attempts to legitimise psychology's scientific status, which is where disciplinary power lies. This is a well-established discursive argument, which I hope needs no introduction. Contrary to many critical thinkers, I do not believe that positivism is in and of itself the enemy of the marginalised or automatically inconsistent with critical thought. Critical scholarship can also be steeped in racist, colonial and imperial logics. Most critical fields of knowledge production have had to confront their whiteness and make space for racial analyses. This includes Marxism, feminism, psychoanalysis, group analysis and psychosocial studies, all of which I draw from.

The kinds of epistemic splits which remove lived or marginalised experiences from constructions of scientific knowledge give credence to dualistic illusions. Naive positivism does promote decontextualisation, which is what I refer to as dissociated knowledge and partial truths. This has upheld white supremacy and adjacent structures of domination and has long deprived society of particular realities and important perspectives. My position is that while there are various ways to know and to access truth, these ways of knowing, if committed to truth, will converge and move in the same direction, the direction of truth. A reflective, contextualised, power-conscious use of epistemic resources is the minimum any ethical scholar should aspire to, across the many formulations of what constitutes evidence.

The notion that knowledge production's principal function is to maintain power structures and thus the unjust social (dis)order is no longer controversial. Although it, in the main, finds in origins in French postmodernist theorists, and particular Foucault, it also continues to find resonance and a home with critical theorists, including postcolonial and feminist scholars. Over the last decade or two, this thinking has been further developed as matters of epistemic injustice and epistemic violence have taken central stage when it comes to liberatory and decolonial thinking. We thus understand better than ever the kinds of epistemic games power plays, and their associated injuries which have long been hidden under the weaponisation of 'rationality'.

My personal politics and praxis seek to uphold these traditions. Consequently, I have stopped seeking to 'evidence' to people racialised as white the existence of whiteness. Not only because doing so positions the white subject as the arbitrator of truth and reality, thus reproducing power asymmetries and associated social expectations of subservience, but because attempting to evidence racism usually leads us straight to processes of gaslighting and 'internal' displacement. This leaves us further harmed by additional acts of injustice, here, in the domain of the epistemic. The enactment, we may argue, of a form of everyday sadistic violence, which is so normalised that it is rarely interrogated, although like most cycles of abuse, expects sadomasochistic unquestioned compliance. This is irrespective of the costs to our minds and our bodies. In fact, it is precisely because of the costs to our bodies and to our minds. This is why sadism is necessarily engaged. What is more, the process of 'evidencing' is not only taxing and harmful, but also is, by and large, a waste of time since, in any event, it is generally an insurmountable hurdle to prove racism to those with vested interests in denying racism.

This is what I refer to as the epistemic shiftiness of whiteness or the associated manoeuvring whiteness engages in to avoid facing itself which make it virtually impossible to 'prove' the very existence of the violence one experiences, in spite of repeated social demands to do so. Samantha's attempt at getting her previous employer to see racism as an effective factor in the relationship with her former South African line manager racialised as white is a perfect illustration of these dynamics. Samantha sought to establish the truth. This attempt did not go anywhere and in truth it rarely does. Even with the direct testimonies of those harmed. Even with evidence of the said harm. Even with video evidence or witnesses to the said harm. Principally this is because that bodily and psychological harm is not formed as harm. And when it is, it compares meekly to the anticipated reputational harm those accused are fantasised to be at risk of sustaining if the harm they partook in was recognised as harm. As Gordon puts it, white supremacy acts as a license that protects the white subject from 'accountability for wrongful actions, whether earned or not' [19].

It is virtually unknown for race-based complaints to be upheld within institutions, and this is so within virtually all social structures. Findings that no one with the most rudimentary understanding of statistics or even just respect for mathematics, irrespective of political position or scholarly orientation, would 'rationally' accept as a true representation of social reality. This state of affairs is nevertheless collectively accepted as 'reasonable', which perhaps speaks of what Gilroy may describe as 'rational irrationality' [20].

Consequently, we know that no one decidedly committed to the comfort of the (dis)order of the social can ever be satisfied that supportive evidence presented to them, regardless of its type, however 'objective', no matter how 'replicable' it may be, is reliable evidence or indeed is evidence at all. Claims that disrupt the (dis)order of the social are treated as though they have no foundation in social reality. That allegiance to the order of things leads to the kinds of problems with thinking and seeing that are sustained by self-deception and amnesia [5, 21, 22]. Consider the following cognitive manoeuvring:

> Both sorts of evidence are used to demonstrate the non-existence of racism. ... When there is a particular piece of overt racism then it is dismissed as anomaly as a one off, an aberration, the fact that this is anecdotal and not statistical is used to render it meaningless, particularly because it is said this evidence being a one-off is not part of a pattern and therefore says nothing apart from itself. On the other hand, when statistical evidence is marshalled to demonstrate that an institution is favouring group A or group B, then anecdotal evidence is used to undermine the statistics. ... It is part of the complexity of racism that things have different meaning depending on which side of the fence they occur. (Dalal, 2002, pp 29–30 [23])

This passage by Dalal highlights what Mills might refer to as 'the epistemology of ignorance'. An obstinate will to misunderstand and to remain ignorant when it comes to white supremacy. In this example,

Dalal argues that both statistical evidence and anecdotal evidence will be instrumentalised to deny the reality of racism, depending on what argument is put forth, at a particular point in time [23]. Constructions of evidence, when it comes to oppression, are always in the service of power. I repeatedly observe adjacent cognitive gymnastics performed in my day-to-day life, when white individuals focus on their subjective experiences in relation to power and 'privilege', when asked to confront the reality of white supremacy. Since they do not *feel* privileged or powerful, they cannot therefore be either privileged or have any racialised social power. This subjectivist position is used to refute the existence of white supremacy as a system irrespective of material realities, hardly refutable social inequality outcomes or indeed any other empirical data on which one might wish to rely. Feelings trump 'evidence'.

However, when the racialised other attempts to speak of their lived or subjective reality, for example, 'I experience you as oppressive' or 'I feel discriminated against', an epistemic shift occurs, an objective turn is now preferred, and performative rationality is employed to delegitimise and invalidate marginalised subjectivities. 'Do you have any evidence?' may be asked. 'Prove it!' will be strenuously ordered. 'Evidence' now trumps feelings.

This is how whiteness shifts epistemically. The white subject's epistemic position moves constantly depending on where threats to their 'truth' lie. Truth being the non-existence of racism, particularly racism that engages the self. Thus, there is a commitment to the invisibilisation of racial oppression and a dedication to the misinterpretation of evidence [5]. The holding onto truth within white supremacy entails a commitment to not seeing the truth. The ultimate function of such epistemic practices, these 'logics' of the self-proclaimed rational subject allegedly wanting to know, is to defend against knowing. Black feminists and women of colour scholars have long written about these epistemic games employed to deny us the capacity to do exactly what we are ordered to do; 'prove', more broadly to speak and to write with authority about our being in the world, thus, to theorise the world we inhabit.

The mundane and more sophisticated ways truth is smothered in everyday exchanges, within epistemic encounters, often means that when we do write or when we do speak, what we write or speak about is rendered strange, if not absurd. In the everyday, this looks like sneers, raised eyebrows and sometimes plain hearty laughter in our face. Most commonly, though, I am met with deafening and disorienting white gazes. But we have continued to think while our thinking was mocked. As Bion might say, while our linking (of objects) was attacked [24].[1] We have long been writing and defying racialised and gendered expectations. We have often theorised under sustained fire. This is how we have continued to shape the social world that shapes us, often borrowing ideas from multiple critical fields, combining them and producing new insights grounded in the ethics of social transformation, of connection and arguably of love.

The struggle for ideas and conceptualisations is also the struggle for land, for safeness and for humanity. Hence, here I unapologetically bring a different kind of evidence to support my theoretical musings. I bring and reclaim another form of knowledge that has often been discarded and devalued: I use stories as tools. Both my own, and those offered to me, mainly as part of the call for contributions, they provide much of the illustrations of the 'everyday performances' of whiteness. They help to give human shape, form and flesh to whiteness. They remind us, once more, that our lives are not theoretical.

Stories have long been used as a tool to resist white normative epistemic and colonial practices and to assert one's humanity. The 'power to narrate' the discarded and the reframing of what constitutes evidence is central to decolonial efforts [25].

In *White minds*, as I tell stories, I rely on current affairs, news reports, historical events and artistic productions. This is an approach to the study of cultural phenomena largely owed to the late Stuart Hall. They provide much of what I reflect on in my 'notes'. This is a practice I borrow from ethnography and make my own. Although all notes and stories are extracted from our collective and shared archives, I somewhat arbitrarily make a distinction between historical notes, cultural notes and autoethnographic notes. Historical notes describe events of significance to our shared history and are usually well-documented. Cultural notes examine artistic productions or racialised happenings in the present. I see these as culturally significant but they are still to become inscribed in the category of history. Autoethnographic notes convey racialised events through my own lived experience. 'Everyday performances' provide illustrations of the phenomena under interrogation from a lived experience perspective, principally of third parties. Usually that of participants to the call for contributions.

These notes on our field of study, which is whiteness, constitute the evidence of the propositions put forth. All human practices (epistemic, artistic, relational, structural, socio-economic, and so on) are interlinked and co-constitutive and, as such, these notes provide deep insights into the cultural reservoir or archives of society. Cultural archives we may say. Archives have been compared to reservoirs with units of meaning containing history, symbols, imagery related to ontological and epistemological phenomena that social actors draw from in their everyday discursive practices [26, 27].

Our archives are responsive enough to accommodate changes and shifts across time and so are in part destroyed while continuing their transmission functions, thus ensuring their survival [27]. They have not only been embedded in discourses, but they have also become integral parts of the psyche. Goldberg has proposed that one of the consequences of Western experiences under imperialism is that Western ways of viewing, talking about and interacting with the world at large became intricately embedded in racialised discourses and 'internal' landscapes [28]. Early beliefs and images become assimilated as part of the psyche so that the 'savage' became a psychological and moral space within the individual that required 'repression, denial and disciplinary restraint', another way to envisage the racialised endurance and maintenance of colonial imaginaries that continue to structure social organisations.

Archives are therefore violently occupied by whiteness and its racial knowledge including premises, assumptions, values and constraints constituting both the self and the other [28]. We draw from this reservoir to relate, to produce art, to make laws, to think and to exist together. Consequently, if whiteness is the central operative system, what is produced within that system should first sustain its very existence. Second, it should provide some evidence of the system. Third, it should expound the system. Connecting to the world, rather than treating it as noise or spurious data and cutting off from it, what I later in the book refer to as social dissociation, challenges much of Western individualism and white knowledge production.

The autoethnographic method is central to the book. Here, too, 'I write myself in' via notes. I inevitably exist in the archives just as much as the archives exist within me. And my experiences form part of the cultural reservoir of society. These autobiographical moments shed light on it and are in turn illuminated by it. As is my standard scholarly practice, I thus deliberately and unashamedly theorise from where I stand in the world, as a result the ideas and experiences I present are anchored in the perspective of a woman racialised as black, and as such there is inevitably a sharper attention to the workings of anti-blackness and, where helpful, intersectional analyses.

I use autoethnography as a tool of social analysis and social theory. Some feminists might say I theorise 'from my flesh', as much of the thinking and writing here derives from the knowledge acquired from my body. Another act of transgression is the re-centring of embodied truths and with that the treating of lived experience as reliable data. So much of Western philosophy has taught us that our bodies are working against us. That the body is the province of chaos. That black and brown bodies are wild, unreliable witnesses to their own experiences and unruly territories to be conquered, occupied and mastered by rational thought, which continues to be symbolised by the white man. Colonial bodies have long been sites for the enactment of white sadism as we will cover in the book. War on our bodies has been normalised. Expected. Rewarded.

And there is, as a result, nothing that challenges the master more than honouring devalued bodies. And so, we must do so as we make our case. In fact, the valuing of our bodies could stand as *the* main case. The ideas that I offer are nonetheless tentative. My understanding of the world, like my understanding of whiteness, has shifted and is still shifting. I am, after all, still a student, primarily of life. We can only ever engage in provisional theories, particularly when it comes to making sense of social structures. In part because the animal we seek to capture is ever so elusive and sophistically mouldable. Like water that it takes great efforts not to lose through our fingers, however determined our half-clenched fists may be. Like water that takes the shape of its container but retains its essence and its composition intact over time. Because too, we are so deeply inhabited by the social world we inhabit, the water we swim in. Some say that as we ourselves change so do our theories. Conversely, as our theories change, so do we.

Note

1. Linking of objects is a reference to Bion's classic work (1959) on psychosis which is expanded upon in the chapter on white trauma. In his formulation, attacks on linking are attacks on meaning making, which impair thinking thus on the apprehension of reality when that reality seems too overwhelming.

1

Whiteness, time and space

> Now he has departed from this strange world a little ahead of me. That signifies nothing. For us believing [*gläubige*] physicists, the distinction between past, present, and future is only a stubbornly persistent illusion. (Albert Einstein, 21 March 1955)[1]

A cultural note

Early in 2021, Netflix released the Oscar-winning short film *Two Distant Strangers*. The film sees the main protagonist, Carter James, a black cartoonist, relive the same morning over and over again. He awakes in bed the morning after a first date, in the apartment of his lover. We see him get dressed and prepare to return home preoccupied with the thought of needing to feed his dog. After a few loving exchanges, he says goodbye, hoping to see the woman he met the night before again in the future. However, this is the morning of his death. Carter never gets to feed his dog or to go home. Instead, when he leaves the apartment, in an act of gratuitous and overzealous authority, a police officer racialised as white stops him. The exchange escalates into a scuffle and Carter is suffocated to death.

The gut-wrenching movie replays the police encounter and murder again and again. Each time Carter is killed he awakes from the nightmare, in bed with his lover. However, this only leads to him soon reliving death and dying as he is killed once more in somewhat different yet similar circumstances, by the same police officer as he attempts to go home.

Powerlessly witnessing the repetition of Carter's gruesome death evoked a strong visceral reaction in me. In part this was no doubt due to the temporal proximity and cognitive salience of the murder of George Floyd, in adjacent circumstances. But perhaps more critically here, the sense of inescapability and Carter's futile attempts at wrestling again and again against the finality and outcome of his encounter with the police felt disturbingly familiar. As I watched the movie, I felt disoriented by the director's use of the temporal. Lost in time. Connected to despair in a way that echoed so many of my own encounters with anti-blackness.

Paradoxically, that vaguely known sense of derealisation allowed me to grasp, albeit mainly corporeally, the significance of the phenomena under dramatisation and thus to come to this realisation: black bodies know intimately the depth of what the movie is portraying, beyond the display of anti-black police brutality. Carter is stuck in a timeless and anachronistic anti-black bubble that is the white (necropolitical[2]) gaze. He is deprived of any possibilities of being outside of it since his existence, his very being, is contingent upon the violence he experiences. No matter his efforts to disrupt the future and to free himself from history, the bubble comes over from the 'past', imprisons him and closes in on him, resulting in his annihilation. The movie consequently has a strong Afropessimist[3] motive in the sense that it positions Carter's death as inescapable and necessary for the material, psychic and symbolic racialised order. It nullifies any chance of subjectivity and agentic power [1]. Proceeding by association, revisiting *Two Distant Strangers* brought to mind the following story, which will add a personal dimension to the chapter's interrogations.

An autoethnographic note

During the COVID-19 pandemic, I went for a long walk with my then husband. My fitness having been adversely impacted by the national lockdown, my lower back was hurting. So, as we were approaching a knee-high brick divider wall, he suggested that I sat down, which I did. The wall I rested on separated some communal gardens and a main road. Once sat, we continued talking for a few minutes. He was facing me. I had my back to the building. We were there for two to three minutes at the most. The streets were unusually quiet, but it was a chilly afternoon. Suddenly, without any warning, my husband was pulling my arm and hurting me as he did so. It took me a few seconds to understand that he was attempting to get me to stand up as he did not say a word. After I stood up, he pushed me behind him and raised the bag of goodies we had just bought up into the air, adopting a defensive posture. It all happened very quickly. It was only when I turned around, confused, that I faced the building and saw a pit bull-type dog charging towards us, at full speed, teeth bared. A white woman appeared right behind the dog. She seemed to be the dog's owner. She shouted repeatedly at me "Do not sit on the wall", then, "Do not sit on the wall, it's the dog's territory".

I was already standing up, but as the dog was still enraged and barking at us, I started to scan my belongings and immediate environment for anything I could use as a weapon in self-defence. I could not find anything, and the dog kept on going. Within a few inches of us, it stops, backtracks, then returns, charging. It goes back and forth between us and the owner, who was four or five metres away. It did this relentlessly: a repetitive pattern of retreat and terrifying advance. Moving away, then coming back full force. It did this three or four times, only stopping when the owner screamed "Enough!" and returned inside the building with the beast behind her. I was standing there, in the middle of the street, unusually silent, and I was conscious I was stopping myself from speaking. I am not sure if it is out of shame, shock or terror. Perhaps I was thinking that protesting might escalate things and increase the risks. The possibility of shame takes me by surprise. I pondered this. My heart was still pounding for a while, even though they had gone, and I felt colder. In the moment, the assault, or threat of it, feels raced. It feels unsettlingly familiar too. In fact, I know that it is familiar even though I had never before been attacked or chased by a dog. We are two years or so post-Brexit, in the middle of Buckinghamshire, but I am in apartheid South Africa. This is where my mind takes my body. I have never set foot in that country.

Time, knowing and remembering

Interrogating conceptualisations and experiences of time is a complex undertaking which cuts across various disciplines including literary studies, history, ontology and epistemology. Though spatiotemporal delineations have been found across cultures, temporal thinking is largely arbitrary [2]. Our conceptual frames and experiences of time are socially constructed, thus culturally and historically located. Still, temporal organisations allow us to structure societies, our lives and to position ourselves within the world, thus, they help us manage our fear of the unknown and of death. The temporal consequently serves metaphysical and ontological functions including the management of terror and the maintenance of ontological security.

Despite theoretical physics, which has long challenged the traditional temporal split within Western thinking, the legacy of Cartesian dualism and modernism's idea of 'progress' is reflected in the dominant conceptualisation of time. A linear and separatist temporal orientation dominates, with time usually constructed as moving in a forward flow from past, to present, then future. Such is the normalisation of this linear time and space framework that differing experiences of the temporal are usually seen through pathological lenses. For example, clinically, the merging of objects from different time points and the 'failure' to linearly orientate the self 'to time and space' is assessed as being indicative of some psychological (or neurological) disturbance, some anxious states or part of the symptomatology of trauma, as seen in dissociation, depersonalisation and derealisation [3, 4].

Yet, even within Western thought and religion, formulations and everyday experiences of time suspension and retrospection, particularly following loss, social change and injustice, are well documented [5]. And other belief systems, for example, African cosmologies, challenge these taken-for-granted temporal boundaries by suggesting that the 'past' exists in a state of constant merging with the 'present', so that what we experience as 'the now' is constantly intruded upon by an ever-present and ever-impinging 'past'. A 'past' inhabited by ancestral entities, suffering and spirits capable of influencing and communicating with us [6].

Whiteness and temporality

The plot of *Two Distant Strangers* and the accompanying autoethnographic note help frame the issues we will attempt to grapple with in this chapter. To start, we will examine the genesis of repeated patterns that colour often violent social interactions. The recognisable rhythm of communication. The enduring motive of social arrangements. The temporal relation between recurrent acts of racial injustice. But also, the strong visceral and embodied experience of familiarity. The intimate knowledge we grasp through our senses which lets us know that we have been here before. That experience of déjà vu is something those of the perpetuating end of injustice and inequality are unlikely to be familiar with, at least not through their body. Yet, it remains something that deeply challenges the collective mind.

All the same, it is undeniably the case that so much of the present not only looks like the 'past', but it also feels like the 'past', and we may even argue that it is the 'past'. That the 'past' and present may be one and the same is an easily arguable case. And while, for some, this is still a radical idea, scholars from a range of disciplines have argued precisely this, one way or the other, for some time. For example, in her examination of contemporary manifestations of anti-black racism, Sharpe has powerfully described slavery's 'continued unfolding' as both constitutive of the contemporary conditions of black lives and as an anchor for the law, the psychic and the material [7]. This is so, despite deformation, reformation and, at times, interruptions. In *In the wake*, she uses the slave ship as a literary device to demonstrate the timelessness of whiteness and the similarities between the shipping of enslaved Africans, the movements of migrants and the so-called refugee crisis, to the policing of black bodies in North American streets and drownings of black bodies in the Mediterranean Sea. This, she proposed, is a reimagining of the slave ship and associated subjugation. She concludes that although 'the means and modes of black subjection may have changed, the structure of that subjection remains'. There is a long tradition within African American scholarship of challenging linear temporalities and to see what we consider different time periods as a continuation of 'past' ones, with the emancipation envisaged and experienced as ongoing enslavement. The plantations are essentially reconfigured as Black Codes or Jim Crow [8].

Temporality is central to analytic thinking. By analytic, here and throughout the book, I broadly intend theories, ideas and practices premised on the existence of unconscious forces and communications, disciplinary fields that are more specifically referred to as psychoanalytic and group analytic. Analytic work clinically involves engaging the subject in deep reflection on events and relationships as situated in and enduring through time. Disturbances in the 'here and now' are understood from the starting point of disturbances in the 'there and then'. It is thus taken as a given that we are fundamentally shaped by 'past' events, experiences and processes, ranging from personal relational histories such as attachment to more macro phenomena such as 'past' social configurations, intergenerational and historical trauma. Despite this, psychoanalysis is still, in the main, needing to turn a critical gaze upon itself when it comes to its reproduction of the colonial imaginary and therefore its entanglement with violent racist systems both in the present and in the 'past' [9, 10]. This is something outside the remit of the present book.

When considering the violence of whiteness thus, and amidst white neoliberal post-racial fantasies, one is faced with several fundamental and arguably intriguing problems or questions, responses to which can easily be taken for granted, but which nonetheless require some elucidation in order for us to set the foundation for the explorations that are to come later in the book. These 'problems' include: the reality that interpersonal racist violence continues to be enacted despite strong legal, societal and moral opposition and overall collective disapproval, at least consciously; the fact that processes and events which we class as 'historical' and locate in this temporal category we call the 'past' continue to rear their heads in our present; related to the second point, the observation that individual social actors and groups become engaged in interactions that so strongly echo and implicate previous generations often appearing to organise or reorganise the social world in a way that mirrors configurations of time periods we deem revolved; and, finally, the realisation that, like Carter, for those of us at the receiving end of white violence, existing within white supremacy can feel like being stuck in an atemporal bubble of repetitive injustice and violence, or indeed like time-travelling into time and spaces never before encountered.

In his formulation of the unthought known, Bollas proposes that the infant can have preverbal awareness of experiences that evade their conscious understanding when it comes to important objects [11]. This knowing is deemed 'unthought' because it is not articulable in words or even capable of being formulated conceptually but it is nonetheless intuitively ever-present in the infant's use of these objects and the fantasies which it may give rise to. It is, we may formulate, as though the infant has knowledge of events which precede their capacity to form knowledge. Extending Bollas' thinking to the realm of the socio-historical and the collective, we may hypothesise that there too exists a form of preverbal collective understanding of 'past' events or processes which sits at the border of the known and the unknown. This is a form of knowledge for what has been significant, wounding or threatening to one's kin group. A knowledge form which is acquired or transmitted in some ways, and can thus be accessed in some ways, independent of personal experience or exposure. A collective and social form of unthought known, which is embodied and evades both rational articulation and the bounds of language but continues to shape the knowledge we form of the world through visceral apprehension and fantasy formation.

Whiteness and white spaces

> They grabbed what they could get for the sake of what was to be got. It was just robbery with violence, aggravated murder on a great scale, and men going at it blind – as is very proper for those who tackle a darkness. The conquest of the earth, which mostly means the taking it away from those who have a different complexion or slightly flatter noses than we, is not a pretty thing when you look into it too much. (Conrad and Goonetilleke, 1999 [12])

> White people in this country will have quite enough to do in learning how to accept and love themselves and each other, and when they have achieved this – which will not be tomorrow and may very well be never – the Negro problem will no longer exist, for it will no longer be needed. (Baldwin, 1962 [13])

The foundational role of race and racism as conceptual categories or fantasies that structure material realities and psychosocial functioning in the West has long been recognised. The two quotes at the beginning of this section, extracted from classic literary texts separated by much time and space, lay the foundation for our conceptualisation of whiteness. They summarise the psychic impulses and psychological defences underscoring racism as well as their material consequences. For Baldwin, self-hate forms the genesis of the shadow phenomenon that leads to anti-blackness. Conrad's heart of darkness was really the heart of whiteness and we are alerted to the fact that this shadow phenomenon was sustained by repression, greed and sadism. These are necessary defences for colonial conquest and capital acquisition.

Analytically, the defence of projection has been central to the formulation of racism, particularly in the context of colonial relations. According to that line of thought, bodies racialised as black or brown are made to carry those intolerable aspects of the collective white mind, including its so-called primitivism, sexuality and moral dysfunction. Racist violence here may be conceptualised as processes of projection and projective identification. It is a breach of psychic boundaries whereby Western fantasies, impulses and desires or its disavowed shadows are forced onto the colonial subject, with blackness in particular being intruded upon, causing it to lose sense of its own subjectivity, selfhood and sovereignty [14, 15]. Of note, in addition to irrational projections of what is split off and disavowed into dichotomous racialised fantasies and the necessary use of the mechanism of projective identification to transform the hated or repudiated object, analytic thinking on racism posits an intolerance for reality or 'pseudo-thinking' in the racist subject [16]. These are ideas which illuminate the epistemic shiftiness of whiteness we described in the introduction and which we will examine again when we consider white trauma and white dissociation.

The first consideration in attempting to understand the colonial logics of psychic disavowal that underscore their figurations and therefore national territorial boundaries, both geographically and in the realm of the imaginary which sustain whiteness, is to ask the question: 'What constitutes the West?'. Hall proposes that the West is, first, an illusory signifier for a classification system that allows us to organise different societies in terms of knowledge and in terms of thought [17]. Second, it is a set of images that represent an amalgamation of differing societies, cultures, peoples and places that function as a system united via 'industrialisation'. Third, this system creates a homogeneity that is employed to compare and contrast different societies and peoples in terms of constructed proximity and distance. Finally, the West provides some criteria around which what is constructed as desirable is attributed to the West and what is undesirable is attributed or once more projected to 'the rest'.

We come very quickly to realise that these criteria are maintained through discursive and ideological means so that representations of the West become formations of what is white. Since what is white becomes what is right, whiteness becomes central to state and nation creation, identity formation and geopolitical relations. In *White minds*, we will use whiteness to refer to the operationalisation of white supremacy. White supremacy is conceptualised here as both 'constitutive of the epistemology of the West and as an invisible regime of power that secures hegemony through discourse and has material effects in everyday life' [18, p 76].

Whiteness is the ways the structure of white supremacy (or white racism) becomes embedded, normalised and inscribed within modes of feeling, thinking, being in and on the world so as to maintain the illusion of white superiority. This thinking decentres whiteness as a phenotypical thus biological phenomena. A scientific myth long debunked. The structure of whiteness, as we seek to argue, equally harms those racialised as white, thus, remembering the machinery in operation, helps locate, contextualise and give meaning to the actions of white social actors within particular time-spaces.

Quijano links whiteness and constructions of race and the creation of racialised others to projects of domination sustained by enslavement, colonialism and the advance of capitalism [19]. Whiteness is therefore, according to him, intrinsically linked to the patterns of resource distributions, power configurations and labour divisions that support the material interests of those racialised as white. Epistemically, Quijano thus similarly traces associated formations of whiteness, its modes of knowing and of producing knowledge to modernity. This is what he refers to as the 'coloniality of power' [19].

In her conceptualisation of whiteness as property, Harris posits that racial identity, the occupation of space or land and property are inherently interrelated [20]. These require the development of particular mechanics of control and exploitation including the extraction of the land, expulsion from land, the occupation of land, as well as segregation and border logics to protect newly created property thus capital. Whiteness as property has therefore functioned as a means to police and administer property and land rights which have, in the context of the US, only been accessible to those with white identities. Trafford, extending on Harris, has argued that whiteness as property is a feature of internal colonialism and the establishment of contemporary geographies of exclusion, marginalisation and segregation in the UK which continue to shape resource allocations such as housing and policing [21].

Attempting to summarise the key characteristics of whiteness, Garner synthesised a large amount of scholarship and identified core themes, as follows: whiteness as terror and supremacy; whiteness as absence; whiteness as values, norms and cultural capital [22]. Whiteness as terror and supremacy map onto the history of enslavement and colonialism and the associated hunger for domination and control, which, however, go beyond brutality and include collective acts of exploitation and of ownership of land and bodies, thus of property, and by extension membership rights and entitlement sanctioned by institutions.

Whiteness as values, norms and cultural capital reveals how it has imposed itself as the default, the yardstick against which other racial worldviews, values or cultures are measured. In this context, whiteness may be seen as humanness and universality; as an unmarked presence. The invisibility of whiteness naturally translates to the white subject struggling to see themselves as racialised. White social actors negate whiteness as a phenomenon worthy of investigation and instead see it as a burden, a source of oppression or discrimination; a threat to the self. From this, the 'whiteness as liability' discourse emerges. This discourse positions white groups as 'the real' victims of racism and discrimination. Framing attempts to better understand whiteness not only as a threat to white groups but as a social threat tells us all we need to know about how fiercely defended the system continues to be.

The specific norms that sustain whiteness have been identified as obsessive self-control and rationality as the preferred way to access truth and independence rather than co-dependence and the repression of emotions. These aspirations serve as powerful templates onto which opposite characteristics may be projected onto the other, leading to binary constructions of 'civilisation' and 'savagery'. The collection of these values afford a form of cultural capital and a sense of social respectability and posited sophistication which create fantasised groups whose 'opposing' behaviours and norms of value may be devalued.

The alleged invisibility of whiteness to the white subject is also something that may seem paradoxical when it comes to thinking about whiteness as atrocious violence. However, it enables us to start to understand how fundamentally necessary this invisibility is to the protection of the system and allows us to anticipate powerful psychological processes involved in ensuring it remains so.

We may, in summary, propose that whiteness designates three main processes. First, the system that ensures the production and reproduction of the dominance and domination of people racialised as white [23]. Second, we may say that whiteness is the root cause of enduring race-based inequality, injustice and oppression. And, finally, that it is the basis for specific patterns of social relations [24]. That is to say it is the basis for particular ways of thinking and, more to the point here, ways of being with the racialised other. Despite these foundational characteristics, whiteness remains, in the main, elusive to bodies racialised as white. Another, we may say, of its core characteristics. Much of the dominance of whiteness is acquired through its normalisation and invisibilisation [25]. It is that which allows it to silently continue to remain woven into the fabric of our society, unchallenged. This is the context of whiteness escaping much of our psychological investigation and elucidation.

Whiteness and racial stratification

A core aspect of whiteness which tends to escape our everyday reflections is its stratification. This stratification refers to racialised social arrangements embedded within social structures. That is to say, the particular order race logics or the logics of white supremacy have become baked into every structure in society, leading to particular pecking orders when it comes to access to resources (material, ideological, epistemic, and so on) based on particular racialised assignments of roles, positions and functions related to their relative inferiority/superiority [26]. How these racialised roles, positions and functions within the system are assigned is complex. They involve race constructions as well as other intersectional factors such as gender, class and both conscious and unconscious, psychic and structural, collective and individual processes.

Crucially, these roles acquire a life of their own. They become empty 'signifiers' with chimeric functions and little connection to the people they are assigned to. Despite this, phantasmagorical racialised assignments have, once more, real material consequences, often life or death ones. They therefore sustain the necropolitical (dis)order. Stratified systems can shift across time and space. However, the overall system they are designed to maintain rarely shifts ideologically or structurally. As an illustration, although there has been movement in those who have been able to access the fortress of whiteness, over time and space, the structure and ideology of white supremacy have remained intact. Further, and crucially, the system of white supremacy is not only built on the existence of two groups; a superior one (a white group) and an inferior one (let's say subjects racialised as others). Things are more complex.

As a matter fact, one of the reasons race logics have been able to sustain themselves is because they have naturalised hierarchical thinking when it comes to racial 'differences' [27]. Differences anchored in scientific racism which made heavy use of debunked methods including observations via the edification of ethno-colonialists' personal journals or accounts and, subsequently, via anatomical examinations using craniology. These methods, which took hold at the height of the colonial project, established human taxonomies ranked in traits and characteristics such as intelligence, beauty, morality, physical strength, adaptability and thus survival potential.

While some groups are placed at the top of that constructed hierarchy, there exist many closely adjacent to them and many (more) inferior ones, differentially constructed. Groups racialised as white are subject to that hierarchisation too, so that each white group is distinctly positioned and constructed within the hierarchy of white supremacy. So, for example, an English person racialised as white is somewhat whiter than an Italian racialised as white who is whiter than a Romanian person racialised as white. Positions in the hierarchy of whiteness are also a function of multiple factors, some economic, some geopolitical, some historical, but largely, still, phantasmagorical. Newly white groups tend to occupy a more precarious position within the structure and are usually located lower down than the longer established white groups

Although skin pigmentation or the absence thereof and associated 'phenotypical' or morphological features are often used as a proxy for the structure of whiteness, things are, once more, much more complex. Notwithstanding the fetishisation of whiteness, the absurd belief in the superiority or even uniqueness of 'white skin' and its enduring association with the West, the reality is that large sections of 'Europeans' racialised as white have darker skin than many Indigenous groups including groups in the Middle East, Asia, North Africa and, in fact, even some Africans racialised as black. In other words, racialised constructions trump 'phenotypes' or, we may say, the eyes will see what the mind has been conditioned to think even when that thinking is fundamentally flawed.

Indeed, we know that social class and wealth in many parts of the world, particularly in Latin America, have historically influenced who has been racialised as white [28]. We know that during the aberrantly brutal apartheid rule in South Africa, racial classifications could change overnight so that it was possible to go from coloured and from 'native', although less commonly, to white. 'Pass-Whites' were those who became reclassified as such [29]. We also know that religion can change the perception of skin shade so that, in the collective imagination, bodies who may otherwise be racialised as white cease to be seen as white once their religion is identified. Irish Catholics' status as whites in England was long precarious because they were Catholics [30]. This is the case today for those who would otherwise be racialised as white who practise Islam and to a lesser degree, arguably, Jews of European descent who would otherwise be racialised as white [31, 32].

Two fundamental implications derive from these points. First, that whiteness does not exclude from its fortress those with 'melaninated' bodies, instead those bodies who are excluded are melanised. Groups who more recently have been racialised as white, including the Irish and 'morphologically' white Jews of European ancestry and most southern Europeans, did not suddenly acquire whiter skin. Rather, their skin upon white racialisation became perceived as white. In many cases, their skin was in fact whitened within cultural and artistic productions so as to sustain the fantasy of homogeneity that underscores the imaginary of whiteness. Similarly, those who are excluded from whiteness who present as morphologically white, such as Travellers and Muslim groups, commonly have their skin darkened within cultural representations so as to emphasise their otherness.

Second, and perhaps more significantly, religious groups can be racialised and stratified within white supremacy. This is central to the (legally and theoretically contested) case that 'Muslims' and indeed 'Jews' are races, and thus to understand why Islamophobia and antisemitism may constitute forms of racism which attract consequent racial violence and hatred, using the concept of 'racecraft' [33]. Focusing on the racialisation of Muslims, Choudhury theorises that since it is racism that produces races and associated racial groups and since the biological foundation of these races has little scientific basis, even though different Muslims are racialised differently, 'the Muslim', as a fantasised category, can and has been 'crafted' as a race [34]. Indeed, attributes shared by Muslim groups have been imbued with racial meaning. An important point that is not without difficulty, since of course 'technologies of power' produce and reproduce racism in the ideological domain which produce and reproduce racialised 'technologies of power' which produce and reproduce psychic organisations which produce and reproduce the 'technologies of power', and so on, the core argument of *White minds*.

Despite whiteness' stratified order, and perhaps paradoxically, the white imaginary that sustains white racialisation, group specificities and intersectional realities are masked, as Frosh argues [32]. In the case of Jewishness, it denies the reality of white otherness, namely here, Jewish otherness, an otherness which white supremacists use, to position 'the Jew' as a threat to white power. Further, white racialisation creates the illusion of racial homogeneity and, significantly, it either minimises or denies the need to include antisemitism and its specificities within anti-racist praxes. Undeniably, the absorption of Jewishness by whiteness, because of the stratified social (dis)order, does lead to competitiveness for perceived scarce anti-racism resources, including affective ones.

It has, though, more perverse consequences. These include the rewriting and revisioning of history and the reimagining of geopolitical configurations whereby the category 'the Jew', imagined as white, by association with white power, and oftentimes simply because of antisemitism, can become inaccurately positioned centrally within modernism's enslavement and colonial projects. At the same time, the central contribution of Muslim Arabs, largely imagined as brown, in the trading of 'black Africans' pre- and post-modernism, is minimised or absent from conversations on anti-black racism. Although the repositioning of 'the Jew' within the history of enslavement of Africans remains in the fringes of racial discourses (revisionism that is mainly supported within sections of adherents and followers of the Nation of Islam in the US), the myth has been employed, among other devices, to pit forms of racialised oppression against others. The pitting of antisemitism against Islamophobia is largely operational in the UK. However, in the US, the 'blacks and Jews' discourse constructs African Americans as fundamentally antisemitic.

While today these polarised and competitive positions often find their genesis in the fragmentations the occupation of Palestine creates, there is a well-rehearsed discursive and political device at play. A device which has been weaponised over centuries, particularly by the ruling or elite political classes to 'divide and conquer'. A device which, in and of itself, is usually loaded with antisemitism, Islamophobia and/or anti-blackness. Yet even though this solidarity has been consistently thwarted [30], there is a long history of interracial and interfaith resistance against strategically divisive tactics through coalition politics. It is true that any thorough psychosocial study of any racism will invariably shed some light on the workings of other racisms and in fact other forms of oppression, if territorial, scarcity and border logics are resisted. However, Lentin reminds us that flattening and homogenising different forms of racism, irrespective of migration trajectories, histories of colonial domination, enslavement and racialised constructions across time and space reduces our capacity to understand the persistent power of race and its continuities as a project [30].

Frosh's intersectional analysis in turn reminds us that 'being Jewish is an attribute of a person that acts separately from whiteness', and that, indeed, Arab Jews, Asian Jews, Indigenous and Pacific-Island Jews, Jews of African descent – some of whom may be 'morphologically' black – exist. He also highlights how processes of racialisation, by massing together multiple identities and histories, necessarily transform, fix and obscure the group subject to that racialisation and, quite importantly, that Jewishness as whiteness has the potential to amplify antisemitism through conspirational and power tropes, which increase precariousness and the risk of violence for all Jewish people and, more so, for those who are intersectionally more vulnerable. Particular vulnerabilities are present in those who occupy lower positions within adjacent socially constructed and co-constitutive hierarchies due to racialisation, class or gender and, perhaps too, those more easily stereotypically identified as Jewish, such as those who practise Orthodox Judaism.

There is a query to be raised at this juncture, although largely beyond the scope of the book, about the construction of Jews, and by extension Israel, as white and therefore European within the structure of whiteness and how this newly 'acquired' and precarious whiteness may have fed into Zionist formations, the creation of the nation-state and the occupation of Palestine in the late 19th century. Palestinians have, of course, been largely racialised as Arab, thus brown, geopolitically and discursively, within the hierarchy, leading arguably to a particular reiteration of whiteness.

Within the racialisation processes of black and brown subjects or, we may say, of more 'distal' racialised groups, hierarchisation is also operational, hence, those higher up the hierarchy are therefore equally capable of enacting white supremacist related violence, at group level, towards those located lower down the stratification. In fact, as we will revisit in Chapters 7 and 8 when we delve into ambivalence and complicity, access and proximity to whiteness requires the acceptance of white supremacy and therefore the reproduction of anti-blackness from all strata of the hierarchy. As Lentin summarises, 'race also relies on creating differences between the racialized, which are reproduced in relations between differently racialised peoples' [30].

Existing within white supremacy implicates everyone in the reproduction of white supremacy. And it is clear that proximity or access to whiteness in that stratified (dis)order protects, but it causes harm too. To the self and to racialised others, located lower down in the hierarchy. Even if proximity and access may be, at least in part, aspirational and indeed chosen. Those who occupy the lowest 'echelons' of that racialised stratification today, those racialised as black and/or as Muslim are particularly vulnerable. Prioritising the safety of those whose bodies are more susceptible to suffocate under necropolitical world (dis)orders is not only an extension of intersectional thinking, but also an ethical imperative.

Mechanisms of reproduction

An exploration of white minds and the temporality of whiteness could not hold unless we could, of course, posit a level of uniformity across white groups, socio-historical contexts in the West and thus across time-spaces. Patterns and common configurations but also shared meaning and symbolism give whiteness this atemporal dimension. The existence of such processes of continuations are subject to fierce resistance. While the claim is not without problems, part of the reluctance to examine these patterns is the endurance of individualism and Eurocentrism as well as deeply held fantasies of exceptionalism, which remain the luxury of the powerful. Those who homogenise others tend to strongly oppose being thought of as part of a collective or cultural group. Insisting on one's uniqueness, negating the grouping influence of socio-historical location and associated racialisation are ways of averting the gaze, as we will see in the next chapter. Another way to protect whiteness.

A focus on whiteness' relationship with time and space is not only fundamental to grasping its homogenising nature, but also to understanding and exploring the micro, meso and macro 'levels' of harm it inflicts, and the mechanics that ensure its continuity as a psychosocial entity. What is proposed consequently is that these form well-rehearsed, practised and recognisable race-based patterns that remain alive and embodied in the present. Consequently, another foundational premise that underscores our project is that racialisation embeds racial fantasies, dynamics and processes within our everyday racialised exchanges through specific mechanisms, and that these mechanisms render whiteness, or at least some aspects of it, atemporal. It is these mechanisms that underpin the violence we will try to explore in each chapter. To help us do this, in this chapter we need to consider some of the conceptual frames and theories available to underpin this thinking. They are numerous and there is no intention here to present them all. Rather, the aim is to use those which I have found the most fruitful in understanding processes of repetition, of continuation and of the permanence of whiteness as a psychosocial phenomenon; accepting that many others exist.

Social scripts

'I was diagnosed with autism in my 40s. It opened up new understanding for me about whiteness because an often-discussed aspect of autism is the use of socially accepted scripts. For example, a script can be a certain way of expressing an idea that is commonly accepted by broader society. Autistic people often get pathologised for their use of scripts, but non-autistic people use scripts just as frequently. The difference is simply that they don't recognise them as such. This much is obvious to me when I witness other white people talking about racism. There are very specific scripts whose purpose is to communicate with other white people in a way that reinforces white comfort. Scripts for asking white people to rejoin white solidarity when they have disrupted it in some way.' (Sonia, white agender, 40s, French American)

Formulating patterns of re-enactment using social scripts enables us to see social relations as performances. Accordingly, we may propose that ways of being and relating that we expect, or that are expected of us, in particular situations, or on particular stages, are performances. Socialisation into roles, and their associated norms, are acquired and transmitted, generation after generation. Through such intergenerational socialisation, we may hypothesise that we learn to perform particular scripts associated with particular racialised configurations. Those performances are not meant to be noted or questioned. Those, however, who for whatever reason are not able or willing to follow the scripts, like Sonia, or who note their performance, are likely to be socially disciplined.

We learn to act, feel and relate in socially sanctioned ways without necessarily realising we are following well-rehearsed ways of behaving, thinking and relating. In fact, we may often believe we are employing our free will and exercising our agency.

From a psychological perspective, the point of the existence of these scripts may be to reduce our cognitive load so that we can invest more resources in situations calling for more sophisticated cognitive functions or that pose greater risks. Psychosocially, social scripts are halfway points between purely psychological formulations at micro level, such as those involving cognitive shortcuts, and more macro phenomena such as cultural reproduction or the repetition of history.

Because scripts are usually performed relationally, they could be said to be located at the meso level of functioning or communication, allowing us to hold in mind individual contributions, structural factors and their intersection: the script performance, while keeping in mind the meso functions of the scripts and the reproduction of 'past' interpersonal communication and relations. Those patterns of communication have macro or structural consequences: social inequality, racial injustice or, we may say, the continuation of 'past' social arrangements. This is why we may see exchanges in operation in the present which may be so evocative of another time or space that they move us into another spatiotemporal point. Rollock, in her interrogation of scripts within academia, crucially notes that the racialised other is rarely the author or playwright of social scripts. They have little agentic power to determine 'the roles, content or direction of what happens on the academic stage' [35, p 2]. As such, they are forced into roles which they perform, while the very existence of these roles, and associated white supremacy enforcing scripts, is denied.

Scripts are a fruitful way to explore the pit bull anecdote and my sense of displacement through time and space. Racialised, canine-mediated violence has a long history. It played a formative role in 'colonial efforts to dispossess Africans of land' in South Africa and elsewhere on the continent [36]. Further, a number of tropes or archetypes are evoked in the exchange between myself and the dog owner. The black body as the alien of the land. As trespasser, even on its own soil. The ferocious dog as guardian of white property or boundaries. The white woman as a covert or vicarious agent of white supremacy. The black body as transgressor in white (only) spaces. Or as moving above its station here while taking space. These tropes are heavily historically loaded and evocative of colonial configurations. We may posit that they have activated associated behaviours, affective states and outcomes in both subject and object. This would help explain the feeling of shame I felt, which I could not rationally explain. Using social scripts as a frame consequently renders visible the heavy symbolism of the exchange, the endurance of racialised fantasy-based roles and the strengthening of social norms and expectations through particular scripts.

Group processes

Within the social sciences there has been some interrogation for decades, if not centuries, of the mechanisms that allow the transmission or the continuation of norms and beliefs within society. There are complex processes which help ensure social actors' alignment with values held within society 'at large'. These are, in part, to anticipate and predict human behaviours. The group matrix is a conceptual tool borne of these lines of thought. It is believed to encompass all communications, conscious and unconscious, 'internal' and external, 'past' and present [37]. Nowadays, the group matrix is thought of as a tripartite communicational field incorporating: the *personal matrix*, which is intended to highlight the more idiosyncratic aspects of our selves such as our psychological traits, relational history and possible interpersonal traumas; the *dynamic matrix*, which in our context may be thought of as the racialised patterns of relationships and communication exchange or dynamics that occur in cross racial exchanges; the *foundation matrix*, which seeks to capture pre-existing configurations, and structures and legacy and meaning we have collectively inherited; and the *social unconscious* [38, 39].

The social unconscious refers to social and cultural communicational arrangements situated at primordial level acquired independently from personal exposure. Rather, it is primarily inherited from collective experiences, shared knowledge/beliefs and symbols/archetypes.

> [The social unconscious] refers to the existence and constraints of social, cultural and communicational arrangements of which we are unaware, as far as these arrangements are not perceived (not 'known'), and if perceived not acknowledged ('denied'), and if acknowledged, not taken as problematic ('given'), and if taken as problematic, not considered with an optimal degree of detachment and objectivity. (Hopper, 2001, p 10 [40])

The social unconscious, as a lens, makes visible the constraints of the social world that we may grasp and enact without conscious awareness, through group inheritance and collective memory. In that vein, it helps us to theorise how whiteness and coloniality may be reproduced within each of those 'levels' of communication and exchange of the matrix. But more than that, it helps us to see how each 'level' of the matrix is co-constitutive of the others. That is to say, memories and fantasies 'located' at historico-symbolic level may, via merging and interpenetration, continue to shape institutional life, structural configurations, relational dynamics and the psychic realities of individual social actors. Durkheim's earlier concept of the collective conscience had already put forth, a century before Foulkes, a formulation as to how individuals come to uphold similar ways of thinking, beings or relating, and how we come together to maintain them [41].

Durkheim described the collective conscience as the sum total of the beliefs, sentiments and attitudes that are shared by the average members of a particular society. This system acquires a life of its own that becomes independent from the individual lives of society's members.

That 'totality of beliefs and sentiments' unifies individuals within society, making society, society. That is to say, an entity of its own existence. The collective conscience maps the relationship between the psyche and the social. Collective consciousness is central to reproducing social institutions such as the education system and the press and thus encapsulates our conditioning within society, our group functioning and the internalisation of cognitive and affective states into which we are born.

Consequently, these ways of feeling and of thinking both exist within each individual and at the same time outside of them, outliving them. The collective conscience, like the social unconscious, posits the existence of collective representations and their embodiment as well as an interdependent relationship between the sociological and the psychological, the individual and the group, the present and the 'past', thus significantly overlapping with group-analytic conceptualisations. However, and most importantly, neither the social unconscious or the collective conscience describe with any degree of precision the particular mechanisms of inheritance, of repetition and re-enactment engaged in ensuring the endurance if not permanence of the social (dis)order; limiting their explanatory power when it comes to understanding the temporality of whiteness.

As I have proposed elsewhere, with the matrix we can nonetheless propose how whiteness may become reproduced within each of those so-called levels of communication and exchange. Crucially, we can see how each 'level' of the matrix is co-constitutive of and therefore shaped by the others. Figure 1.1 is a schematic representation of the matrix [39].

Figure 1.1 provides a visual representation of how historical and symbolic forces (the social unconscious) shape, social structures and configurations (the foundation matrix) that permeate relational functioning (the dynamic matrix) which in turn shapes our psychological landscapes (our personal matrix).

Figure 1.1: A representation of the group matrix

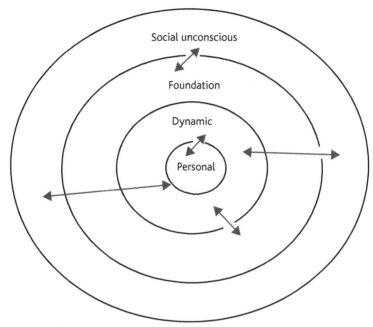

Source: Kinouani (2021)

The matrix challenges Eurocentric individualist and separatist orthodoxies. Although Figure 1.1 is an attempt at both operationalising and visualising these multidirectional communications, each so-called level is porous and interpenetrable. As such, they cannot exist independently.

Repetition compulsion

Repetition compulsion is a concept extracted from classic Freudian theory. Freud saw in repetition one of the most fundamental features of the psyche [42]. His formulation of repetition compulsion was based on his clinical observation that 'forgotten' and repressed emotional experiences often reappeared in the patient's life as symptoms. Psychic manoeuvres or mechanics that therefore ensured the continuity of such experiences as psychosocial entities. Making links with the 'past' to discover from the patient's free associations 'what he failed to remember', or the initial situation which had given rise to the symptom (and was continuing to cause disturbance), required filling 'gaps in memory' or in forgetting to overcome the defence of repression [42, p 157].

The compulsion, he believed, originates from the fact that the painful experience cannot be remembered as something belonging to the 'past'.

Repetition compulsion thus speaks to the impact of trauma and of overwhelming experiences. How might it serve us as groups, as societies or as individuals to repeat what caused us harm, pain or trauma – here, racialised? The precise reasons for repetition compulsion remain a matter of theoretical debate. Freud, in his 1920 essay *Beyond the pleasure principle*, proposed that the death drive, or humans' innate disposition towards destruction and annihilation, leads to the re-enactment of a painful 'past' through our actions. However, it has also been proposed that we feel compelled to repeat the 'past' to foster a sense of consistency or continuation, to create a sense of safe unsafeness because what was painful is, in some ways, known to us. That we repeat to 'work through' the traumatic experience, desperately seeking a different outcome from the one we have obtained in the 'past'. Or simply to exercise power and control over events which might have created unbearable powerlessness and helplessness.

Although initially conceptualised as an individual defence, Freud's thinking has been extended to groups within group analysis, so that it is now believed that groups feel equally compelled to repeat 'past' wounding events or patterns and, thus, to transfer 'past' social configurations, arrangement and feeling states onto present situations, in a way that reproduces the 'past'. The concept of equivalence – group transferences – has been used to define this phenomenon [43]. Through equivalences we may propose that we collectively recreate our oppressive, colonial and imperial history. We repeat over and over what we may seek mastery over, socially. Within racialised configurations an important interrogation follows. Surely, whether the compulsion to repeat is considered an individual or a group process, we need to ask ourselves whose trauma is being repeated when it comes to racial injustice and violence, or, in other words, who is the agent or subject of the repetition. A complex question which invites us to consider racial trauma beyond traditional boundaries of 'victims' and perpetrators and leads us to explore intersubjective factors.

Summary and resistance

In this opening chapter we have considered different conceptualisations of whiteness and started to explore it as an atemporal phenomena orientated towards repetition, re-enactment and continuation. We have seen that for those at the receiving end of white violence, the embodied sense of déjà vu, of having been there before, deeply challenges how we tend to think about time and space and requires us to rethink the Western temporal delineations of 'past', present and future. We have examined how deeply evocative everyday encounters with whiteness can be for the racialised other. Plenty of theories exist to help us formulate that sense of embodied familiarity in the midst of the unknown. We have covered three: social scripts, group processes and, in particular, the group matrix; as well as repetition compulsion. The latter introduces the centrality of trauma to our undertaking. The idea that individuals, groups and society work together to recreate 'past' situations, particularly those within which they have been traumatised, lies at the core of the book. This means that historically significant collective events, mass atrocities and injustices have huge influence on the way we operate in the present, such as how we communicate, interact and arrange social systems. This realisation raises several fundamental questions for social justice, equality and liberation. How might we resist the pull towards the familiar, towards what we call the 'past' and stop the re-enactment of previous harm? How might we resist whiteness' continuation of what has already been? I tentatively suggest that the first step to obtain different social outcomes is to see and recognise the patterns, configurations and scripts we find ourselves caught up in. Disrupting these patterns requires being prepared to confront them directly. This is a significant challenge given the psychological structures these very social patterns give birth to and need to sustain. Once seen and held in mind, there is additionally, at least from an analytic perspective, the need to 'work through' and reclaim disowned unacknowledged collective wounds. These include processes of naming, of grieving losses, including self-concept-related moral injuries. Engaging in sustained reparative work over 'past' injustices is necessary to change over time what constitutes the 'past'. Thus, the creation of new presents requires acting mindfully and arguably more consciously in the world. Thus, in a way, deliberately directed towards social and racial justice. A new world order requires the disruption of the quotidian, of the mundane and of the micro. That is to say, acting in a way that is less scripted and socially determined is one way we may propose to transform the macro structure of whiteness. In the next chapter, we consider how the white gaze functions to fix the other in time, in fact to take it back to a fantasised 'past' so as to maintain the social (dis)order. We also examine ways we may attempt to subvert that gaze.

Notes

[1] Albert Einstein on lifelong friend Michele Besso, in a letter of condolence to the Besso family, 21 March 1955, less than a month before his own death; Einstein Archive 7-245.

[2] Necropolitics essentially refers to the existence of a social order based on the central requirement that some people must die or experience death-like living conditions ('deathworlds') in order for others to live. The decision as to who can live and who must die is reliant on (necro)power. The conceptualisation of necropolitics is attributed to Achille Mbembe and is further discussed and referenced throughout the book, notably in our formulation of sadism (Chapter 4).

[3] According to Wilderson III, to which Afropessism is attributed, anti-black racism or anti-blackness is fixed, permanent and required for the running, organisation and maintenance of white civil society. This regime of violence against black people is framed as a form of ontological negation or death; a state of perpetual enslavement which robs the black subject of their personhood and therefore of any possibility of existing as human in society.

2

White gazes

'Look, a Negro!'
It was an external stimulus that flicked over me as I passed by.
I made a tight smile.
'Look, a Negro!'
It was true. It amused me.
'Look, a Negro!'
The circle was drawing a bit tighter. I made no secret of
my amusement.
'Mama, see the Negro! I'm frightened!' Frightened! Frightened!
Now they were beginning to be afraid of me. I made up my mind
to laugh myself to tears, but laughter had become impossible.
I could no longer laugh, because I already knew that there were
legends, stories, history, and above all historicity, which I had
learned about from Jaspers. (Fanon, 1952, p 84 [1])

Although popularised by Lacan, it was another French intellectual, Sartre (in *Being and nothingness*), who formulated the impact of the gaze [2]. Specifically, Sartre put forth subjectivity's entanglement with the perception of others, since what is perceived, including other people, is turned into objects by our gaze and becomes defined by the gazing subject [3].

Sartre sought to critique Descartes' individualism in the formation of human subjectivity which he saw as distancing the subject from its relational context [4]. With his interrogation of the gaze, Sartre aimed to highlight the influence of the social on the subjective. Lacan further developed these ideas. Extending on from how infants relate to their reflection in mirrors, he proposed that during infancy we come to master a sense of self-awareness through the mirror [5]. Accordingly, human beings go through a process of acquiring self-representation through the reflected image they see of themselves in actual or symbolic mirrors usually; the gaze of others, and primarily that of their caregivers. This gaze allows the creation of a mental or 'internal' representation of an 'I' as the infant attempts to identify with the image which is projected onto them. Lacan later extended his theory from infancy to adulthood and set it as a theory of human subjectivity and identity. In summary, for Lacan, our subjectivity, our perceptions of our selfhood, are fundamentally relational since the mirror stage conceives our identity as contingent upon external objects.

In turn, Fanon elaborated on these formulations and applied them to the formation of subjectivity within the colonial situation. He did an unparalleled study of applying the Lacanian gaze to processes of racialisation. In the short extract which opens this chapter, one of the most famous passages of *Black skin, white masks*, he is describing the phenomenology or the lived experience of being fixed, consumed and displaced in time and in space, by the white gaze. In it, we can see Fanon unpicking in poignant detail the embodied or 'corporeal' effect of black racialisation. What he refers to as the racialised body schema. The felt sense of being displaced through time and space due to the internalisation or 'epidermisation' of whiteness. This too is an experience of being turned into an object, albeit a particular kind of object. An object whose existence, by way of myths, fantasies and anxieties or racial schemas, precedes the essence, the very being, of the black subject while permeating its very core. An object that is 'chewed up' and returned to a mythical primitive, savage Africa. In the passage we therefore get a sense of how the white gaze is, according to Fanon, historicised and cannot be separated from the colonial imagery which swallows a sense of reality and Fanon's very subjectivity. In Fanon's work, we have an evocative articulation of the white gaze and the power it holds to shape, if not transform, the object of its scrutiny. The white gaze, we may therefore say, is a device that stops the clock in that the colonial or black subject is unable to move in time and in space. As such, the white gaze makes 'moving on' from historical trauma virtually impossible.

While links between the Fanonian gaze, Sartre and Lacan's ideas are widely made, the influence of De Beauvoir on Fanon's phenomenology of racialisation, which is undeniable, is frequently absent from racialised theorisations. However, *The second sex* was published three years before *Black skin, white masks*, in 1949, and De Beauvoir was a close contemporary of Fanon. In her book, which is an oeuvre on how women become the other, the feminist and philosopher theorises that the category of woman is man-made. First, it is man-made in the sense that, as she famously opens the book, 'one is not born a woman but rather becomes a woman' through trauma-loaded discursive practices. Practices which she proposes map onto developmental biological processes such as menstruation and 'sexual maturation' or the painful initiation of girls into sexual intercourse. Put differently, it is socio-political processes rather than biological ones which create women.

Second, and crucially, taking up Sartre's formation of the subjective, she proposes that women come into existence through the othering male gaze. A gaze which reduces women to the status of objects because it is men who are the seers, the gazing subjects. Her central idea of 'becoming flesh' – which clearly maps onto Fanon's epidermalisation – proposes that as they become women, girls' bodies are snatched away from them by the male gaze: 'The young girl feels that her body is getting away from her … on the street men follow her with their eyes and comment on her anatomy. She would like to be invisible; it frightens her to become flesh and to show flesh' [6, p 333].

Contemporary race scholars have integrated the impact of the white gaze on everyday racial dynamics and on the temporality of racialisation, drawing from a phenomenological reading of Fanon, whose theorisation on the white gaze he mainly initiated in the French context, and in dialogue with De Beauvoir's formulation. Yancy writes: 'It is a particular experience to have one's body confiscated without having physically been placed in chains' [17, p 20]. In his encounter with white women in elevators in white America, Yancy explores the experience of being confiscated from himself. Of having his black body snatched away from him by the white gaze. An experience he historicises and links to processes of enslavement and, in particular, the confiscation of African bodies to fulfil European capitalist modes of production. Confronted with the distorted meanings of blackness as a toxic, loaded signifier which is reflected back at him, he sees himself imagined as a criminal and as a threat '*in deed*', in the absence of any threatening or criminal action. He experiences the fear of a white woman, who 'shifts nervously … [as] her heart beats more quickly'. He sees her 'clutch her purse closely to her', he is a witness to the anxiety she feels 'in the pit of her stomach' [17, p 21]. The white woman's panic at the mere presence of blackness in the elevator – the elevator effect – a blackness embodied by a man, deprives Yancy of the presumption of innocence. To be seen as criminal in this elevator is therefore not to be seen at all. For the black subject, the encounter means disappearing in space as he is not witnessed. For the white one, Yancy hypothesises, time disappears in space, the encounter feels like eternity as blackness is experienced as an omnipotent force, occupying every breathing corner of the elevator.

While, here, Yancy focuses on the 'bodily repertoire' and affective responses underpinning the racialised use and experience of time and space in the US, Ngo, in the Australian context, examines the discursive processes, including white ignorance and forgetting, that render white bodies temporally present and futural in orientation, free from the legacy of the 'past', while affixing the racialised and postcolonial subject to the 'past' [8]. She first proposes, like Fanon, that the black and/or brown body continues to be tied down to mythical and primitive pasts today, a 'past' maintained by public imaginaries since the process of colonialism itself requires the racialised other to be constructed as 'an earlier expression' of humanity, a group lower down the evolutionary chain than those racialised as white. Second, she notes that postcolonial bodies' identities are constantly framed in terms of 'past' orientation because of whiteness' preoccupation with their ancestry as illustrated by micro-aggressive questions: 'Where are you from originally?'

'Where did your parents come from?' Finally, and critically to her argument and in line with Fanon's, the 'past' to which these subjugated subjects are fixed is not in fact a 'past' that is recognisable to them, that is to say, it is not their 'past' since it is mythical and constructed by white projections.

For Yancy, Ngo and Fanon, the 'Africa' or 'blackness', which is projected on racially othered bodies through the white gaze, is both a time in history and a space in the geopolitical sense. Africa becomes a space-time, one that is nonetheless always imaginary. It is imagined as primitive or criminal; as dangerous and debased. Bodies, space and time are therefore intrinsically linked. It is through space that bodies express themselves and act in and on the world, it is through space that bodies can therefore experience the world, that they can come to be, and become free to move or be held immobile by other bodies. It follows that without space there can be no subjectivity, communication or power relations [9], or, as Ahmed puts it: 'Bodies are shaped by this contact with objects. What gets near is both shaped by what bodies do, and in turn affects what bodies can do' [10, p 153]. The policing and ordering of the category of space, actual or fantasised, allows whiteness to become inscribed within particular geographies [11]. Geographies it then inscribes in the black or brown subject, and this policing, Ahmed further argues, 'holds' through habits [10]. Public spaces, spaces where white, black and brown bodies interact, are therefore shaped by the habitual actions of bodies and how these have been conditioned to move in particular spaces.

A cultural note

Star Wars' black actors have spoken about the racism they experienced upon being selected to perform in the movie franchise, including John Boyega and Kelly Marie Tran. More recently, Moses Ingram spoke out about the harassment she experienced when she was offered the role of Reva Sevander in *Obi-Wan Kenobi*, the 2022 Disney series about the return of the Jedi. Referring to the hateful comments she received, she stated that 'there are hundreds of them, hundreds' in an Instagram post [12].

The resistance, if not hostility, to black and brown bodies inhabiting Space, and science fiction more broadly, we may argue, is resistance and hostility to imagining the racialised other, first, as inhabiting the future, while being preoccupied with paranoid thoughts about them colonising the future, and second, and consequently, being in existence in the present. As stand-up comedian Richard Pryor astutely commented in his routine which touched upon the absence of blackness in the 1976 sci-fi movie, *Logan's Run*: '[I]t's set in the future there ain't no black people in it! White folks ain't planning for us to be there' [13]. And if whiteness does not want us in the future, we may add, it is because it does not want us 'here', in the present [13]. In fact, it is because it requires us to remain relics of this 'past' with no futural existence. There is a disturbingly long trail of actors of colour who have been subjected to racial abuse and harassment for taking up roles in sci-fi films or, being cast to inhabit Space. The bordering of space, which is also the bordering of the imaginary, necessarily leads to the bordering of Space in the extra-terrestrial sense. The white gaze, we may argue, continues to function to police these geographies and spatiotemporal realities by habit, leaving little room for the objects of its gaze to experience and imagine themselves outside of the borders it imposes. As such, we can argue that the policing of space is the policing of bodies, and the policing of bodies is also the policing of time. This interconnection, which here is mediated by the white gaze, means that each 'entity' can therefore explicate the others. And thus, whiteness may express itself, be experienced and understood through bodies, movement and through space; all of which have the potential to tell us something important, if we pay attention, about interdependent subjectivities as well as about socio-political arrangements, 'past' and present.

In summary, through its gaze, the white subject manipulates, shapes, controls and oftentimes displaces the object. Experiencing one's reflection through racialised mirrors is different from seeing one's reflections through the gaze of loving subjects. Oppressive gazes lead to self-alienation and a fragmented sense of self. They lead to a form of ontological death as the objects of the gaze experience themselves as 'non-beings' [1]. As things [14]. And, as the ultimate others [6]. In any case, this gaze bars us from experiences of mutuality and reciprocity which are central to what renders us human.

Everyday performance

'On Wednesday mornings, once a month, I'd walk into a meeting of the entire faculty. Often, I was late, as I lived further away than most of the other (older, mostly white) faculty. Often, I was the only faculty member of colour in that space. I blurred my eyes as I sat down. Once, the only empty chair in the double circle of chairs was in the front row. I felt the heat in my body as the gazes of my colleagues bounced off my skin. Was I metallic? In the break, a colleague asked: "Are you okay?" in a concerned tone. And then: "I saw the look on your face when we were speaking about diversity issues." In that moment, I understand that the many arrows or vectors, the many gazes I felt passing through me, slicing the air around my body, came from progressive colleagues as much as the colleagues who were angered that their syllabi were being interrogated for the lack of any bodies (presences) that did not resemble them. It was too much. I sometimes had the same feeling when I walked into a restaurant with my family. En masse, everyone (white) looking up from their plates, towards where we were standing at the door, waiting for the waitress to seat us, then away.' (Aisha, Asian woman, 40s, US)

This story offers a contemporary lived experience of the white gaze as an intruding force for black and brown bodies. Fixating white eyes here are seen as piercing the structure or boundaries of the mind and body of the object, leaving them inhabited, occupied and transformed. In Aisha's story, the gaze was activated by the discussion on 'diversity'. She is the only person of colour in the meeting room. All sets of white eyes in this room turn on her as the only person of colour in the space and in the process put the spotlight on her otherness. She becomes self-conscious. She has been colonised. A well-intentioned, albeit arguably paternalistic, colleague asks how Aisha is. They could have asked what was happening in the room or whether the white team was OK. Instead, and no doubt out of 'care', they continue to fix her as the object of their collective gaze, the source of the disturbance or pathology in the room. The one needing rescuing or saving.

Doing so naturally increases Aisha' sense of displacement, her body self-consciousness and colour-awareness. That embodied self-consciousness creates a kind of ontological malaise or a malaise in her being in that white space. She recognises that disturbing embodied experience. Like many of us, she has been there before, albeit in other settings. The meeting of the gaze freezes her in time and space and take her to a place of vulnerability and space precariousness. That freezing of us in time and in space is paradoxically a mechanism of white escapism. By locating the focus or disturbance on Aisha, the group escapes its own sense of incompetence and ignorance. The group essentially flees itself. It attempts to flee its whiteness.

The white gaze as a white shield

We have seen that the white gaze creates a form of prison. For Fanon, this is the inescapability of blackness for bodies racialised as black. The white gaze, however, also has structural consequences beyond the psychic and beyond the normalisation of racial stereotypes or colonial tropes. One of these consequences has been that relative lack of attention paid to the psychological worlds of white groups, which we have started to problematise. This absence is neither coincidental nor innocuous and because, as we are about to see, it serves numerous functions for the protection of whiteness, we may posit that discursive mechanisms are silently in operation when whiteness is not seen and named. In other words, not being seen and named is a device, possibly the main one, that allows whiteness to be reproduced silently and invisibly. This is a device that locates otherness or 'difference' and thus disturbance onto those with less social power, here the racialised object. It repeats the experience of embodied racial trauma.

Consequently, focusing on the psychological functioning of black and brown groups reproduces colonial schemas by continuing to position us as exotic objects of curiosity. Traditionally, as we have covered in the introduction, the scholarly gaze has been white [15]. It has put its focus on what it has naturally found to be strange and intriguing from an unquestioned normative position. The racial figurations of Others have inexorably relied on the white gaze, its fantasies and, with them, the power to sustain emotional, structural and interpersonal 'them and us' divisions which have barred us from the power to self-define [16].

By ensuring no scrutiny can be placed on the gazing white subject, the white gaze makes it impossible for white subjects to fully know themselves. This absence of scrutiny is a direct correlate to the lack of structural accountability that ensures not only that social inequality and violence can flourish unchallenged, but that they become naturalised and objectivised. The normalisation of racial inequality is achieved, in part, through the framing of inequality as either accidental – often overtly but disingenuously – or as the product of legitimate if not inherent differences in merit, talent and aptitudes (usually more covertly but often with more conviction). As a powerful projective mechanism, the white gaze therefore acts as a black screen or, as Fanon may say, a white mask. Not only does it fundamentally construct the identity and subjectivity of the other, thus denying their sense of self, but it also helps to ensure white subjectivities remain impenetrable.

The white gaze thus produces and reproduces the structural arrangements that maintain white power. These white supremacist structural realities in turn come to further shape the internal landscapes of white subjects, in particular, their internalised racial superiority which has the effect of making the white gaze all the more potent. The internal–external boundary comes into question. In other words, the white gaze is both cause and effect of white superiority, which requires meritocratic thinking and more indirectly racial essentialism to justify race inequality. Put another way, by implicitly stating there is 'nothing to see here', or that 'this is all about you', the white gaze excludes itself as an object of interest, investigation and scrutiny. It further feeds into the psychological functioning of white groups, specifically here reinforcing supremacist worldviews, without the need to explicitly express supremacist worldviews.

Still, the reasoning to explain social outcomes remains, really, the same. Some groups are simply less than 'us'. Or, at best, social outcomes and inequality are self-generated and have nothing to do with 'us'. The white gaze, we may therefore say, is a fiercely defensive gaze. It is a gaze that acts as a shield and makes it near impossible to not only understand processes that sustain race inequality in society, but, affectively, it also makes white hearts equally inaccessible when it comes the harm of whiteness. In the meeting, we saw how fixating Aisha in the group's gaze essentially allowed it to avoid facing itself and therefore its need to know about the 'diversity' issues at hand. Aisha existed in the space to act both as distraction and redirection.

A cultural note

On 29 March 2019, and reporting from Green Park in Westminster in the vicinity of large Brexit protests and rallies, senior British journalist, Jon Snow, commented on the street disturbance he was witnessing by uttering the following words: 'I've never seen so many white people in one place' [17]. This simple and factual sentence, since it was overwhelmingly white people who took to the streets in the pro-Brexit demonstrations, provoked collective anguish and anger. These ten words triggered one of the highest numbers of complaints the broadcast regulator Ofcom had ever received. The regulator investigated and eventually cleared Channel 4 News of any wrongdoing [18]. It found in its ruling the comment to be 'sufficiently contextualised' despite having 'the potential to cause offence'. Channel 4 News stated it regretted the offence caused by the 'unscripted' remark.

A contemporary piece of British political and media history that is bound to leave many readers incredulous, and which certainly requires a little exploration. It is extraordinary that a white journalist calling a group of people racialised as white, white, could trigger such an intense national response. It is even more extraordinary that Snow's comments were even deemed to have the potential to cause offence to the same people who would not think twice about referring to, say, people racialised as black as black people. The response to Snow's words, in and of itself, is an arresting manifestation of whiteness' desire to remain nameless and invisible. It provides a contemporary example of how whiteness resists being the object of gazes. More than that, it illustrates how deep collective anxieties are. When it comes to white racialisation, these anxieties are never too far from the surface in contemporary Britain.

An autoethnographic note

About ten years ago, a group of white women came together to make a complaint against me in a higher education setting. The essence of their disgruntlement was that I was taking too much space, that I was talking about race too much, that I was intimidating and that I was 'not aware of my own power'. Of particular note, the group also shared some collective fantasy that I was 'writing all the time' and thus feared I would write badly about them. At the time, I had not written anything but academic assignments.

I was thinking about becoming a writer, but clearly I was not one. Yet the grossly paranoid fear of the harm my non-existent words had the potential to cause them was already present in their mind, if only unconsciously. I too was imagined as a threat. A threat to be neutralised, contained, gagged. Their fear of my writing felt alien to me. I could not connect with the power they saw in me and to what I had become in their imagination. I was disconnected from my own power. I now write. And I have been writing about race. The incident ironically acted as a motivational force. It is difficult to argue, thus, that the group of white women had not picked up something accurately. Even if their move may have been drenched in misogynoir and a mixture of reality and fantasy. Still, perhaps they saw something I did not see in myself. They intuited something about the potential of my words that I did not recognise, the mirror image they were projecting onto and into me did not align with my self-concept.

The fear of being seen by me and then of being exposed and thus through my words of being seen by others, brings to the fore a different aspect of the mirroring phenomenon. The paranoid fantasy that I could expose them is, we may argue, evidence that there were parts of themselves they were struggling to connect with too. Parts they did not want to see. Not least of all, their disavowed racism and aggression. But also, we may argue, their wish for power and the disowning of such a wish, for more space and, perhaps too, a desire for a capacity to write which resulted in what was essentially, at least in part, an envious attack.

This anecdote also speaks of whiteness' fear of the black gaze, consequently of the gaze being reversed. Because the direction of the gaze has always been the direction of power as we have argued, and 'to look a white man in the eyes … is to forget one's place in the natural scheme of things' [7, p 222]. The act of reverting the gaze is an act of subversion. The oppositional gaze, an expression first coined by bell hooks, seeks to do just that. To challenge and disrupt the racialised (dis)order maintained by images of blackness that perpetuate the sorts of 'stereotypes' which legitimise and lead to anti-black violence. In effect, to be an image is also to be fixed in time and often in space. The oppositional gaze aims to create spaces where blackness can exist outside of the constraints imposed upon it by the white gaze. It seeks to free blackness so it can move through artistic, visual and cultural productions. And since moving through artistic, visual and cultural productions is to exist in alternative imaginaries, the oppositional gaze creates spaces which in turn make it possible for blackness to simply move through space.

We may say the fear of being seen by me speaks of that oppositional gaze which today cannot expressly or directly be ordered down. This fear, we may argue, rather than being exclusively fantasy-based, is in fact reality-based. The white subject is haunted by the fear of being seen as racist, which really translates as the fear of being known and therefore, by extension, the fear of themselves. Perhaps we can start to understand how the colonial gaze was always a way to stop the colonised subject from seeing. And undeniably, for centuries, colonised and enslaved bodies have been ordered to 'lower their gaze'. It is unlikely that this demand was only an enactment of status or the wish to crush defiance and opposition. There was always a plea in this order. Please do not see me for what I am. And, perhaps too, I do not want to see my own reflection in the mirror that is your eyes. The fear of being seen links to the fear of black anger [19]. If one knows intimately that anger is a legitimate response to subjugation and injustice, then being seen as oppressive would also mean risking being exposed to that rage. That is to say, being seen also implies seeing reality. The white fear of confronting black and brown rage does not only lead to the fear of associated oppositional gazes, but also to the pacifying of anger and by extension the maligning of anger which won't be pacified.

My autoethnographic and cultural note illustrate how the fears of being recognised and being met are significant in the psychosocial organisation of whiteness. A fear closely related to the desire to remain in the shadows, unnamed and unmarked, here as protection from the risk of revenge. There is arguably nothing that perpetrators of violence or oppressors fear more in the objects of their violence than their memory, thus their capacity to remember the harm that was caused to them, the anger and, with it, the associated wishes, if not impulses, for justice, retribution and/ or reparation for the wrong they experienced. The fear of revenge or the fear of death is therefore intricately linked to resistance to justice. The white gaze is therefore a useful tool both psychologically and structurally to prevent justice.

White fears when it comes to black anger force us to rethink power. The socially sanctioned and loudly applauded act of forgiveness for racism, colonialism or imperialism, we may say, is an act of social control and psychic sanitisation. The social expectation of forgiveness from the racially brutalised is fundamentally a self-sacrifice demand, in the sense that the black or brown body is expected to bypass their grief, mourning and sense of injustice to maintain the social (dis)order as well as the 'white psychic equilibrium'. The structural function of these defences which are in the service of the white racial equilibrium is defined as: 'A social, historical, and cultural location where whiteness is insulated from critique and the importance of race is largely ignored by white people. The expectation of the white racial equilibrium is one way white people define their whiteness, and this expectation protects white supremacist epistemologies and ideologies' [20]. We are expected to silence if not bury and repress the impact of racial violence and therefore to beautify the ugliness of racism. And so too often we learn to split off from it as we mirror white dissociation.

Another autoethnographic note

Imagine that you are spending time together with your peers as an undergraduate student, on this occasion the location is a quiet corner of the university library. Among your comrades is a young white woman. You are about the same age, somewhere between your late teens and early 20s. As it is the start of the year, you don't know much about her, but you do know already that she is particularly fond of black men. More than fond, in fact, she has a ferocious sexual appetite for them. You know this because she systematically recounts her sexual adventures of the previous weekend each time you meet, and the men she discusses are always black. In the group you are the only black person, in fact the only body who is not white in your cohort.

As she describes in the most intimate of details her sexual encounters – where they laid her hands on her, where she placed her body on theirs, how they moved, 'what she made them do' to her in front of an audience of mildly aroused and wildly curious young white women – you feel deeply uncomfortable. But you do not say so. It's hard for you to understand what in the spectacle on display is disturbing. Nor can you quite articulate how degrading you find the scenes portrayed but you feel it deeply in your body. You are still young, after all, and perhaps anxious to fit in. You have not yet been exposed to sophisticated scholarly ideas around race, the exotic, fetishisation, racialised sexual phantasm. You hardly even understand white supremacy. Still, in the superficially jovial but sexually charged atmosphere, you note that you get more than your fair share of gazes and stares from the orator. It feels to you as though you are the main audience for the performance. You say nothing. It will take you years to even grasp some of the dynamics and phenomena at play.

We could spend much time thinking at length about sexual encounters between women racialised as white and men racialised as black. Although we would no doubt have plenty to say, plenty has already been said about this. Instead, let us focus on the complexities of relations between women racialised as white and women racialised as black. We may get some sense of these relations through the experience shared in the autoethnographic note. That is to say, we will attend to the quieter phenomenon, which is adjacent to the louder sexual fetishisation and adds an intersectional dimension to the white gaze. The repeated stares directed at me in the group as the body, who happens to be racialised as black and gendered as woman, provides rich material to expound the very particular kind of feminised gaze directed on that situated object that was me, as I was made to witness narratively the retelling of these sexualised encounters.

The white female gaze

Although it tends to be discarded from our usual theorisation, the micro yet rich encounter between me and the white woman storyteller via her furtive yet insistent gaze reminds us that oppression is a sexualised project. In this story, we have a clash of liberatory agendas. We have a white woman, albeit young, who it appears is reclaiming for herself sexual desire, attraction, erotic wishes, wants and needs, loudly and unapologetically. An act, it would seem, of sexual liberation, a gendered transgression, for certain. But that act of sexual liberation is messy. It is messy because it is bound up in racialised oppression and in the enactment of a double subjugation. A subjugation that is both racialised and gendered. It is a form of subjugation directed both at the object of her fetishised sexual desire, the black men, and the object of her gaze in the white space within which she retells her sexual tales, me.

The objectification of blackness and the rearticulation of racialised sexual constructions or chimeras are at the core of anti-black racism and colonial logics in that space. Here we have the usual use of black subjects as objects of white narcissistic supply for the purpose of self-aggrandisement, gratification and sexual consumption.

Much has been written about the sexualised foundation of white supremacy. Many scholars have studied the links between sex and racial subjugation. The black or colonial body has long been constructed as a repository of white groups' unacceptable sexual desires, drives, wishes and wants.

According to Fanon, for example – an idea we will revisit later in the book – the fear of the fantasised unbounded sexual power of men racialised as black leads to neuroses in the men racialised as white which are rooted in a fear of sexual inadequacy or impotency [1]. It is this same racialised sexual phantasm, he argues, that gives birth to acts of atrocities towards black men, such as castrations physical and symbolic, so frequently found within colonial and racial violence. Further, white supremacy has required the use of misogyny-loaded sexual violence to sustain the status quo and so it is vital that we remember rape culture's entanglement with white supremacy. It is, for example, through systematised rape and breeding practices (also rape) that the system of enslavement kept going. Colonial 'punishment' has always included sexual degradation and torture. Similarly, cultures of 'concubinage' normalised in the colonies, the bypassing of sexual consent when it came to colonialist–colonised intimate 'encounters'.

Stories of the screams originating from 'rape camps' consisting of women held hostage and sexually brutalised by colonial agents if men failed to meet ivory or rubber quotas in both Congos, are passed on intergenerationally, are still being told. They are corroborated by historians [21]. This is just a tiny snapshot of the macabre relationship between the (racialised) necropolitical and the sexual. We could quite easily argue that racial violence is always sexualised violence and perhaps even that the sexual charge is loaded in necrophilia. And arguing that racial violence is sexualised violence also means arguing that white women engaged in racism will enact sexual violence.

However, while reflections on the gaze on racialised and gendered grounds are long-standing, there has been extraordinarily little interrogation of the gaze integrating intersectional thinking [22]. What is being argued is that the white male gaze is not experienced as, say, the black male gaze. Similarly, the white female gaze is not quite the white male gaze (and how these gazes are experienced is of course going to be dependent, to some degree, on the object's positionality and history). Gender figurations and social expectations mean white women claiming race-based power or sexual power openly or enacting them aggressively is gender-transgressive, creating the need for more complex subtle enactments. While white men may find it near impossible to avoid sexual harassment claims if they were to be too overly interested in the sexuality of a black woman peer or colleague, white women, most likely, can get away with such sexual intrigue, which take us to the intersection of whiteness and patriarchy in the genesis of rape culture.

Rape culture has been defined as:

[A]n environment where sexual harassment, sexual violence and rape are expected, normalized, excused. Rape culture is said to be perpetuated through complex devices including misogynistic language, the objectification of women's bodies, and the glamorisation of such violence. (MYMU, 2022 [23])

In summary, according to the Equalities Act, harassment is conduct that has the purpose or effect of violating your safety or dignity. Conduct that intimidates, humiliates or degrades, here on the ground of sex and/or race.

Everyday performance

I met a black woman. She was distraught. She worked in a school, as a psychologist, and used to wear knee-length skirts. She explained that she had received a formal invitation to attend a meeting, the purpose of which had not been defined. When she joined the meeting, she was greeted by a 'panel' of managers who wanted to discuss her wardrobe. She was warned 'informally' in that meeting by her 'superiors' – who comprised only white women managers – against wearing skirts. She was shocked and unprepared for the conversation as her skirts did not breach the school's dress code. When she asked why she was being singled out for wearing skirts, given women staff were routinely wearing them too, she was told that she had 'a different body type' which was 'more sexual' and could distract the students. Once more, hard to imagine that a group of men, white or not, alluding to a black woman's physicality being a potential turn-on, would not attract well-founded accusations of sexual harassment, at the very least. Hard to argue too that positioning this black colleague as the body to be restrained, contained, policed and held accountable for some fantasised sexual misconduct is not an enactment of rape culture.

Considerations of the white gaze have in the main excluded white women from its performance. Likely because the white woman's body is, through patriarchy, subjected to the male gaze. Partly due to cisheteronormativity and the notion that sexually abusive relations can only take place between a man and a woman, with the (cishet) man being the only possible sexual transgressor imaginable. Partly also due to white patriarchal notions of innocence, purity and virtuosity which continue to protect white women from accountability. But looking back at my own lived experience and having spoken to hundreds of black women about this phenomenon, I can say without hesitation that I have experienced more sexualised harassment at the hands of white women within institutions than I have at the hands of men of any racial background. Without a shadow of a doubt. And I know through my conversations over the years with black women that I am not alone in this experience. In fact, I believe it may well be the rule rather than the exception.

The harassment enacted mainly through the white woman's gaze is not accounted for, it is, in the main, invisibilised. It is therefore not even considered harassment. Let alone sexual harassment. But, from curiosity about 'sex with black men' in work contexts to other intrusive sexualised questions in higher education contexts all the way to sneers, the disregarding of personal boundaries, non-consensual bodily contact with our body or hair, constant gossip or enquiries about the shape of our body, the colour of our body, the hair that grows or does not grow out of our body, or even the weight of our body, the sexual component is unmistakable yet not seen. Or it is seen but not named and thus not owned. And, even though these behaviours are as much of a sexualised nature as they are of a racialised nature, their sexualised dimension, it seems, cannot be tolerated.

I suggest it cannot be tolerated because it deeply challenges cisheteropatriarchal notions of female sexuality. It also challenges racialised formations of white womanhood. The gender or race of the person engaging in sexual harassment or in reproducing rape culture is irrelevant to these forms of domination being in operation. Denying white women's capacity to enact a sexualised white gaze is a socially sanctioned device that helps white women, as a group, to disown their sexual agency and continue to position themselves as passive, submissive and innocent objects within racialised relations, sexualised configurations and within society at large. It is disavowing their power and capacity to also commit sexualised violence often, more covertly – though not always. Perhaps this is perfectly illustrated by the furtive yet insistent stares I experienced from the white woman as she described her sexual encounters with men racialised as black. Through the white female gaze, patriarchy and whiteness meet and keep racialised misogynistic structures intact. However, the phenomenon we are grappling with is not unique to the relations of these two social groups. We could posit, outside of a racialised lens, that cishet women routinely sexually harass trans, queer, lesbian and bi women. Non-disabled women sexually harass disabled women, and so on. That sexual harassment is so prevalent within power relations indicates something about the centrality of rape culture and its transmission across time and space. This is a disturbing reminder of how so much of how we relate to bodies deemed other is violently sexualised.

Summary and resistance

Interconnections between the psyche, history and society are partly mediated through the white gaze. The white gaze fixes the other. This experience of being fixed is embodied and deeply evocative for the objects of the gaze. It is embodied experience that is so loaded that it often leads to nausea, to an existential malaise and a sense of displacement in time and in space. As a result, the white gaze is an intruding and colonising force. Deep and disowned fears, we have proposed, hide behind the white gaze, and as such we can see that the white gaze also functions as a shield. The fear of being seen, which is heavily underscored by the fear of anger in the object of white violence, does not sit too far away, according to Baldwin, from self-hate. The white gaze serves critical structural functions, this is both a cause and effect of psychological and structural realities. And so, the psychic and the social are in turn shaped by the gaze. Beyond individuals, the white gaze enables entire white societies and white groups to continue to be blind to their own functioning. Nowhere is this truer than when it comes to white women's contributions to this gendered and sexualised gaze which has escaped theoretical scrutiny. The white gaze thus renders the white subject alien to parts of themselves. It blocks alternative truths and insights which can only come about by the use of an oppositional gaze as invited by bell hooks. Shifting the gaze is occupying space differently, moving differently and in effect simply being able to move. This freedom of movement is in turn linked to the redistribution of epistemic power. As epistemic power is co-constitutive of other forms of power, since the suppression of black women's ideas has been critical in maintaining social inequality [24], defining and theorising whiteness from the embodied perspective of black women not only shifts the direction of the gaze, but it also has important consequences beyond the epistemic. It reorganises psychic and social structures that impact on and shape our existence. And so, reclaiming the power to know and expressing what is, will also invariably be reclaiming institutional and structural power, thus reorganising the material. Consequently, our insistence on speaking what we see, on giving names that stick, here in relation to whiteness, is not only oppositional, transgressive and defiant of the white gaze, it is in fact a transformational act. For those racialised as white, words that disrupt the white gaze will deeply disturb the self. Staying with that disturbance is necessary to engage in processes of resistance. In the following chapter we explore the links between envy and whiteness and interrogate the role of envy in day-to-day white performances.

3

White envy

What are you without racism? Are you any good? Are you still strong? Are you still smart? Do you still like yourself? If you can only be tall when someone is on their knees, you have a serious problem and I think white people have a profoundly serious problem and I suggest they start thinking about what they are going to do about it. (Morrison, 1993 [1])

A cultural note

The year 2018 saw the release of the long-awaited superhero film based on the Marvel comic of the same name, *Black Panther*. *Black Panther* is the first film in the Marvel cinematic collection centred on a superhero of colour: black prince King T'Challa. The movie, which is set in the imaginary African location of Wakanda, also sees a virtually all-black cast defeat its enemy, avoid colonial invasion and successfully head a global technological revolution. Although the film can and has been astutely critiqued for its use of Western colonial motifs and significant capitalistic imaginary, its cultural significance is indisputable. Commensurate with this significance and the storyline which portrayed black subjects beautifully, and as agents of their own destiny, was the black joy that instantly erupted upon the release of the movie. By black joy here I simply mean a shared and collective sense of joy among groups racialised as black originating from the same event.

Black Panther brought a significant sense of euphoric pride in black groups across the diaspora, and although I focus here on the UK, videos of celebrations and joyful communication and dances shared on social media from across the world suggest that joy may have been global. With that joy came a significant backlash. I have observed it mainly online through the racist comments and abusive trolling of those seen to be happily tweeting about the movie or singing its praises. Anonymous social media accounts and identifiable figures came forth en masse as a reaction. Many, it appeared, worked hard to spoil the moment, deriding it, mocking the joy and even racially abusing those expressing it. It is clear that the hate-filled responses were not only acts of opposition to the quality of the movie, or forms of critiques, as it may be tempting to propose. Any astute observer would have recognised in the intensity of the bitterness and in the relentlessness of the attacks that these responses were detraction and opposition to black joy. I wish to suggest that the racist trolling and harassment campaigns were symptomatic of something significant. Here I posit white envy, which the chapter will attempt to explore.

As a society, we find talking about envy difficult. Possibly as hard as we find talking about sex. There is still a taboo around both subject matters. The two are intricately linked, at least when it comes to whiteness. Envy and sex continue to affect race relations. Envy is the direct product of our history and continuing racial stratification. It took many years for me to be able to broach the subject of envy and name it as a factor and a dynamic in many of my encounters with whiteness and to come to the conclusion that envy lies at the very core of my experience of racism. This envy is in part sexualised and I had to allow myself to think seriously about the everyday expression of this dynamic. A peer recently shared with me that, upon reading the parts of an academic article of mine which named white envy to a white woman, she exclaimed to him, full of anger and outrage, that I was an 'imbecile' not deserving of a doctoral qualification for believing such a thing, since no sane white woman could ever be envious of a black woman. Perfectly demonstrating, of course, the very thesis of the article she sought to critique.

Everyday performance

'The experience I will share raised so many questions and feelings about my whiteness – one of quite a few incidents that has eventually led me to now focus my art practice and PhD research on revealing and interrogating whiteness as anti-racist "activism". I'm a white woman and I was out in Manchester one evening with my black boyfriend (this was the early 1990s and we were both students at the university – we later married and had two children). At the bus station waiting to go home we were targeted by a group of drunk young white men who started hassling us verbally with racial slurs ('n' word-lover) and overly aggressive behaviour. They were incensed at the sight of an interracial couple. I tried to intervene, but they surrounded my boyfriend, knocked him to the ground and kicked him. This was going on in full view of everyone at the bus station. No one did anything. The men stopped when their bus was leaving. My boyfriend was kicked badly in the eye, and we had to go to A&E. Luckily, he suffered no long-term physical damage. The men were eventually prosecuted, we had to go to court, and they received a fine. In terms of my feelings about this it's a powerful mix of guilt, shame, anger and responsibility. I'm so aware that it wouldn't have happened if he hadn't been with me. It's made me feel like I have a latent power that can be exploited against my will. Although the men threatened to hit me, they didn't, which summons feelings of fragility, innocence and all the things that have made white women so dangerous to black men over the centuries.' (Emma, white Italian woman, 40s, England)

As illustrated by the opening quote by Morrison, racism is needed. Not only to construct white self-concepts but to keep existential angst at bay. Envy fulfils this broader function. There is much in this 'everyday performance' story that has strong historical echoes. The social transgression of a black man–white woman romantic entanglement. The brutalisation of the man racialised as black by a group of men racialised as white. The hostility triggered by the confrontation of this 'mixed couple'. The theme of sexualised envy, which we'll return to later in the chapter, dominates. Apart from the prosecution of the white assailants, the anecdote, which took place in the 1990s, could well have happened half a century ago, if not a century earlier. Similarly, while the racist assault took place in urban England, it has echoes of the lynching events taking place in some places, namely the Deep South of the US. The story reminds us of the centrality of sex in racist violence and with that patriarchal constructions of white women as property to be protected from lustful and sexually aggressive black men which continue to have a solid hold on white imaginaries. This is particularly evident when the man racialised as black in some other ways appears to transgress social expectations and thus his place in the racialised stratification.

A cultural note

A decade and a half or so ago, a 'mixed' (cishet) couple was murdered in rural France. The husband was black. He was a doctor. He was also one of the few doctors practising in their village and, simply, one of a few people racialised as black. His wife was racialised as white. They had, I think, two kids. Everyone was killed. When the killer, a white man, was caught, he explained fairly calmly that he simply could not stand seeing the family doing so well and that looking at the kids 'always looking nice and well dressed' was causing him distress. When this tragic event occurred, I was already living in England, and the affair was big news in France. I remember discussing it with my sister who was also living in rural France, whose family was similarly the only black family around and who was doing equally well materially. I have occasionally revisited this story as I grappled with understanding envy in racism. It struck a chord and had a chilling effect partly because it contained the essence of a dynamic, albeit an extreme expression, that we recognised and have experienced at more micro and everyday levels.

A historical note

The People's Grocery Store was an African American store in Memphis, Tennessee in 1892 [2]. The store was owned by Thomas Moss, a family man and valued member of the local African American community, and two of his friends. Memphis, which was the fifth-largest wholesale grocery market at the time, saw escalating racial tensions after the Civil War as people racialised as black sought opportunities for economic emancipation. Upon its creation, the People's Grocery Store was instantly successful. It not only brought capital to the local African American community but also helped build a sense of pride and racial optimism. The store found itself in competition with a nearby white-owned grocery store belonging to William Barrett. Barrett's store had been in operation before the black-owned store started trading. The success of the store created resentment and bitterness in white residents. And, as its success grew, so did Barrett's hostility. Race relations deteriorated. Taking advantage of these racial tensions and, under false pretences, a group of white residents, supported by law enforcement, orchestrated an attack against the store, but, as staff at the People's Grocery Store, who were not eligible for police protection, anticipated the attack, they had arranged for armed men to watch and protect the store.

Altercations followed and led to a shootout between white and black residents, during which three men racialised as white were shot. This self-defensive posture by the black store owners and their clear willingness to take to arms to defend their interests and their safety took the white community by surprise. It struck terror into the hearts of white residents. A terror in part fuelled by anti-black sensationalist headlines and, no doubt too, by this evergreen fear of black payback. Eventually, Barrett fabricated a story and alleged that police officers had been shot by black residents in their line of duty and that staff at the People's Grocery Store were plotting to seek revenge on white groups. As a result of this conspiracy story, Moss and his associates, together with more than 100 black residents, were arrested and jailed. A few days later, on 2 March 1892, a mob of 75 white men wearing black masks dragged the owners of the People's Grocery Store from jail and lynched them in a railroad yard. It is reported that Barrett and his associates then acquired the People's Grocery Store for a fraction of its worth.

Lynching has long been used as a tool of social control to maintain that stratified social (dis)order and to therefore keep African Americans in positions of subservience and submission [3]. It was, therefore, instrumental to uphold the racial stratification of society via the use of terror. Typically, a lynching event would involve dubious criminal accusations, usually of sexual transgression, an arrest, and a lynch mob, supported actively or passively by law enforcement officers. The public administration of violence by grotesque torture was usually followed by death by hanging. One of the most gruesome and disturbing facts surrounding the practice of lynching is that the sites of racist mob violence where black bodies were subjected to unimaginable and grotesque torture were sites of joy and entertainment for white groups. The unspeakable suffering which was inflicted on the victims of lynching led to deep feelings of joy, evidencing the presence of sadistic impulses within racist violence.

It was Ida Wells-Barnett's systematic analyses of lynching in the US at the end of the 19th and early 20th centuries that exposed the story of the People's Grocery Store [4]. Her examinations provided empirical evidence linking white violence to economic envy and white supremacy. In other words, Wells showed that lynching was also used as a tool to enforce economic subordination to protect white economic interests. That is to say, lynching was a tactic employed not only as retaliatory acts following alleged sexual 'misconduct', but it was also used to protect white power and to push back against the economic advancement and progress of black citizens. During this period, racial tensions were rife as African Americans challenged socio-economic configurations and their place in racialised hierarchies by seeking financial autonomy and independence. The People's Grocery Store's tragic ending may seem incomprehensible today. That it may be so tells us how far removed from our everyday reality and, arguably from contemporary race relations, these acts of gross brutality appear to be. The temptation, therefore, to discount, dismiss and deny that this history continues to be alive today may be hard to resist.

Our exposition of the temporality of whiteness in the opening chapter challenges this idea. A recent essay examining the 'lynching trope' has also argued just that. It proposed that the logic, discourse and practice of lynching have been adapted in the 21st century in ways that are central to the democratic project. And so, although popular texts often represent lynching as memories from a revolved period of history in order to appeal to white post-racial temporal fantasies, and a rhetoric of erasure and atonement, the practice remains. Patterns of contemporary state violence from police brutality and mass incarceration to state executions have all been seen as the reformation of lynching practices, making, once more, the case for the atemporal nature of white violence as 'it foregrounds the time of anti-Black violence as an accumulation and continuity, a ceaseless and imminent violence, that recontextualizes how lynching culture continues to create suffocating conditions for Black life' [5].

An autoethnographic note

> Group analysis is particularly concerned with the permeation of the individual by the dynamics of her social context. In a racist society the dynamics of racism will be internalized by all its members. We should expect this dynamic to emerge in an analytic group and should be prepared to analyse it. (Blackwell, 1994, p 1 [6])

As part of my training in group analysis, I set up a group to support people of colour composed of women and a non-binary person. The group aimed to promote their wellbeing, tackle isolation and facilitate socio-political reflections or what we might refer to as conscientisation. Each selected member spoke of the desire to meet others with similar lived experience, to feel connected and to make sense of ongoing experiences of oppression. Analysands collectively struggled with experiences of marginalisation, mainly through racism, but also often intersecting with misogyny, Islamophobia, queer- and trans-phobia. Links to envy and competition in the domestic and public arena were often made. Throughout the year-long intervention, contents dipped from the socio-political to more 'personalised' concerns. Experiences of sexual abuse quickly emerged. This created significant resonance in analysands, many of whom later disclosed their own history of sexual violence. The themes of intrusion and boundary violation became recurrent. Not only through the 'disclosure' of sexualised violence and rape but through stories of breaches of personal boundaries. In session six, unexpectedly, and in the middle of the session, an agitated white man abruptly barged into the group space, a serious boundary violation in analytic practice. He reported having been informed that the group premises were left unattended and that he feared that I was a burglar. Extraordinarily, and although he found me sat in a circle of chairs surrounded by patients, he proceeded to question me in front of the group. His anxiety was not appeased by this sight. This, in turn, created a significant level of anxiety in members or analysands. A group member, who was Muslim, fled as she had removed her veil, was exposed and was thus trying to hide. Of note, this was a staff member with concierge-related responsibilities who, two sessions prior to this incident, had mistaken me for the cleaner. I was the only black clinician.

This autoethnographic note brings together many of the themes we have explored in the book so far. White territoriality, paranoia, whiteness as an intruding and displacing force, and the white gaze as surveillance and border control. All of this may be linked to envy. Being imagined as the cleaner, we may remember, echoes once more the bin anecdote I shared at the start of the book. We posited a racialised and gendered role associated with social expectations of servitude and subservience from bodies formed as other, particularly those of women racialised as black. In addition, we have the trope of the black subject not only as the trespasser into spaces possibly imagined as 'white only' but as a criminal. A thief. Another heavily racially and anxiety loaded projective archetype evocative of Yancy's phenomenological description of the white gaze in the 'elevator effect'. I too am disappeared in space [7]. As I am interrogated and criminalised, I am not witnessed for who I am.

There is much more that could be said about this rich encounter with whiteness in the clinic which may crystallise the co-constitutive nature of structural and psychological phenomena, using group analysis. As we have seen in our introduction to group analysis and the group matrix and, as reiterated by the words of Blackwell at the start of this section, group analysis is not only concerned with studying the dynamics, communication and processes within the clinic for therapeutic purposes, it is equally concerned with examining the permeation of configurations that exist or have existed in the wider socio-political situation, within communication, within the relational and, crucially, inside our psyches [6].

To that end, groups are believed to operate at three levels; at structural, process and contents level. Structural configurations compose the very architecture of the group, here the group setting. Process is concerned with fluid and dynamic communication in a particular space, the interactions between group members, between group members and me, or between the intruder and myself. Contents refer to the actual storied narratives, what are discussed in the sessions [8]. We note the striking parallel processes within all three levels of group functioning. Specifically, as the group was recollecting memories of boundary violation, mainly through the theme of sexual abuse and thus bodily intrusion (contents), a white man intruded into the group setting (structure), a space exclusive to women and non-binary people of colour. The intruder, who positioned me as the intruder, proceeded to question the legitimacy of my presence and my intentions in front of my group of anxious patients, embodying the policing of borders or boundaries that edifice white territoriality. Further, by exposing the Muslim woman who had removed her hijab to the male gaze, he re-enacted sexualised violence (process). Put differently, the healing and conscientisation efforts of a group largely dedicated to processing the harm of whiteness and misogyny were interrupted or derailed, if only temporarily, by a white man, re-enacting whiteness and misogyny, sexualised racism. An act we may formulate of (compulsive) repetition, thus of retraumatisation.

It is also of poignant note that the Muslim analysand was the most distraught. There was, for her, a double assault, a double intrusion but a triple re-victimisation. She was both intruded upon by the white man entering the group space without our consent and without warning and she was intruded upon when she was forcibly exposed. She was therefore subjected to racism, misogyny and Islamophobia, at a time when gendered anti-Muslim sentiments were rife and the 'question' of hijab was a prominent one in society, through racist and sexist interrogations about whether Muslim women choosing to cover their face and/or hair was compatible with British values and whether Muslim women should still be afforded the right to wear the hijab in public [9]. These interrogations were partly triggered by the contemporaneous ban on Islamic face coverings, in public, in France, and news reports of Muslim women being required to unveil in public [10]. Opposition to the wearing of the hijab and the desire in some sections of society that Muslim women be similarly unveiled permeated the group.

We can see that even the tasks of setting up and sustaining a clinical group, analytic or psychological practice, engages macro-level transactions and relies on both the negotiation of material realities and psychic phantasms likely culturally inherited (back to the social unconscious). These tasks, often referred to as 'dynamic administration' within group analysis, are consequently influenced by power, by social and economic restraints and social positioning, which, in turn, co-shape the psychic landscapes and psychosocial realities of all involved.

More directly relevant to the consideration of envy of the present chapter, an uncontained white man compromised the containing function of the group. The presence of these racialised maligning and disparaging tropes, in the context of me being the most senior clinician and member of the team, takes us back to whiteness as property. We may see here attempts at policing the clinical space, indirectly thus my body and those other bodies racialised as black and brown occupying that space, the analysands. By extension, we may hypothesise an attempt at restoring, if only via the unconscious, racialised stratifications in that clinical space. A contestation, arguably of my role and/or of our collective existence in that space, which may be read as another envious attack.

Black jealousy – white envy?

Whiteness' relationship with black joy reveals the atemporal presence of white sadism. Black joy, we have seen, continues to lead to the activation of white envy as responses to the film *Black Panther* documented. Put in a nutshell, seeing joyous and carefree black bodies in relation to the movie attracted vitriol and white resentment. Echoes of the bitterness that led to the People's Grocery Store's deadly ending and the bloody murder scene in the French countryside are impossible to ignore. The malice. The disturbance caused. The anger. The resentment. It all looks and sounds familiar. As though, once more, we have been here before. Black joy disturbs, I would propose, partly because it is humanising and as such transgressive of the social (dis)order.

In everyday terms, envy refers to painful or resentful awareness that an advantage is enjoyed by another, together with a desire to possess the same advantage, often by malice. Envy is, therefore, the desire to have for oneself a quality, possession or other desirable objects belonging to someone else. In analytic thinking, envy has a more specific meaning. It is believed to be an expression of the death instinct that exists within us all, and which drives us to want to destroy all that is good that we desire in others [11]. Angry feelings triggered because another person possesses and enjoys something desirable – the envious impulse being to spoil it. Through these ways to think about envy, and the notes we shared, we can now extract common themes. Desire. Longing. Bitterness. Resentment. Destructiveness. Death.

It is often assumed that the racialised other wants to be white and, therefore, that they envy white people, and there is no denying that a desire for whiteness exists in the racialised other. The desire for whiteness has been astutely articulated by Fanon. Evidence of this is not hard to find, even today. We can observe it in assimilation-centred cultural practices. In the idealisation of whiteness. In the skin-whitening epidemic affecting most of the globe or, again, in the seeking of white sexual partners by people racialised as black or brown. The wish to be white is more commonly understood as internalised racism; Fanon refers to this as Black neurosis [12]. A neurosis is the intense anxiety produced by wishes, ideas or impulses, things about us, the world or others we have pushed far away from our conscious awareness. Things we are thus so scared of that we cannot express or contemplate directly or consciously, and which, as a result, create within us a conflict, distress or disturbance.

This wish to be white, or this black neurosis [12], is not, however, a psychological pathology. Rather, it is a reflection of socio-political arrangements. It is essentially a wish to be seen, the wish to be free and the wish to self-determine. It is also a wish to escape that enforced sense of inferiority. It is, thus, power that the colonised or the racially oppressed desire rather than whiteness per se, having come to believe that only by becoming white will they be treated as human. Become human. The internalisation of racism is, therefore, a natural psychological consequence of asymmetric power configurations. It is a manifestation of the cultural and historical trauma of white supremacy.

To claim that the white subject and, by extension, those with more social power in society may be envious of racialised others, and in particular of those with less power, or in other words, to say that 'the haves' envy 'the have-nots', challenges much of what we have come to believe about the social and about the psychological. This proposition is not only counter-cultural, but it also fundamentally challenges white superiority and racially stratified social configurations. A superiority that is presumed to be so obvious and so natural, that, of course, it follows in the white imagination that the racialised other would have very few aspirations beyond turning white; after all, who would not?

For white groups to be so strongly convinced that they are objects of envy is, in fact, a manifestation of their internalised white supremacy. This sense of superiority is both cause and effect of their internalised racism. When one becomes so wedded to the idea of one's inherent and indisputable superiority, such a worldview becomes 'common knowledge', objectivised. It leads to women racialised as white deriding the idea that they may harbour some envy towards women racialised as black. In a nutshell, to posit the existence of a pernicious form of envy in the white subject towards bodies racialised as black or brown is a challenge to white supremacy and to whiteness. Nonetheless, the position I am taking in this chapter is precisely this. Envy is not uniquely the domain of the subjugated or the oppressed. Envious feelings experienced by the white subject vis-à-vis the black one, and those racialised as other more generally, exist. The envy that groups racialised as white feel towards groups of colour is fundamentally different to what has come to be described as envy in the postcolonial subject, or black or brown envy.

Although it may be tempting to propose that both parties are envious of the other and, therefore, suggest an equivalency or bi-directionality, I do not believe that we can sustain that there is one. Instead, white envy, I propose, is the residual of white supremacist logics. Envy is often compared and contrasted to jealousy. But envy can be distinguished from jealousy in critical ways. To be envious is first to feel an absence of something in oneself. It is, second, to feel afflicted by the existence of that actual or fantasised something in someone else. Third, it is to experience a drive or impulse to destroy that something or that someone possessing that something. In other words, it is feeling deeply disturbed that another entity possesses something we so desire for ourselves, but one which we believe is out of reach for us.

Jealousy, on the other hand, has been defined as the malign feeling, which is often experienced towards a rival, for the possession of that which we greatly desire, as in love or ambition. Envy is a similar feeling towards another. However, in envy, we feel we cannot obtain what we covet. This is significant. There is, thus, an important although arguably subtle distinction between envy and jealousy. When we experience jealousy, we experience a fear of loss or a sense of deprivation which we cannot tolerate; we, therefore, seek to possess the object triggering the jealous feelings. When we experience envy, on the other hand, there is a sense of being bereft rather than deprived. We do not believe that we can obtain what is envied. We, therefore, make no move to possess but to spoil. To destroy. To kill whatever or whomever contains the object of one's envy. In doing so, we seek to rid ourselves of any trace of that feeling of lacking or absence and the sense of inadequacy it produces. This is an important distinction when it comes to racial dynamics. It is the difference between seeking to possess and seeking to destroy.

Moss' success created a deep sense of lack and inadequacy which we may posit was too much to bear for his competitor. It disrupted his sense of superiority and, thus, the racialised social (dis)order. It led to an almost obsessive desire to cause him harm in order to return to a sense of equilibrium psychically and to restore the status quo: the superiority of white residents. To destroy Moss and his achievements was thus to rid themselves of this sense of inadequacy which indirectly threatened their masculinity and, by extension, sexuality. One may say the violence was performed to punish those black men at the People's Grocery Store for challenging whiteness and reminding white men of racialised insecurities in relation to their own sexuality. This, I would posit, is the crux of white envy. I do not believe this drive to destroy the goodness in others – that one so desires for oneself – accurately conceptualises the black or the brown subject's relationship with the white subject or with whiteness. Historically and contemporaneously, this cannot be sustained.

According to Fanon, the fear of the constructed unbounded sexual power of bodies racialised as black leads to neuroses in the white man which are rooted in a fear of sexual inadequacy or impotency. This envy lies at the centre of race relations. In other words, the white man, despite claims and behaviours to the contrary, is envious of the black man's fantasised 'primitivism' and its associated constructed sexual potency. This envy breeds racial paranoia. Exaggerations and deformations of the other (and particularly here of his alleged monstrous sexuality) feeds both sexual anxieties and fears of persecution in groups racialised as white (for example, imagined risks of rape and other acts of sexual violence). This paranoia perpetually legitimises the need for violence against men racialised as black. Sexualised fears are also, at least partly, projective since historically, of course, the direction of sexual violence has been from groups racialised as white to groups racialised as black and towards racialised others rather than the other way around.

As illustrated by the fact, rape was used as a tool of colonial subjugation throughout European empires. This sexualised envy can also easily be evidenced by the torture of black men during acts of lynching and other acts of colonial violence. Castrations, genital mutilations, molestations. Further, there is a long although often forgotten history of women racialised as white exerting domination and violence onto women racialised as black due to envy borne out of rivalrous relationships or sexual competition. Black women slaves were after all often the forced 'mistresses' of slave masters, albeit non-consenting ones. They were also the breast that often fed white infants. The wet nurses. Black women were thus, if only metaphorically, pitted against white women for the affection of white children and the sexual attention of white men.

Since the white psyche needs to project onto the racial other undesirable aspects of itself that have been discarded, these may eventually be wanted back, thus evoking the possessiveness of jealousy. However, even though this lack and the absence of these parts may be experienced painfully, these parts cannot be re-claimed, which would be an enactment of jealousy, since they are unacceptable. What to do? Destroy these parts in the other by harming or seeking to kill the object possessing them. This is envy. Contrary to white self-representation, which is, to a large extent, dependent upon projective colonial constructions and specifically the posited existence of inferior or 'primitive' beings, which white groups are superior to, the racially subjugated, more generally, have not located, at least not at collective or group level, unwanted parts of who they are onto white bodies. That is why I do not believe that we are threatened by the dismantling of colonial formations. If anything, such dismantling would set us free. Hence, why there is really no bi-directionality or equivalency in racial envy and why it is more appropriate to speak of white envy rather than of racial envy. The key difference here is the drive to be the white other as opposed to the drive to annihilate the black other, because being the black other would entail integrating parts of the self that are simply too intolerable. The key distinction between jealousy and envy.

The politics of envy

Populist narratives such as 'economic anxiety' sell the notion that far-right groups have gained popularity in Britain because the concerns of the working class have been ignored. This alleges successive governments have ignored the concerns of the working class and prioritised the needs of migrants and people of colour [13]. These ideas speak to the same dynamic. The working class is said to feel disenfranchised since all resources to tackle inequality are taken away from them. This ignores the reality that 'working-class people' and 'people of colour' are not mutually exclusive categories, that class oppression and racism, as has been widely theorised, intersect and mutually co-create and, fundamentally, that poverty and deprivation disproportionately affect people of colour. In fact, the latter comprise the largest part of the working class proportionately. The working class is, therefore, primarily racialised as black and brown. Still, and even if fundamentally fictional, the imagined political focus on the concerns and needs of the groups most adversely affected by class oppression, the alleged prioritising of the racialised other in the allocation of welfare resources, continues to create uproar, anger social tensions and rationalisation for racial hatred.

That uproar tells us that the imagined prioritisation of non-white groups, however illusory, is still socially transgressive. That it challenges the natural (dis)order of things. And that the natural order of things is white priority. Only within this ideological system would those racialised as white be presumed, expected or required to come first, to be centred, to be prioritised above others with similar if not greater needs. It is worth noting at this point once again that the 'divide and conquer' tactics of the white bourgeoisie are similarly implicated in these social tensions and continue to be exploited in the political arena particularly in relation to border control discourses [7].

Some empirical evidence has found that resentment and envy towards multiculturalism and immigration are the most significant emotional responses underlying xenophobia and racism towards migrants. We are, therefore, clearly in the same murky waters of white envy. In November 2016, political commentator Van Jones described Donald Trump's electoral win in the United States as a 'whitelash' [14]. The journalist aimed to capture the dynamic of retaliation that followed what was perceived to be a significant step towards the advancement of equality; the election of Barack Obama, a president racialised as black, the first person of colour to ever take residence in the White House. The term quickly entered political conversations and even made it into the Cambridge dictionary, which defines 'whitelash' as a strong negative reaction to a change or recent events by white groups against the success and achievements of black groups. Whitelash is consequently an act of rebellion or resistance towards racial equality and a form of protest against the shifting of the racialised social (dis)order. Whether social and geopolitical configurations actually shifted with the election of Obama is highly contestable, but, of course, facts matter little here. What matters primarily is the imaginary that the social (dis)order, white interests and power were being conceded.

The dynamic of whitelash has been posited to be central to far-right and far-right-adjacent political parties and ideologies making a return in 'Western Europe' and in the US. However, whitelash has a long history. All waves or attempts at social change led to mass backlash and to whitelash. President Trump, nonetheless, seized the opportunity, as illustrated by his campaign slogan, 'Make America great again'. An effective dog-whistle phrase, steeped in imperial nostalgia seeking overtly to legitimise white supremacy and the 'good old days'. It symbolised a longing to return to the time when 'we used to treat them really bad'. It speaks of whiteness seeking foreclosure and entrapment in the 'past'. A 'past' where everyone knew their place or could be put back in their place, violently, if necessary, if they ever attempted to move 'above their station'. When power did not have to be shared. And, when words did not have to be minded. Also, a time when bodies racialised as black frequently hung from trees.

In the UK, similar responses have been amply formulated and led, it has been argued, to the toxic and violent Leave campaign that secured Brexit. A campaign which relied heavily on racialised images, symbols and discourses, as illustrated by United Kingdom Independence Party posters of bodies racialised as brown – widely imagined as Muslim in the collective imagination – on boats making their way into Britain. This was a campaign capitalising on fears related to the so-called 'migrants crisis' and the Islamisation of the country [15]. The success of the Brexit campaign can thus also be interpreted as a form of backlash from groups racialised as white for what was perceived to be changes to the colour of power, to the demographic composition of the UK and its identity.

However, even before Trump and before Brexit, these same dynamics and fantasies had been noted. In *Policing the crisis: Mugging, the state, and law and order*, Hall et al analysed the hysteria and moral panic created by widespread fears of rising crimes and, in particular, the fear of 'mugging' of the 1970s [16, 15]. These are discourses which dominated the political arena and media reporting during the decade. Even though these fears had no foundation in reality, they quickly unleashed xenophobic hatred, anti-black sentiments and hysteria over migration, multiculturalism and integration. Anxieties symptomatic of deep-seated concerns, which Gilroy saw as the manifestation of a historical crisis [15]. A crisis which largely sprang from the loss of the British empire, its colonies, the emergence of radical racial resistance movements and socio-economic precarity in the working classes. These socio-political anxieties led, according to the theorist, to an era of 'authoritarian populism' crystallised by the rise of Thatcher who, like Trump, promised the anxious masses to put the 'great' back into Great Britain [15].

We can therefore see that projective concerns over sovereignty, economic precarity and implicit competition for perceived scarce material resources have historically been racialised and sit at the core of the dynamic of whitelash. They may thus be formulated as safeguarding or gatekeeping what is imagined as belonging to white groups, and which has been taken or is at risk of being taken by the racialised other. Consequently, white resentment, white priority and white envy all feature in the dynamic of whitelash. In that sense, although the dominant political narrative of the Leave campaign was based on taking back border control in relation to European Union migration and being free from Brussels-based bureaucrats, hate crimes increased towards those visibly different and native. British citizens of colour bore the brunt of this violence. The real objects of that resentment, we could argue, were once more subjected to constructions of white nationalism and white Britishness.

Penal and punitive border discourses are not only a postcolonial affliction. Their legitimisation through expressions such as 'economic anxiety', we can argue, are, therefore, simply political manoeuvres to sanction white priority and, therefore, the need to respond with hostility or to punish those who dare to move above their station and step out of their designated territories, by restating the terms of the racial contract. The discourse of economic anxiety thus functions as a tool to restate the racially stratified social (dis)order and its associated psychic equilibrium, in part by feeding off envy and resentment linked to capitalist and material concerns, concerns nonetheless intrinsically linked to racialised competition, competition which is really, for the most part, non-existent.

White envy led residents racialised as white to feel animosity towards Moss and what he possessed. It resulted in him and two of his associates being lynched. White envy has led millions of others to decry these so-called progressive policies seen to benefit those racialised as black or brown, in some contexts, often leading the white working class to vote against their own class interests, in an attempt to assert racialised power and priority. White envy again makes it difficult for so many to witness black joy, even over something as mundane as a movie.

Summary and resistance

Complex and historically loaded envy-based dynamics are triggered within the white psyche and within social structures when bodies racialised as black or brown, for whatever reason, transgress expectations that deem them inferior in intelligence, in beauty or in talent. We have seen that white envy is heavily sexualised in part due to colonial formations. White groups continue to feel collectively challenged in their sense of superiority and entitlement because such racial transgression calls for changes to social configurations, changes to psychic organisations and to the redistribution of power, sometimes real, often imagined. The sense of threat and precarity in relation to whiteness as property is weaponised structurally and can lead to the acting out of retaliatory or defensive political moves to ward off eternal feelings of competition vis-à-vis the envied object. White envy, when activated, will attempt to reassert white priority and the racially stratified social (dis)order, often through attacks and violence. More ubiquitously, though, through more socially acceptable and more indirect ways of saying don't you dare stand above me. My comfort, or joy or success should come first. Do not challenge my place in the hierarchy. I am entitled to what you have. And, if I cannot take it from you, I will destroy you or at least spoil it for you.

This is the crux of white envy. Sometimes these feelings are not uttered as statements. Sometimes there are no statements. Only performances. We observe them in the relocation of the envied or transgressive body racialised as black and brown to some mythical primitive places. In us being reminded that bodies who look like ours are poor. That bodies who look like ours are full of dirt, that bodies who look like us are starving. Afflictions which are largely mythical but, in any event, are presented in an ahistorical and decontextualised manner, separated from white power, interests and actions. The reality, however, is that envy is an attempt at escaping pain associated with loss and feelings of lack. White envy is therefore fundamentally an expression of distress. Envious subjects often experience more suffering as a result of their envy than their envied objects, at least psychically.

Tolerating distress is therefore central to tackling white envy before that envy is acted out. Envious attacks, we may argue, are a way of discharging that distress by transferring it into the objects of white envy. Hence, distress tolerance is likely to be helpful for those who have a tendency to feel overwhelmed by feelings of lack and find them so unbearable that even mild challenges to their sense of goodness trigger disproportionate responses and lead to them resorting to projective violence. Helpful strategies to resist envious feelings include self-compassion and gratitude. The capacity to show ourselves kindness and nurture ourselves when we feel lacking or inadequate and the practising of gratitude so as to connect to what we have, can be effective tools of resistance. They can help white subjects resist greed and regulate that sense of perpetual illusory deprivation which is the root of racialised competition and leads to violence interpersonally and structurally. Both gratitude and self-compassion thus are emotional and cognitive states which have the potential to reconnect white groups to their own humanity and by extension to humanity at large. In the next chapter we consider a closely related psychological dynamic: white sadism, specifically, the experience of gratification, often sexualised, that one derives from the suffering, humiliation and pain of the racialised other.

4

White sadism

My years in academic psychology have, beyond the shadow of a doubt, been the most distressing years of my adult life. ... Whenever I reflect on these times, it is the faces of white middle-class women I see. Smiling. (Kinouani, 2021, p 14 [1])

A cultural note

In May 2020, the world was shaken to its core when the videoed killing of George Floyd by white police officer Derek Chauvin in Minneapolis took place. This act of extraordinary yet banalised police brutality resulted in possibly the largest wave of global protests and riots in living memory. For several months, and across the world, hundreds of thousands of people took to the streets in anger, despair and distress, dissenting at what seems like unrelenting police violence against black bodies. In the US, largely peaceful but resolute protests were met with largely violent repression. Scenes of protesters being roughly handled, aggressively apprehended, hit with batons, tear gas or rubber bullets by a heavily armed and militarised police force were repeatedly spread across our screens. Via national news, on our social media timelines, and for many of us in our dreams too. In the midst of the chaos, I tried as much as I could to spare my mind from witnessing the events too closely. I avoided the video like the plague. It took me several months before I found it in me to watch the infamous recording. But for the need to write the present chapter, I do not believe that I would have had any inclination to do so. Like many, across the globe, the mere written description of the events leading to Floyd's death, the incessant news reporting, were tortuous enough. They were triggering enough. The word trigger has unnecessarily become controversial, in large part because of right-wing media pundits who have, over the years, perverted its original meaning and taken it as symptom of what they describe as a manifestation of 'snowflake' culture allegedly infringing on the capacity to speak freely. But understanding psychological triggers is important to understanding the effect of whiteness on all of us. We speak of triggers when we are dealing with trauma. Triggers are specific stimuli, such as scenes, smells, noises which take us back to a painful and/or traumatic event. They are the body's way of protecting us and registering that the stimuli we are exposed to in the present is alarmingly similar to that which accompanied violence we endured in the 'past'. The impact white violence continues to inflict on the racialised other remains to be fully accepted, and deriding the existence of triggering effects is a way to deny that very violence and the pain it causes. There is also something worth interrogating in the mindless if not habitual consumption and specularisation of black pain and violated black bodies arguably amplified in the age of social media, which speaks deeply to the theme of the chapter. We cannot deal with white sadism without dealing with black pain and their relationship within white supremacy.

The footage of Floyd's last moments show the police arriving at a scene responding, we are told, to a call alleging that Floyd had used a fraudulent 20-dollar bill to buy some cigarettes. We are distant witnesses to the police approaching Floyd's car and knocking on his window a few times and then, within seconds – 25 seconds, official documents indicate – Floyd having a gun pointed in his face all while being repeatedly asked to show his hands. We see Floyd show his hands without resistance. The weapon remains in his face, nonetheless. Naturally, this aggressive demand at gunpoint is followed by what seems like an immediate fear response by Floyd, together with some apparent confusion: "Please, please officer I did not do nothing, what did I do?" We hear and see him repeatedly plead "Please do not shoot." Completely unmoved by Floyd's distress or fear, there is not even an attempt to reassure him from Chauvin nor to de-escalate at this point. Floyd is asked to get out of his car and shortly after to get into the back of a police van. At this point, his fear and distress become much more pronounced. He is somewhat agitated. "I am claustrophobic," he repeats, as he resists getting in the van. Again, his distress is ignored. More pleas ensue. He is met with hostility then we watch a small scuffle. Floyd is wrestled to the ground within seconds and here starts the tortuous last few minutes of his life, the infamous death scene. Chauvin places his left knee on Floyd's neck as Floyd lays face down on the floor. Again, Floyd pleads several times:

'I can't breathe.'
'I can't breathe.'
'I can't breathe.'
'I can't breathe.'
'I can't breathe.'
'I can't breathe.'
'I can't breathe.'
'I can't breathe.'
'I can't breathe.'
'I can't breathe.'
'I can't breathe.'
'I can't breathe.'
'I can't breathe.'
'I can't breathe.'
'I can't breathe.'
'I can't breathe.'
'I can't breathe.'
'I can't breathe.'
'I can't breathe.'
'I can't breathe.'
'I can't breathe.'
'I can't breathe.'
'I can't breathe.'
'I can't breathe.'
'I can't breathe.'
'I can't breathe.'
'I can't breathe.'

This is the number of pleas jurors who watched a long video taken by a bystander witnessed. Floyd is seen and heard pleading for his life 27 times [2].

Each of Floyd's pleas is ignored. Trivialised in fact. "It takes a lot of oxygen to talk," Chauvin retorts at some point. For seven minutes and 46 seconds, official records show, Floyd gasps for air. Still officer Chauvin keeps his knee firmly on Mr Floyd's neck as he continues to struggle to breathe and repeatedly and continuously begs for his life. At one point, he is calling out for his mother and, seeing other police officers approaching, he is heard muttering "You're going to kill me." Chauvin's colleagues are around. Three of them. They watch in complicit silence. None of them intervene. Floyd is now seen bleeding from his nose. Still no intervention. He starts to complain that his tummy is aching, to no avail. Passers-by and witnesses grow concerned and are heard imploring Chauvin to get off Floyd's neck. One black onlooker screams "Look at you! You are enjoying it." Floyd becomes silent. He is now unconscious. Even in this state and completely immobile, Chauvin does not release his knee from Floyd's neck for another couple of minutes. His pulse is finally taken after it appears this is requested by an alarmed passer-by. There is no pulse, we hear. An ambulance is eventually called to the scene. It arrives and Floyd is taken to hospital. He is pronounced dead, it is reported, upon arrival. In the spring of 2021, Chauvin was convicted of murder. A rare event for a law enforcement officer.

In Chapter 3 we examined the central place of envy in the psychosocial structure of whiteness. In the present chapter, we will explore sadism. Sadism is closely related to envy's impulse to destroy. Nonetheless, sadism also departs from envy in important ways, which we will consider. The chapter discusses the theoretical underpinning of sadism, including its origins and clinical conceptualisations. It will then historicise the connection between sadism and whiteness, illustrations of which will be provided in support. On this point, it is argued that imperialism and colonialism, and the associated mode of production and relations, relied on sadism. From this historical context, we once more hypothesise that an ongoing relationship between sadism and racism has remained, which has become institutionalised. We use case studies within our contemporaneous context to make that case. This connection, it is proposed, is evidenced by the brutal anti-black violence witnessed within law enforcement, correctional and medical practices. Making once more the case for a continuing presence of the 'past' via the persistence of older modes of organising the world and relating to the black body.

"Look at you, you're enjoying it!"

I watched the last moments of Floyd's life like a detective observing every move Chauvin made. In fact, before I sought out the video, the question which was going through my mind was, will I see it? Will it be there? Will I find evidence of it? The 'it' here is sadism. When I started the footage, I could see the white testosterone-charged confrontation. We see state-sanctioned power used as a weapon, it hyper-masculinises the white police officer in a way that feels compensatory. We see a tall, large black man reduced to sobbing like a child, in a state of terror, begging for mercy and at one point asking for his mother. Pleading for his life amidst ego, power and whiteness. Ego, power, whiteness and masculinity.

It would be hard for anyone to miss the power struggle on display. A power struggle that really is nothing but a fantasy in Chauvin's mind. There is no doubt that the painful power asymmetry between Floyd and Chauvin feeds the spectacle. It is Chauvin's show. What may be harder to notice in the video is the rejoicing, the clear gratification, the pleasure Chauvin appears to be deriving from being in this position of necropower. It is more diffuse and for most of the video difficult to pinpoint and locate precisely, but it is written everywhere. It can be perceived through Chauvin's body language, his proud demeanour and utter disregard for every single plea to remove his knee from Floyd's neck. Silent and unnamed for most of the video. Still, it hits you right in the guts as you watch the interaction. Then, a black witness screams at Chauvin, possibly hit by it too, "You're enjoying it!" And so here it was. Sadism had been identified and it had been confronted directly. The enjoyment Chauvin derives from the painfully protracted murder of Floyd, his public torture and lynching, are noted live. One of the most chilling moments of the deadly encounter.

African Americans have been found to be 3.23 times more likely than white Americans to be killed by the police during routine encounters [3]. The overwhelming majority of these deaths are preventable. Contrary to popular belief, risks are far from lower in the UK. In *I can't breathe: Race, death & British policing*, an inquest found people racialised as black to be seven times more likely to die than people racialised as white following restraint by police [4]. Risks are even more elevated for disabled people racialised as black and/or those experiencing mental health crises. Additional data suggests female officers are 27 per cent less likely than male officers to 'exhibit extreme controlling behaviours such as threats, physical restraint, searches, and arrest' in the line of duty when interacting with citizens. Research also suggests that even after controlling for differences in assignments, police officers who are women are significantly less likely to use force than male officers, they are also more likely to display empathy and more likely to de-escalate fraught encounters. In addition, suspects who are arrested by women police officers are much less likely to be injured [5].

These findings highlight that the relationship between policing, racism and violence is also mediated by gender, reminding us of the toxic intersections between whiteness, masculinity and violence in fostering police culture. Further, it once more brings into the equation competitive fantasies and, thus, the dynamic of sexualised envy we covered in the previous chapter is closely related to the enactment of sadism.

Defining sadism

The word 'sadism' finds its origins in the name of the Marquis de Sade, a French aristocrat not only famous for his writing and its violent sexual and pornographic content, but also for acting out his violent fantasies on children and women from lower socio-economic classes [6]. In his literary works and, it is reported, in his life too, De Sade promoted perversion and indulgence in pain to achieve sexual excitement and enjoyment, which he described with the most meticulous precision.

It was at end of the 19th century and posthumously that sadism became adopted as a term both within and outside France. The word was mainstreamed at the start of the 20th century when it was appropriated by psychiatry in Austria and, in particular, by Freud [7]. The definition of sadism used then has not changed significantly; it refers to the experience of sexual pleasure which results from exercising or witnessing cruelty in the form of bodily violence afflicted on others. Central to sadism is, therefore, an innate desire to hurt, destroy, wound or humiliate others in order to create pleasurable sexual sensations. In other words, sadism is the urge to make someone suffer and to degrade them for some form of gratification.

Although the initial conceptualisation of sadism remains centred on sexual gratification, and the libidinal arousal created by the infliction of pain, the definition of sadism is not constrained to sexuality or sexual impulses or even perversion. Similarly, although from its inception as a conceptual framework, sadism has been thought of as a deviancy or as psychiatric dysfunction, evidence suggests sadistic traits exist on a spectrum or continuum and can be found within non-clinical populations and indeed entire cultures.

For example, members of the general population or non-clinical samples have repeatedly been found to have sadistic traits, with those individuals scoring high on verbal aggression, enjoyment of violence and the consumption of violent media content tending to score the highest for sadistic tendencies [8]. Three psychological origins for sadism have been suggested according to researchers: sensation seeking; threatened egotism; and the pursuit of thrills and excitement [9]. Sensation seeking contributes to the appeal of violence, and it implies that the desire for excitement may compel some individuals to try out new experiences, making them act aggressively and impulsively [10]. On the other hand, threatened egotism refers to a perceived threat to one's self-image or status. Such threat is posited to make vulnerable individuals develop violent behaviour in an attempt not to lose face. The pursuit of thrills and excitement includes planning and executing mischief or anti-social activities to feel pleasure.

This theoretical framework links sadism to the adjacent concept of narcissism. Equally fruitful in reviewing Chauvin's behaviour. The apparent need to maintain face at all costs, the hypothesised grandiose need to be respected or feared, the egotistical display of power, the repeated failure to show empathy and compassion towards a pleading, distressed, then dying Floyd. We observe the centring of Chauvin's needs and wants at the tragic expense of the needs and life of the black man.

Fromm proposes that sadistic personalities find pleasure in controlling others [11]. He distinguishes three distinct types of sadism grounded in one's insecurities and social impotence: physical; sexual; and mental [8]. From this framework, Chauvin would have been motivated to inflict pain and suffering on Floyd because of insecurities related to lack of control, power and potency. This view would be consistent with Fromm, who described sadism as the desire and tendency to control the lives of other human beings absolutely and unrestrictedly [11].

Everyday performance

'As a senior manager at a nonprofit organisation that served victims of domestic violence and sexual assault, I, along with another black woman, asked the organisation to review its policy on mandated reporters. At the time, every person that interacted with a client, from the receptionists to therapists, was required to report the client to Child Protective Services if they suspected her of child abuse.

Since child abuse has a level of subjectivity and the area's Child Protective Services was known to disproportionately separate children of colour from their mothers (black and Latinx), we were advocating for a review of the policy with the hope that it could be limited to the clinical staff to make that determination. We were assured that the executive team would review the issue, and we could have a discussion.

After several weeks of asking for a response, we were each called into a meeting with the Associate Executive Director and the Executive Director, both white women. This meeting was unexpected. We were told that the organisation was going through a restructuring and that both of our positions were dissolved. Under the new job description, I was no longer qualified for the job. The other black woman was told that although she was a lawyer, they needed another lawyer with a more considerable skillset than hers, so they decided to do a national search, but she was "free to apply". I will never forget the smiles of satisfaction on their faces. Both enjoyed the ambush.' (Krystal, African American woman, 50s, United States)

Krystal's everyday encounter with white sadism exposes multiple levels of violence in a form of sadism which here is enacted by women racialised as white. It is a form of sadism that is therefore feminised, composed and courteous. All the same, it appears, deliberately malicious and all smiles. In the opening quote, extracted from *Living while black*, I share one of my own encounters with white women's sadism in academia. I recognise that smile. It featured too. It has inscribed itself indelibly in my mind. Such smiles, in the midst of distress, rarely fail to indicate sadism. However, if we were in doubt, we may recognise sadism here in the institutional manoeuvring of the 'letting go' of the women racialised as black, the kinds of retaliatory violence designed to keep subjugated bodies in their place. Silent. Compliant. Silent and compliant is in the face, it would seem, of institutional and structural harm. What we have here is the covert disciplining of a pair of women racialised as black. The added humiliation of inviting the lawyer to reapply for her job, the narcissism evidenced by the resistance to being challenged, the absence of any sign of empathy or compassion at the distress and damage created. It is not the workers alone who will be harmed, but entire families, including children. Quite poignantly, the themes of family separation, through the displacement of children and the displacement of women racialised as black, who sought to interrogate those separations and displacements, reinscribe and re-enact the politics of the plantation and their associated sanctions for perceived transgressors. For those who dared to question the master.

Colonial discipline and cultural sadism

> A retired concessionary company manager told France's fourth-largest-selling paper, *Le Journal*, that his firm routinely forced Africans to deliver ivory and rubber to them by 'tying them down and whipping them 50 times with a chicotte' – a cruelly ingenious lash made of raw, sun-dried hippopotamus hide, twisted to form hundreds of razor-sharp spokes. 'After each blow, the victims screamed in pain, their blood spurting out'. The next day, 'they returned with ivory and rubber'. (Berenson, 2018 [12])

Colonial configurations and master–slave dialectics are particularly important at this juncture. There is plenty of evidence that suggests colonial and enslaved bodies became the site of debauchery onto which white sadism could be acted out with impunity [13]. The systems of enslavement and colonial extraction relied on the dehumanisation of Africans and on inflicting upon them unspeakable pain [14]. The infliction of pain was rationalised, naturalised beyond any question, since the social (dis)order and, thus, white economic interests were absolutely dependent upon black suffering and black pain. This matters a great deal. It means that black and brown suffering lie at the very core of capitalism and, thus, the modern world. As Mbembe summarises, whiteness-induced black blood stains the entire surface of modernity [15].

In the 'new worlds', the super-humanisation of bodies racialised as black was required to maintain the entire socio-economic system that fed the cycle of violence. It was, after all, because bodies racialised as black were deemed to be more robust and able to withstand the most hostile of environments, living conditions and painful treatment that they became the ideal candidates forced to work the fields of 'new worlds'.

Once in these worlds, it became necessary to rule by fear and terror to exercise the kind of social control which could sustain mass submission and subjugation. Ruling by fear and terror cannot be achieved without the administration of pain or the threat thereof. Illustrations of the ruling through the mechanisms and practices of white terror can be observed in punishment practices. The quote in Berenson's article was a contemporaneous account of a colonial officer in Congo-Brazzaville [12]. It reveals widespread disciplinary practices in the small French colonial territory employed to coerce Africans to meet extraction quotas. 'The spurting out' of Congolese blood functions to fatten France. Other well documented capitalism-mediated acts of torture include: the mandated castration of enslaved subjects found guilty of escaping or assaulting their white masters throughout the new world; the raping of women with bottles filled with pepper and water; colonial subjects being sodomised with foreign objects, animals and insects; captives being surgically operated or experimented on without anaesthesia; colonial subjects, including children, being amputated or mutilated if they failed to meet natural resource quotas or pay colonial taxes [16]. These practices are documented throughout colonial empires.

Humiliation was central to the upholding of the colonial project. The enactment of humiliation is observable through acts of public discipline and audience-mediated whipping, rape and other sexualised violence intended to act as deterrents and dissuade other individuals from seeking liberation, freedom or emancipation [17, 18, 19, 20].

The boundaries between violence as social control and violence enacted for sadistic gratification are bound to become blurred. In other words, socially functional violence or violence to maintain the social (dis)order and psychically functional violence or violence for pleasure or gratification become, we may expect, one and the same. While it may be tempting to posit that white slave masters and colonialists exclusively inflicted pain to protect their economic interests, over time, there is little doubt master–slave and colonial relations encouraged the development of sadistic expressions and tendencies.

The normalisation of extreme violence, we might expect, would encourage sadism, so that if imperial and colonial systems relied on the infliction of pain for socio-economic purposes and such violence became necessary to maintain the social (dis)order, some psychic adjustments would necessarily need to follow, requiring a transformation of the white psychic landscape. Such psychosocial reasoning may be sustained as follows. First, the more dehumanising and torturous the conditions of enslavement or colonial subjugation were, the more terror and violence were required to quash dissent and resistance, the freedom impulse, to enforce compliance. Hence the more pain was inflicted.

Second, since sadism alone would turn the object of one's violence into a tool or a commodity required socially, the process of violation is bound to become naturalised, further detaching the white subject from the humanity of the object of its violence, an expected evolutionary or adaptive response. The social need for violence, then, perpetually co-creates the psychic disposition for the expression of sadism, which in turn further breeds the free expression of sadistic impulses.

Third, escalating sadistic violence would naturally require more elaborated defence mechanisms for the violence to be tolerated and sustained. More elaborated dissociation, rationalisation and denial, in turn, fostering further distance and disconnection between master and slave and making it easier to carry out sadistic acts.

Finally, since engaging in sadistic practices becomes necessary for individuals to gain power within society, such practices become aspirational

[16]. Over time, the process of habituation would likely come into play. Where master and slave become habituated and fixed in that co-dependent violent relationship, with each stuck in correspondingly sadistic and sadomasochistic ways of relating, virtually unable to escape these roles and scripts. The binary distinction between sadism and sadomasochism, however, requires some interrogation. If we believe that dehumanising others is the ultimate act of self-dehumanisation and that violence harms those who enact it too, then white sadism also presupposes sadomasochism or gratification from self-inflicted pain and suffering in the white subject.

A cultural note

In the previous chapter we encountered a disturbing envious attack, the murder of an entire family at the expense of the welfare of the community. In the *Underground Railroad* series, this dynamic is put under sharp spotlight [21]. The main protagonist, Cora, essentially having ran away from her plantation, finds herself hiding in the roof of a kind enough white couple, under the harshest of conditions. She is in the roof with another runaway slave, a young teen fathered manifestly by a white slave owner. She is eventually discovered, which leads to fury being unleashed onto the white couple who provided refuge to her. When she is found, she keeps quiet about the other girl hiding, hoping she might remain safe in the roof. At the very last moment, an aggrieved Irish housekeeper, who appears to suspect someone else might be in hiding and, out of sheer anger, torches the couple's house with the mixed-race runaway still hiding as the flames start to consume the house. Cora, who still has not revealed there is another slave in hiding, becomes distraught while the Irish servant visibly rejoices. But tragedy quickly strikes (back at) the small white community. The house catches fire and becomes almost completely engulfed in flames within minutes. It's a wooden house. Houses in the village are built in close proximity and are also wooden. The inferno which started with the couple's house quickly devours the neighbouring houses, pretty much the whole street, then the whole village. Devastation hits. The crowd realises what the house cleaner has done. It's too late. They turn on her. The 'mixed-race' enslaved girl manages to escape the flames because of the brouhaha of the village erupting in flames.

This cinematographic illustration of the folly of whiteness is stupefying. It renders, in the most visual and arresting way, the depths of the irrationality and depravity of racial hatred. The fire represents whiteness' self-inflicted suffering and trauma arising out of pure sadism. We can thus propose that self-inflicted pain would not endure but for some disowned gratification, unless the pain we inflict onto the other makes our own more tolerable. It is commonly uttered within contemporary discourses, and when contemplating the violence that the enslaved Africans and colonial subjects, particularly insurgent ones, were subjected to, that they were treated like animals. This is in fact inaccurate. Although the enslaved were transported and bred like cattle, and colonial subjects were deprived of most rights reserved to white human beings, a significant difference has remained throughout history between the treatment of animals and the treatment of enslaved and colonial bodies. All evidence suggests enslaved Africans in particular were, in many respects, treated in a way that markedly distinguished them from the treatment of animals. At the collective level, we have little evidence of socially sanctioned sadism or torture enacted towards animals or evidence of collective gratification derived from the mistreatment or torture of animals as foundational to Western societies at any time in history. We have, in fact, across European nations, many accounts of animals being spared pain and suffering, across the centuries. To this day, many argue that collectively the suffering of animals triggers more empathetic and compassionate responses than the suffering of humans racialised as black or brown. At best, the latter activates indifference and at worst a form of enjoyment via spectacularisation and voyeurism. It is common for animal welfare rights campaigners to make use of racist and anti-black tropes in their activism [22].

Everyday performance

> I am a torture survivor and I claimed asylum in the UK. I was detained because I was seeking protection. I wasn't a criminal, but I was being treated like one: I couldn't and still can't understand why. When I came to the UK, I was in a bad physical and mental state. I could not trust any authority anywhere and thought that I might be tortured again. Being detained brought back memories. The sound of the locks, the footsteps, the four walls, the not knowing what was happening – this was all mental torture. The detention guards and health staff were not able to respond to my physical and mental needs resulting from my torture. (Borry, 2020 [23])

The story of Borry is extracted from a Freedom from Torture campaign to abolish immigration detention centres in the UK. It exposes the layers of normalised state-sanctioned violence. Immigration detention centres continue to be in use and have become a normalised part of the state border control apparatus. I worked in Yarl's Wood, one of the largest detention centres in Europe, as wellbeing lead, a few years ago. I am still to fully digest the level of trauma and suffering my body was exposed to in that space, which I have no doubt I still carry in my body. Detention centres are ultimate zones of non-being, Fanon might say. Zones where one is forced to disconnect from everything that makes one human. The ability to connect to others, the opportunity to experience mutuality and the capacity to make meaning. They are places where 'the walking dead' can freely be sadistically tortured. They are, we may propose, the ultimate site of necropolitical violence [24].

Necropolitics positions others' lives as disposable and sacrificeable in the interests of, first, protecting the vitality of the powerful and, second, protecting the racialised social (dis)order. Elsewhere, I have argued that it normalises murder since murder is not constructed as murder: those killed cannot have been murdered because they are not seen as human [25]. The suffering and slow extinction inflicted on their bodies is rendered legitimate, if not virtuous, in the name of control, security and sovereignty [24].

Necropower or the power to decide who can live and who should die relies heavily on the infliction of pain. Death here follows suffering. There is no dignified or peaceful death. Pain therefore lies at the centre of the necropolitical project. The ultimate means of hierarchisation of lives – who can live and who can die – therefore also entails who deserves to suffer and who should experience comfort based on their socially ascribed worth, in the context of whiteness, based on racialisation. As a result, racialised bodies are often forced to exist in death-worlds. Worlds within which conditions of existence make self-harm, harm, suicide and psychological suffering the norm. And given that ontological death precedes physical death, annihilation always looms near in these spaces situated at the border between life and death. Such places include detention centres where those fleeing persecution, war or conflicts, often orchestrated by Western nations to sustain neocolonial interests, are forced to exist deprived of freedom, of much human contact and are fed just enough to remain alive. The very existence and tolerance of these places of torture within nations premised on moral superiority points to the institutionalisation of sadism to sustain the racialised social (dis)order.

Sadism, the social unconscious and the group matrix

We saw that imperialism and colonialism created cultures that allowed sadism to flourish; they created a sadistic culture. Sadistic cultures created within society will permeate social structures and institutions. We can expect that they will become instruments themselves for the operationalisation of racialised sadism. In this vein, the re-enactment of sadistic violence within social systems, such as immigration control, the police or healthcare systems cannot but be natural consequences of these sadistic cultures. These must be seen as another residue of colonial and imperial sadism maintained collectively by white psyches and social structures, which may be conceptualised as an extension of the mind.

Structural sadism casts light upon why black and brown subjects continue to be the objects of more violence, humiliation, pain and control than white groups within social structures. Law enforcement officers continue to misuse their power against people of colour, or subject them to unnecessary violence [26]. Police brutality has proved that sadism can quickly come into play during the policing of bodies racialised as black and brown. There is a large volume of documentation of police violence against the descendants of the enslaved and colonised within all postcolonial nations. For example, as we covered earlier, we know that men racialised as black are much more likely to be brutalised or murdered by the police than men racialised as white. The murder of George Floyd evidences how those with state-sanctioned power continue to torture black bodies, almost, it would seem, despite themselves and seemingly for pleasure. Of course, Floyd is just one of the many brutalised black men who died at the hands of the US state and in other countries, the UK included. These events and the acts of black suffering routinely captured on smartphones support the link between sadism and racism, in today's world too.

Another contemporary illustration of the expression of structural sadism is evident within correctional facilities. The facilities reportedly designed to protect the public from dangerous elements of their communities have, instead, become places of torture and violence where sadistic and socially malignant behaviour towards African Americans often jailed for benign offences and/or without due process, can act as fuel for sadistic impulses. Given the use of prison labour as virtually free corporate labour in the US, the troubling relationship between pain, deprivation of freedom and capitalism is once more made, here in the present.

Much has been written about the school-to-prison pipeline, how the disproportionate harsh policing, excluding and sanctioning of youngsters of colour from poorer backgrounds within schools eventually leads to incarceration in their youth. Preparation, some argue, for their mass imprisonment, something which is required to keep the prison-industrial complex going [1]. Institutionalised white sadism may be used to make sense of these apparently intractable inequalities. It could be argued that sadism and racism collide within the criminal justice system to repeat the trauma of collective suffering and pain for a section of society which has been designated to suffer in order to gratify whiteness and, like 'there and then', maintain the status quo.

We do not have to dig that deeply within medical structures to discover today further evidence that supports the institutionalisation of white sadism or empirical evidence that bodies racialised as black and brown continue to have pain and torture inflicted on them in plain sight. Nowhere is this more evident than within the management of pain in medical settings. A large body of research evidence documents troubling relationships here too. We know that those racialised as black, including children, are much less likely to receive pain medication. Racial bias in pain perception and treatment continues to afflict the lives of millions of people racialised as black who present for support to healthcare professionals. This area of research demonstrates that the white subject, whether they may be drawn from the general population, medical students or experienced medics, continue to hold false beliefs about the existence of biological differences in pain thresholds between patients racialised as white and black which means the black subject can endure pain without feeling pain. Beliefs which mean they continue to be blind or dissociated from black pain. This may be framed as an enactment of sadism.

In Chapter 1 we introduced the Foulksian group–analytic formulation for the social unconscious as further developed by contemporary group analysts. We saw, in summary, that the social unconscious refers to the constraints imposed by the historical, the social and the cultural, constraints that we either lack awareness of, deny or take as non-significant or operative which nonetheless shape social arrangements and relational configurations. The social unconscious allows us to see how 'past' or historical use of sadism now constrains the relational, the structural and the psychosocial. Thus, sadism towards the racialised other, through collective memory and group inheritance, has become almost compulsorily acted out within the postcolonial nations.

The social unconscious provides the imago, archetypes and racialised figurations such as blackness as dangerousness or as superhumaness culturally and collectively inherited [27]. Similarly, the group–analytic matrix [27], also encountered in the opening chapter, may help formulate white sadism. These inheritances are central to the operationalisation or the institutionalisation of racialised sadistic cultures (in the foundation matrix) which may be supported by social discourses, legal instruments, policies and practices. Institutional and ideological arrangements in turn shape relational exchanges and communication (and vice versa) between social actors cross-racially in the domain of the everyday. Hence, people racialised as white are socialised/ habituated into the tolerance/acceptance of and indeed come to experience forms of gratification from black pain (the dynamic matrix). Finally, at the 'level' of the personal, racial figurations, racialised fantasies, scripted relational exchanges and institutional/ideological practices will acquire personal meaning by connecting to individuals' psychohistory, such as their neurotic tendencies, character traits, relationship with authority, control, conformity, etc. (the personal matrix), so that the black object also becomes loaded with what is personally meaningful and disavowed. So we can expect some variation in terms of what blackness will represent in the individual fantasies of white social actors. We may posit, as per the representation of the matrix, bidirectionality and co-constitutiveness between all 'levels' of functioning/communication so, once again, the historical, the symbolic or discursive, the structural and the psychic are connected in a perpetual loop that feeds white sadism and ensures it remains alive today.

It is worth reminding ourselves at this point that these so-called levels and the boundaries that sustain our visualisation of the group matrix are believed to be illusory. As Foulkes suggests: 'The borderline of what is "in," or "outside" is constantly moving … there is no clear-cut frontier between inside and outside, as little as between reality and phantasy' [27, p 184].

Whiteness and ontological pain

As we have repeatedly argued, racial hatred has long been posited to be a form of protection against those aspects of the self or the world one cannot tolerate. Thus, projection is also protection against the contemplation of uncertainty, powerlessness and mortality. Some of our most primal anxieties. In the context of colonialism, there is little doubt that the black or colonised body acted as a mechanism to gain control and mastery over a world which was unknown, undoubtedly terrifying and, in many ways, hugely unpredictable. The use of sadism may thus be offered as a strategy to keep these feelings at bay. That expressions of sadism and, in particular, in relation to anti-blackness closely revolve around fears of black sexuality is once more relevant. The compulsive sadistic and sexualised violence against the body racialised as black constitutes, we may argue, a fear of desire for that body. This is a defence against sexual attraction or lust, as often what is feared is desired. If so, sadism may have acted as sexualised repression in a context of puritanical, evangelical and Christian chastity.

Questions therefore arise in relation to the possibility of the white subject existing outside of the object of its gaze. Or, as Morrison asked us to consider, what would whiteness be if it were deprived of racialised others. If it were deprived of the capacity to brutalise the colonial and postcolonial subject. Undeniably, if the brutalised object comes to be brutalised to manage that sense of lack, including that capacity to connect to joy, outside of sadistic enactments, something we encountered in the previous chapter, then the existence of the racialised other is required for the white subject to cope with their own existential angst.

This is a proposition that Steele considers and links to emptiness [28]. Steele proposes that anti-blackness in essence acts as a 'white Armour' posited to have come into existence to ward off painful feelings of emptiness which lie at the core of the white subject. Baldwin had already suggested that without its hated objects whiteness would fall into a world of meaninglessness, if not nothingness, as white identities are so profoundly constructed from the racist figurations of blackness. As Reed has poignantly more recently rearticulated, disinvestment in white supremacy would leave nothing short of an empty vessel. 'An empty vessel of white fears, anxieties, and desires'

[29]. Disinvestment in whiteness cannot, therefore, be achieved, I would add, without the white subject finding and sustaining ontological meaning in alternative ways.

Summary and resistance

There is a close if not intimate connection between sadism and racism, both in historical and contemporary times. Numerous definitions and conceptualisations of sadism exist to help us understand humans' relationship with power, control, pain and white supremacy. All generally imply the derivation of pleasure from subjecting others to humiliation and suffering. We have posited that sadistic urges which needed to be heavily mobilised during enslavement and colonialism have now permeated the white psyche and most of our social structures. The normalisation of sadistic cultures which came with modernism has now therefore become institutionalised. Evidence supporting the connection between sadism and racism in contemporary times includes the treatment of postcolonial bodies within law enforcement, border control, policing and medical practices. In light of the postcolonial and post-imperialist sequalae of sadism, there is a continuing need to remind our collective mind and, particularly, white minds, that the racial other does experience pain. That we are not immune to suffering physically and psychically and that the dismantling of structural racism cannot happen without addressing sadism.

However, it is equally crucial that we accept that there is a form of racial suffering in existence in the white subject. One that sits at his very core. Refusing to see this deep malaise is not only inconsistent with the theoretical case we have made, but it also fundamentally reifies white omnipotence, thus supremacy, as well as problematic notions of separatism. We saw that disinvestment in whiteness for the white subject is likely to be fraught and resisted in part because of the ontological functions white supremacy fulfils reminding us of the sadomasochistic dimension of racism. We posited that liberation from whiteness for those racialised as white may only be achieved if alternative ways to finding existential satisfaction and meaning are found. Finding connection in the world is another way to be in the world, which may help fill that existential emptiness. Since sadism is sustained by dissociation, contact and intimacy can act as resistance tools. Connection and relationships alone will not dismantle white supremacist structures, but their absence deprives the white subject of the opportunity to connect differently to the world, thus to connect differently to themselves, which is required to imagine alternative ways of being with others. Seeking mutuality and reciprocity with the racialised other may sound like an elementary and perhaps even naive prescription, yet, if it were so, we would not be functioning within largely segregated, bordered and gated world (dis)orders. Contact requires entering the experiential field of the other to meet them there. And most fundamentally it requires being willing to be close enough to the other, to be touched psychically and physically. However uncomfortable this proximity may be to initiate and sustain. In the chapter that follows we explore trauma. But not trauma as the consequence of whiteness for the other. Rather, we examine it as a consequence for white minds.

White trauma

'In this country in 15 or 20 years' time the black man will have the whip hand over the white man.' ... I am filled with foreboding; like the Roman, I seem to see 'the River Tiber foaming with much blood'. (Powell, 1968 [1])

A cultural note

It was on 20 April 1968 that Enoch Powell, the prominent member of the Conservative Party, made his now widely known and infamous speech, 'The Rivers of Blood' [2]. A speech which was so drenched in paranoia, racialised imaginary and hate that it would inscribe itself into British memory and remain the object of sustained political analysis. It provoked repulsion and fascination in equal measure for decades to come. Powell's speech shook the nation largely because it employed discourses and devices which, until then, had been seen as the province of far-right politicians, white nationalists and extremists. The speech contained powerful imagery describing an apocalyptic Britain on the brink of black annihilation. Metaphors included, of course, the spreading of white natives' blood, Britain 'heaping up its own funeral pyre' under the watchful eyes of 'wide-grinning piccaninnies'.

The contents of the speech, which in many ways normalised within the UK mainstream the politics of racial paranoia, continue to make many of us recoil. I have attempted to fully re-read the entire text and considered incorporating larger extracts for a closer analysis in the present chapter. However, so strong and visceral was my response to the words I was reading, in the end, I simply was not able to. My will to read was overcome by a sense of repulsion which, no doubt, activated my own trauma-loaded response.

Another cultural note

On 17 June 2015, the same paranoia-filled 'logics' led to the mass shootings and murder of nine African American church-goers in Charleston by 22-year-old Dylann Roof. During his trial, it was found that Roof had wanted to start a 'race war' [3]. That he had dedicated hours to bemoaning and writing about how evil black people were. This belief in the threat posed by blackness was unshakeably held in the absence of evidence of him having been hurt by a single black person. In his own statement to the FBI, Roof confirmed he had never suffered harm at the hands of a person racialised as black.

In fact, there was evidence of him appearing to have sustained friendships with people racialised as black for most of his life. Despite this, Roof, who was said to have been radicalised by neo-Nazi propaganda, grew increasingly convinced that 'black-on-white' violence was threatening not only his life but the very existence of people racialised as white. 'Blacks' became, in his imagination, deadly enemies to be annihilated pre-emptively. Ticking time-bombs to be neutralised, to defend the very survival of the white race. Although Roof's paranoid ideation may seem extreme, and Powell's political apocalyptic vision may be excluded from the realm of the banal and the ordinary, evidence of quotidian expressions of the same phenomena is relatively easy to find, as illustrated by the experience which follows.

An ethnographic note

Towards the end of 2018, I met with a friend of mine. I was invited to her art gallery where I met a friend of hers for the first time. He was a middle-aged white English man who had successfully set up his own business following a career in banking, despite his working-class origins. He was a warm and open man and we clicked instantly. We bantered and took turns critiquing the artwork on display. The atmosphere was relaxed as we settled down for a glass of wine. Then the subject shifted to immigration and race and things took an unexpected turn. He recounted being accused of racism by an Asian man for whom he had turned down a mortgage application. With some agitation, he described what he thought was an attempt by the client at using the 'race card'. He subsequently spoke of a Jewish man becoming angry over Christmas decorations in the branch. He lamented this 'intolerance' as he, an English man in his 'own' country, had to tolerate 'Jewish decorations' on the streets of London. He went on and on. The rant ended with him discussing the threat of a foreign invasion, England's unrecognisable face and the fight the country was required to lead in order to preserve its culture and identity. I could feel my blood pressure rising. My temples were starting to slowly throb. I also became conscious I was having palpitations. But, as he carried on, I deliberately shifted my focus outward by attending to the emotions and feelings on display in him. I noted the obvious anger. Mainly, though, it was terror and paranoia that dominated. These feelings were palpable, however disconnected from reality they really were. I experienced his hate-filled words as an assault on my body, which came out of nowhere, as though out of space. I knew we had become a vehicle for the articulation of something which is still taking form in my mind but which I was certain, even then, went beyond us as individual racialised subjects. It struck me that his terror and anxiety paralleled mine. It struck me too that, while I could pay minute attention to the internal worlds unravelling and intersecting in the gallery, both mine and that of my interlocutor (my body was at the receiving end of this racialised violence dished out as speech), he was completely oblivious not only to the impact of his words on me, but of his own affective state of activation. He was, in effect, completely cut off from his body and from mine. He was the one in that white bubble.

Exceptionalising the contents of Powell and Roof's worldviews is tempting. The art gallery anecdote, nonetheless, forces us to refrain from doing so. It illustrates how so much contemporary ethno-nationalist border control discourses have normalised the same themes and beliefs in much of the general population. And how paranoia-filled migration imaginaries become acted out relationally and are felt once more viscerally. That they lodge themselves in the body means they have health implications and will affect the welfare of the repository of this hatred, however delusional, it may be. The complex interplay between reality and fantasy, and the blurring of psychic boundaries between the affective states of social actors, is one of the hallmarks of trauma activation.

Whose trauma?

In Chapter 1 we contemplated the Freudian principle of repetition compulsion. We posited, then, that part of the complexity in seeking to apply this thinking to the repetition of racism was that it was not always clear whose trauma was being re-enacted. There is a tendency to consider trauma as the burden of survivors of atrocities and injustices and/or their descendants. The current chapter seeks to challenge this notion and to draw attention to an idea that is still controversial. The notion that trauma is not uniquely the province of survivors and victims of atrocities but that, on the contrary, abusers, perpetrators of violence and oppressors can experience their violence as trauma or be traumatised by their own violent acts and, thus, come to be harmed by the harm they cause and engage in. Or, in other words, committing heinous or unjust acts has the potential, and does often, cause psychological injury to the perpetrators. While we tend to see trauma through individualistic lenses, as is often the case for all processes under whiteness, entire groups of perpetrators, societies, states and nations can suffer from their engagement, in contemporary or historical atrocities. Put another way, severe violence has severe consequences for those who do serious harm. These consequences can manifest psychosocially and culturally. Hence, the trauma-related effects of whiteness on white groups likely goes beyond the harm sustained by survivors as individuals.

I propose that using a trauma lens to examine the impact of white supremacy on groups racialised as white is an important step to building a full picture of the legacy of colonial and racial violence and thus gives us a better understanding of processes of repetition, re-enactment and acting out. In the remainder of this chapter, I will suggest that key trauma-related psychological processes – paranoia, fragility and aversion – are derivatives of white supremacy-related trauma for groups racialised as white and that these are central to the reproduction of whiteness. This trauma remains by and large unaddressed, even though it is part of the cycle of white violence. The proposition I am putting forth is consistent with many non-Western collectivist philosophies which see the intersubjective and the interbeing as foundational to both human subjectivity and social phenomena. These ontological beliefs provide some epistemic grounding in the idea that we may call intersuffering. If the Southern African philosophy of Ubuntu is best understood by the axiom 'I am because you are' or 'we are because you are' [4], intersuffering may be encapsulated by 'I suffer because you suffer' or 'we suffer because you suffer'; highlighting the universal connection, bonds that unite us and, here, we may propose, bonds of pain.

When it comes to understanding oppression, the idea that oppressors are compromised by the oppression they engage in is not new. The idea of 'toxic masculinity', for example, has entered our collective consciousness and public discourses. Toxic masculinity speaks of the damaging ways in which boys, men and masculine presenting bodies, are gendered and socialised within patriarchal systems. The social coercion to perform masculinity has, some have argued, led to particular ways of relating to the self and to others and, in particular, the suppression of emotions, the enacting of dominance and aggression [5]. Gender differences in relation to intimacy, connection, propensity to violence and reduced self-awareness, among other characteristics, have been posited to be part of patriarchy's harmful socialisation within cisheteropatriarchy. Thus, constructions of manhood, of masculinity which provide structural and relational power to those gendered as men or masculine, also carry hefty costs, to themselves. It is primarily in the domain of the psychic that such costs have generally been explored and perhaps the most significant cost of masculinity might be suicidality, violence, we may formulate, turned inwards.

We have known for a while that men are far more likely to take their own lives when compared to their women counterparts, all things being equal. In the UK, where suicide is still the most common cause of death for men under 45, the suicide rate for women is a third of that of men. The same pattern exists in most Western countries. The disparity is in part believed to be due to the stigma surrounding psychological distress, the social pressures of performing 'masculinity' and the gendered restrictions related to help seeking and vulnerability. hooks, in *All about love*, reminds us that masculine identity requires the repression of feelings and socialisation into loneliness, pain as well as the development of a false self sustained by dishonesty and self-deception. Learning to dissociate from feelings so as not to feel is a cultural expectation of those gendered as men within social structures, from authority figures and oftentimes even in the domestic arena. Estrangement from feelings necessitates estrangement from others as well as estrangement from the self, all of which is required to remain unaffected bystanders to the harm and pain caused to others. It justifies violence towards those with less power.

That masculinity can lead to such estrangement and to the ultimate act of destruction and self-annihilation, highlights the seriousness of issues of self-alienation. Here too the subject encounters difficulties with the image of the self one is projected back to from society's mirrors. This false consciousness, or false self, which is required to conform to a society that still demands, by and large, strict adherence to these gendered norms and roles and which violently polices and restricts freedom of expression, thought and action along gender lines, kills. It kills others and it kills men themselves. Men, in other words, are raised to raise monsters within themselves, monsters which then become a risk to themselves as subjects.

It is thus generally accepted that patriarchy and its associated systems of domination harm men possibly as much as they harm others, although differently. The idea that the white subject may be harmed by whiteness is not as widely articulated. It remains much more contentious. In part this is because white psychological functioning is still positioned as the healthy norm as we have argued. It is accordingly those who are directly harmed by whiteness, who for the most part are conscious of this harm, who have tended to be imagined as deviant, pathological or vulnerable. In line with such constructions, white 'allies' continue to see anti-racism and racial justice work as a favour they do to others 'less fortunate than themselves'. The harm of whiteness is therefore located outside the self. A perspective which provides supply to white narcissism and fantasies of omnipotence. Instead, of course, dismantling whiteness for the white subject is fundamentally a favour they do to themselves. An inescapable realisation is bound to arise from self-awareness, auto-recognition and consequently appreciation of the harm whiteness poses to itself.

The latter proposition has existed in the anti-fascist and postcolonial literature for some time. What came to be termed imperialism's 'boomerang effect' by post-war intellectuals – an expression coined by Arendt – theorised that empires used colonies as training grounds or laboratories to develop methods to be later employed in the metropolis as means of social control and stratification [6]. Arendt herself posited that imperial processes of racialisation and territorial expansion provided the foundation for fascism and totalitarianism in Europe.

Césaire has similarly proposed the same as he wrote about the hypocrisy and duplicitousness of Europe whose sense of moral superiority was edified in the face of colonial atrocities on overseas territories [7]. His argument that 'no one colonises innocently' and 'no one colonises with impunity' resonates. For Césaire, in his attempt to civilise the 'savages' through the use of violence, the colonialist in fact enacts and displaces his own savagery and sadism, which are allowed to run errant. These displaced impulses not only dehumanise the white subject in the process of their enactment, but they also nurse a monster eventually bound to turn inwards, to return home. Césaire saw torture and brutality enacted on colonial territories as laying the foundation for the Holocaust on European soil.

A severe disconnection or split must necessarily exist within the white psyche to allow white minds to continue to engage in racial violence, to be complicit in the same, while feeling untouched. Such dissociation is necessary to protect the collective white self-concept which revolves around moral authority, superiority and benevolence. A process that Fanon has posited relies on cognitive dissonance. Cognitive dissonance is the intense discomfort that is produced when we are presented with evidence or information that challenges some core beliefs we hold about ourselves, others or the world. To minimise this discomfort, we tend to engage in a range of cognitive distortions or gymnastics that leave the core belief intact, in order to discharge the dissonance. In other words, we would rather discard evidence that requires us to change a core belief than discard the core belief rendered defunct by the evidence. Hence, racialisation necessitates the white subject to operate in a state of false consciousness. It requires the development of a distorted view of the self, others and the world, to sustain unjust and violent world (dis)orders and violent relational configurations, where the self must be thought of as independent from white supremacy, possibly engaged in anti-racism and, of course, seeking to do good as one fundamentally is.

Everyday performance

Dear Guilaine, please see the reflection below. I am sorry if it is painful or disheartening for you to read this. It's from about three years ago. I was supervising in the NHS and received a minor complaint from colleagues against a Black supervisee. I tried to explore the situation in supervision with her – asking what happened from her perspective, but this didn't seem to be useful. Finally, it came to my mind, and I asked without thinking on it further, 'Is it because they (the complainants) are White?' I saw that this was the first time I'd said something which came close to the mark, but there was also a communication from her that I had broken a boundary, however naively. I was now in territory that I was ill equipped to explore. And as she replied, 'Of course it is', along with it came the realisation that although I had positioned myself as outside the conflict, as the helper in this situation, there was now no escaping my Whiteness in that room and the harm it meant to that supervisee. And that part of my Whiteness was to have intruded on her experience and named something that I then had no ability to work with. I felt my heart racing and hot tears coming to my eyes as I also felt a new emotion, anger, and a desire to defend myself, even though it was she, and not I, who was most hurt by the interaction. Perhaps it's best to end here. We both left the service shortly afterwards. I've reflected a great deal on my Whiteness ever since and my complicity in racism. (Stephanie, white woman, 40s, England)

Of all the contributions I received to illustrate the everyday relational performances of whiteness, this was possibly the most difficult to read. As we saw in Chapter 2 on white gazes, the story Stephanie brought to the call for contributions has strong echoes of my own experience of existing within white (women-dominated) spaces. Although the contents of the complaint against the black supervisee is not known to us and, in fact, need not be known for us to consider the inequalities and dynamics the anecdote exposes – we do know that professionals racialised as black and brown are significantly more likely to be the recipients of complaints by both clients and colleagues in most professional settings – since the themes it makes us a party to are central to our formulation of location of disturbance, scapegoating, white complicity, shame and distress, thus, potentially, trauma.

Stephanie, it is clear, initially saw herself as the benevolent helper attempting to resolve the complaint against the black supervisee. A kind of manoeuvring which was naive and extracted from structural and group realities as well as Stephanie's own contribution to the racialised crisis. The sort of unreflective or unthinking saviourism that often springs from white innocence. Stephanie's 'help' was thus rightfully met with silence and resistance. Perhaps because the black trainee, aware of the power asymmetry in the relationship, the supervisor's limitations when it came to understanding whiteness and its workings, understood she was in a precarious position. When it finally hit Stephanie that race was operative and that she, as a supervisor, was part of the group disturbance, she continued to locate in the black trainee, an act of racism in and of itself. As she did not have the capacity to reflect on the race dynamics at play, strong emotions were activated in her, emotions she could neither bear nor contain. She names anger and distress and describes her embodied responses: her heart races. Her autonomous cerebral system is in threat mode. She feels the need to defend herself because she feels under attack in her integrity and her self-image as a benevolent, innocent, well-intentioned 'helper'.

White innocence, violence and 'basic assumptions'

Connecting to the disturbance the black trainee was forced to carry alone in what may be adequately described as scapegoating, Stephanie is distressed to the point of tears. The same tears we encountered when I too forced a white woman to confront her complicity in racialised harm, in the bin-dumping anecdote which I described at the very start of the book. The distress I have no doubt is genuine here, too. I propose nonetheless that underlying that distress is a deep sense of shame. And that regardless of its authenticity, Stephanie's distress is socially functional. We may even argue that this affective turn is a common power move in that it deprives the black subject – here the trainee – of support, and it protects structures of power by positioning the supervisor, if only symbolically, as the wronged party or, at the very least, the party needing care and attention. The trainee racialised as black is forced, we may argue, into a caring role. This occurs by reinscribing relationally and institutionally what Hill Collins may refer to as the 'controlling image' and expectation of the mammy. We observe the racialised and gendered (misogynoir) social expectation of the indefatigable nurturer of well-intentioned white souls, particularly white women and white children that typifies the 'good black mother' and, in actuality too the good black woman within white patriarchy.

By shifting the direction of accountability or the gaze toward the black subject, here the trainee, Stephanie increases risks of structural harm and violence for the more precariously positioned party. In summary, in a moment of shame and self-awareness acuity, the main repository of the group racialised disturbance is left alone and, likely, more structurally vulnerable because of the white subject's momentary affective and largely narcissism-based vulnerability. The trainee's vulnerability, however, is primarily located in the material even though it likely finds its genesis in the unconscious functioning of the institution.

Bion's thinking on group processes and, in particular, his formulation of the 'work group' and the 'basic assumptions group', is particularly helpful to explicate that increased institutional vulnerability [8]. His formulation proposes the existence of two groups, or we may say two institutions, within each group or institution. These are a group/institution which operates consciously, aware of the tasks at hand (here maybe the need to support the trainee), and in parallel, a group/institution whose functioning is phantasm based. This is where the neglected, hidden and buried parts of group members collide and behave unconsciously, often by acting out feelings of anxiety and, in doing so, derailing the explicit or conscious purpose of the 'work group' (perhaps by seeking to exclude or punish the black trainee). This 'shadow group', or shadow institution, is a hidden reality. This is a reality that exists in parallel to the conscious functioning of groups and institutions and which can be triggered into violent 'fight or flight' mode by the identification of a 'common enemy' within the group or institution.

A black trainee 'causing' distress to a white supervisor or white peers, even if that distress stems from their resistance to facing disavowed parts of themselves, can easily become vilified, pathologised or otherwise positioned as an institutional threat. When sufficient anxiety is aroused within a particular context, the 'basic assumptions group' has the potential to overtake communications and interactions, engulfing conscious functioning. It is this engulfment of the 'work group' or work institution by the 'basic assumptions group' or the 'basic assumptions institution' that means the trainee is vulnerable to further group violence, group analysts may formulate. Here of course, the 'basic assumptions group' is liable to springing into operation by the positioning of the Black subject as an institutional threat.

This is in part because of the racialised disturbance, which is located in her, and in part because institutions remain quick to reify and protect the sanctity of white womanhood and associated figurations of innocence. Perhaps too by being positioned as the originator of white distress, the black trainee transgresses racialised and gendered expectations of emotional servitude and thus easily slots into another colonial archetype, that of the dangerous black body needing control, restraint and discipline. The intersections of these factors mean that, within a matter of moments, the black trainee can be turned into the common enemy, the victimiser, and be treated as a traumatising object rather than as the traumatised subject, which arguably circles back on white trauma and consequent dissociation from reality.

Victimhood, trauma and resistance

Using trauma as a lens to consider the impact of whiteness on people racialised as white as illustrated, some may argue, by the fragility of the supervisor's response, provides a micro illustration of post-war and postcolonial thinking on the murky if not illusory boundaries between victims and perpetrators. Yet, this application is not without contestation. Contemplating whiteness or any social phenomena more generally under a trauma frame presents some challenges. Beyond broader limitations related to the psychologising of white supremacy and the risk of individualising social and political structures, many may see in this approach an imperial expansion of psychiatric thinking – thinking which even 25 years ago was still equally contested. And therefore, the shifting of psychiatry into the domain of social theory. Such a move certainly has important moral, ethical and possibly legal consequences; consequences for how we may come to define victims and formulate victimhood. Consequences in terms of how we may think about suffering and validate the truth of that suffering. Consequences for how we may or may not experience compassion towards the said suffering and consequences for repair and reparation. Of particular importance to the present, while trauma conceptualisations, or trauma as a regime of truth, may visibilise some forms of suffering, it has the potential to lead to the silencing of others through associated politics of proof and the propagation of clinical reasoning [9].

I have witnessed these reservations when attempting over the years to have conversations on the subject of white trauma with those around me. And, although the idea can initially attract a captive audience, these conversations seems to go in two predictable directions. White individuals I have come into contact with, in the main, seem to have difficulties relating to the idea of them being traumatised. Although some were taken by it, usually those associated with the mental health field. For those outside there tended to be much more resistance. I have formulated that perhaps something about trauma calls those individuals to connect to the less powerful and more vulnerable parts of themselves which may challenge white narcissism and grandiosity, the defensive sense that they are able to remain perpetually unscathed by racial violence. On the other hand, people of colour can be equally perplexed and suspicious of the idea. Anger is not an unusual response. Mostly this anger appears to be activated by the idea that such a frame would centre 'white fragility' and/or create false equivalencies rendering their trauma less likely to be attended to.

These anxieties are not without foundation. Threats to white power and interest are susceptible to be experienced as violence, as humiliation and as trauma. Such subjective realities are liable to be weaponised to ensure the re-centring of whiteness at best, and, at worse, may place those who challenge white structures and those with less social power at risk of being positioned as the 'real' perpetrator of violence, the racial oppressor. The real racist. These manoeuvres and rhetorics have been acted out aggressively socio-politically. They have been central in the rise of neo-fascism and imperial nostalgia which boosted Trump's win and the Brexit vote in Britain. The use of white trauma as an explanatory model, it may be argued, has the potential to embolden discourses of white victimhood and adjacent ideas of white disenfranchisement. Culturally sanctioning the edifice of 'white feelings' and consequently providing further cushioning around the affective comfort of the white subject at the expense of the confrontation of both the affective and, more importantly, material realities of race inequality for the racialised other.

Given these risks, it is right to consider the ethical case for examining white trauma. The raison d'être of *White minds* is the absence of theorisation vis-à-vis the internal worlds and psychosocial functioning of white psyches in light of centuries of racial oppression and mass atrocities. This legacy includes the afterlife of trauma, or at least what we today have come to form as trauma, white groups might have suffered as a result of their active and passive participation in oppression. The residuals of exposure to overwhelming experiences and to violence, be it vicariously, indirectly and well as more directly, need attention. Equally, there are significant risks in refusing to consider resulting responses that may in effect cause relational harm and support the reproduction of social dysfunction. As a clinician, it is simply impossible to read the 'Rivers of blood' speech and miss the terror, the paranoia, the delusional thinking it contains, in the same way the profoundly misdirected anger and psychological distress displayed earlier in the art gallery anecdote lend themselves, if only theoretically, to a trauma interpretation.

We also know that, historically and throughout all imperial and colonial engagement, terror has existed on both sides of the power divide. Slave owners were haunted by the belief that they would suffer the very fate they had imposed upon black groups. The colonial subject was fundamentally formed as a dangerous and terror-inducing being, in part because of the atrocities they endured. The projective anticipation of rebellion, retaliation and payback have terrorised the hearts of countless white generations. They have led to unspeakably brutal repressions throughout history, providing evidence of material consequences to the association between racial paranoia, psychological overwhelm or terror and racial violence albeit as defensive enactment or projection. Functioning which not only lay at the core of current trauma conceptualisations but likely engender racial trauma or at least wounding, at mass level, onto the object of that paranoia. A trauma framework, as a result, does have the potential to offer psychic and structural insights it would be unethical to discard, insights which may in effect help us to disrupt the endurance of the 'past' into the present to which analytic formulations may contribute.

Trauma: some analytic concepts

A significant analytic contribution to the conceptualisation of trauma of relevance in the context of whiteness focuses on fragmentation of the psyche [10]. Accordingly, trauma is thought to result from overwhelming experiences which overtake our capacity to make meaning. Events deemed traumatic according to that line of thought are those that our psychic defences cannot cope with, giving rise to significant internal disturbances and conflicts.

Freud's contributions to our understanding of trauma, despite much controversy, remain with us [11]. For example, his formulation of repetition compulsion we encountered in Chapter 1, and his thinking on repetition is closely linked to the defence of repression [12]. In essence, repression occurs when we block or disallow to reach our consciousness material we find intolerable, or which may cause psychic overwhelm. More technically, repression is used by the ego as a defence to help to get rid of anxiety so that the disturbing knowledge is warded off our conscious awareness and in a way forgotten. Another core Freudian conceptualisation of trauma relates to the phenomenon of intrusion. Trauma here is imagined as forced entry or as forced merging. This is why at the heart of the traumatic experience is thought to exist a blurring of the then and now, a blurring of time and place boundaries and a blurring of objects. Trauma as boundary transgression and intrusion is helpful to explain experiences of reliving, repetition or 're-experiencing' commonly found in those with significant trauma histories.

Bion's formulation of trauma centres on containment [13]. Containment here has a specific meaning. This containment function is fulfilled in our early relationships – usually with our caregivers when they are able to tolerate, process and give back in manageable form unbearable feelings that we cannot put into words. Here, trauma is seen to be the result of unresponsive caregivers, or important others and their inability to contain the fragments, the chaos or the dread, of the infant. The core containment function beyond infancy entails tolerating projected unbearable feelings that we struggle to articulate. In other words, containment allows meaning and sense to be made out of beta elements which are these fragmented and overwhelming experiences – this is what he refers to as the alpha function – and allows unbearable experience to be made intelligible, laying the foundation for the capacity to think, to mentalise and to acquire knowledge.

His work on psychosis further elucidates Bion's formulation of containment. His theory of 'attacks on linking' proposes that psychotic parts of the mind, of those parts which cannot bear confronting reality, will direct destructive and sadistic attacks on the links made between objects such as between 'past' and present, between events and meaning, between objects or between mind and body. Here links may be thought of as the intellectual connection which allow meaning making. 'Attacks of linking' are, in essence, believed to be the result of ruptures in communication, failed containment and thus the disruption of developmental processes. Attacks on linking disable the non-psychotic part of the self, compromise knowing and, in particular, make apprehending reality virtually impossible. When we attack 'links' we aggressively attempt to destroy meaning so as to avoid reality to emerge.

Bion's formulation of trauma thus centres knowledge and the capacity to know which are only possible through adequate containment [14].

The main clinical and psychoanalytic theorisations of trauma pose a number of challenges for the study of groups and society. First, they tend to extract trauma from socio-political contexts or, we may say, they individualise trauma and fail to engage with the collective dimensions of overwhelming experiences and their resulting wounds. Second, and perhaps more critically, they are blind to the harm of racism, not only on individuals but on collectives and, crucially, on both white individuals and white groups.

Still, even though this thinking may not neatly transfer onto our study of whiteness and white minds, they do assist in making a case for the necessary exploration of white traumatisation within white supremacy. For example, Bion's work on psychosis is fruitful to think about white defensiveness when it comes to the contemplation of racism. A refusal to confront reality. Eurocentrism's individualism may be formulated as an attack on linking. A response originating from the psychotic part of the white psyche to evade these connections or links which are necessary to make meaning, connecting between these split entities or phenomena as we proposed in Chapter 1, such as the links between the 'past' and the present, the individual and the group, the psyche and the social. Further, these analytic frameworks invite us to hypothesise a collective racial trauma 'syndrome' in white groups in effect and implicated in the capacity to grasp reality. A case scholars from a range of disciplines have indeed made.

Contemporary empirical evidence exists that suggests that offenders with a history of violent crimes have higher rates of 'post-traumatic stress disorder' [15]. And this remains so even for those without trauma histories prior to offending. In other words, committing violence against others renders us vulnerable to trauma responses and this is consistent with the empirical literature on trauma and offending. Further, we know from years, if not centuries, of clinical observations and empirical investigations, that military personnel, soldiers and those involved in combat and conflict zones also are at increased risk of experiencing trauma-related distress irrespective of which adversary side they fought or defended from. This is so even when acts of violence were committed in self-defence. It seems clear that violence and trauma are not subject to the kind of boundaries we rigidly impose onto the perpetrator–survivor divide. A divide that seems all the more blurred once we consider less individualistic formulations of trauma.

Collective trauma

A social psychology perspective on trauma moves trauma considerations from individuals to group level phenomena [16]. In moving us beyond liberal, hegemonic discourses that tend to individualise and extract it from socio-political and material realities, such collective scholarship sheds light on the impact of trauma on whole cultural or ethnic groups, entire societies or nations within particular spaces and at particular times. Collective trauma frameworks propose that trauma goes well beyond the lives of direct survivors or direct witnesses of the distressing events or atrocities in question. Rather, it continues to be remembered by entire groups however far removed from the actual event or events, it is believed through a process of transgenerational transmission.

Trauma as a group phenomenon, and as conceptualised by group analysts, is often understood in relation to meaning making and identity formation [17]. An event which is collectively experienced as traumatic markedly shifts how we make meaning of the world and transforms both our sense of who we are and that of others. Essentially, it forces us to redefine our relationship with the world and our worldview. Of particular note, collective trauma transforms how the world is perceived and experienced by both survivors and perpetrators. As such, collective trauma is believed to be a focal point of group identification; an important context through which group members comprehend their social environments and locate themselves in the world at large. This transmission of traumatic memories to descendants of trauma survivors is believed to be achieved through a number of means, many of which we have covered, including cultural archives, group processes, social scripts and group equivalences which support processes of identification with the original 'perpetrators' or survivors' groups.

The concepts of chosen trauma and chosen glory speak to those processes [18]. They refer to the mental representation a group holds of itself following collective traumatic experiences. These representations are deeply linked to how the group thinks of itself. Contrary to what 'chosen' implies, here choice is not involved in trauma. Instead, it is suggested that memories are drawn upon, to construct and form a sense of group identity. This process is believed to be collective and primarily unconscious. Chosen traumas are therefore collective, shared mental representations of traumatic events which are unresolved or incompletely mourned. And because they are not completely mourned, they are transmitted to subsequent generations to resolve. It is believed that they will continue to be handed down until the trauma they underscore is processed and its associated wounds healed.

Chosen glories are also shared mental representations of collective experiences related to historical events. They are equally critical in shaping a particular's group identity but create a sense of group pride. Chosen glories allow members to rally around a sense of collective triumph, success, brilliance. Every nation, society and even institution will have their own chosen trauma and chosen glories. The fundamental problem we have when considering whiteness is that chosen traumas and chosen glories often clash or are frequently one and the same. That is to say, chosen glories, the celebrated historical events which lead to pride, are also at some level the very source of trauma. And conversely, what is consciously held in contempt is also connected to white groups' sense of accomplishment, triumph and glory in terms of group identity. Take for example, the UK's involvement in enslavement. This clearly carries great shame and likely trauma on the one hand in white groups, because processes involved, such as genocidal violence, torture and rape, clash with more conscious group chosen glories such as in the boastful narrative of 'we ended the slave trade'. Or, again, consider empire-building, which is both trauma-laden and a source of pride. The conflict between glories and trauma leads to ambivalence, the denial of the harm caused and sustained and indeed resistance to letting go of that which is a source of collective pride. This is even if letting go would help support collective healing and repair.

Summary and resistance

Trauma, despite its contested history, remains firmly with us when it comes to thinking about human suffering. Although using trauma as a lens to build social theory has significant limitations, more recent theoretical advances and empirical findings can illuminate the psychosocial functioning of whiteness. We have seen that trauma has no firm boundaries when it comes to time and space and that analytic formulations of trauma challenge these 'common-sense' physical and psychological lines of demarcation between perpetrators and survivors. Although white supremacy cannot be reduced to psychic functioning, let alone to white traumatisation, the hesitancy to employing trauma as an explanatory framework to consider the harm of whiteness on the white subject is denying that they may be experiencing a form of wounding as a response to their active and passive participation in white supremacy, and because of the associated wounds they have collectively caused others. This belief is arguably symptomatic of the kind of separatist ideas that form the foundation of uncritical Western thought. Not only is this inconsistent with various non-Western ontologies, but it is also inconsistent with commonly observed white responses to race-based material which show evidence of overwhelm, hence a failure to contain, digest and metabolise what challenges the sense of self and the sense of one's being in the world. These responses are evocative of many conceptualisations of traumatisation at individual and at collective level. It is consequently not in our collective interest to ignore the harmful impact of violence on white groups, it is certainly not in the interest of the racialised other. Unaddressed harm or trauma may well lead to racialised violence, and intergenerational transmission, thus the continuation and repetition of cycles of harm, further traumatisation in groups racialised as black and brown, as well as the reproduction of structural inequality. To resist the relational and structural consequences of whiteness-related trauma and for white groups to address their collective wounds, integration must be centred. Integrating a disavowed part of the self, disavowed memories and disavowed histories and thus resisting repression or the collapsing into terror-based fantasies of annihilation. This cannot happen unless the white subject is prepared to connect to vulnerability. Interrupting the transmission of the trauma related to the disowned and to the discarded would require white groups and society more broadly to tolerate the truth of colonial atrocities. It would require them to bear witness, to accept the wrong they are implicated in and the associated suffering in the 'past' and the present. This is fundamental to support recognition and reparation both for the self and for the other [19]. Although demands for reparations are strenuously opposed in society, for any form of meaningful repair to be sustained, however limited it may realistically be, it must take place in all the domains affected by the index violence and injustices. As such, there can be no genuine repair that excludes the material. In the next chapter, we examine white dissociation, a mechanism integral to trauma, which poses further challenges to truth, repair and reconciliation, and we also suggest strategies of resistance.

6

White dissociation

> I was socialised ... not to see myself as connected to racism and certainly not to see myself as connected to race. In other words, I did not have a sense of a racial identity. Today, I understand that I move through the world always and most particularly as a white person. I have a white frame of reference and I have a white experience. And part of being white is to have that be invisible to ourselves and to be able to live our lives without ever acknowledging that, to see that as non-operative. (DiAngelo, 2017 [1])

Di-Angelo's words provide a white context to Eddo–Lodge's book *Why I'm no longer talking to white people about race*. Specifically the racialised context to the disconnection that can follow cross-racial exchanges. As a woman writer racialised as black, Eddo-Lodge refers to 'the gulf of an emotional disconnect' which translates to recognisable difficulties in being seen, heard and understood. She names what people racialised as black often experience when they attempt to articulate matters related to race. In the previous chapter, we proposed that whiteness may be reiterated through unprocessed traumatic responses, responses which might continue to be transmitted from generation to generation. In Chapter 4 we have seen that lynching was used as a method of social and economic control. We referenced the grotesque pictures of lynching scenes on postcards which depicted jovial and carefree white audiences posing next to black bodies, often hanging, in pieces, from trees. Reconciling the joyful mood of these audiences with the gruesome violent acts committed may seem impossible, even after the examination of sadism. Dissociation and splitting offer analytic tools to help do just that.

Splitting and dissociation

> The intoxicating influence of Whiteness creates a vapid space in which thinking is impeded – defended against. (Dennis, 2022 [2])

The defences of splitting and dissociation which keep white ignorance and white benevolence intact in fact strengthen the case for white trauma. But since maintaining the status quo requires some disconnection from the status quo, the distance created by splitting and dissociation illuminates the temporality of whiteness and its links with dominant ideologies and epistemic practices in the West. Therefore, they help us to better grasp the processes that allow dualistic and associated logics and the constant rearticulation of the 'past' into the present. At the same time, a reconstruction of that 'past' via revisionism, so it is not faced in the present.

Splitting is often described as polarised, binary 'black and white' thinking; the defence is, in reality, more complex. Explaining the genealogy and evolution of the concept is beyond the scope of this chapter. However, a summary is proposed in what follows to situate our reflections. Splitting is central to Klein's object relations theory. According to the theory, splitting is one of the earliest manifestations of the death instinct. It is developed in early infancy to manage overwhelming anxieties primarily related to the fear of persecution. The fear of persecution leads to the development of mechanisms to protect the ego, key among these is the splitting of internal and external objects, emotions and the ego. In simple terms, splitting involves separating objects (mainly here objects refer to important people) into all good and all bad parts and repudiating or repressing the anxiety-provoking bad parts, in what Klein termed the paranoid-schizoid position [3].

The paranoid-schizoid position, for most of us, is followed by the depressive position. In the depressive position, splitting is reduced, and a more balanced and integrated view of reality can be achieved. Part-objects become whole objects and from this springs the capacity to repair and form authentic connections.

Put more simply, we are able to integrate both good and bad aspects of ourselves, others and the world. Klein's object relations theory remains controversial, particularly her theorisation that aggression and sophisticated ego functioning in infancy not only exist, but they also lay the foundation for the human capacity both to form fulfilling relationships in adulthood and to access and hold onto reality. Importantly the theory has implications beyond infancy and, as the term suggests, the paranoid-schizoid and depressive 'positions' are not phases or permanent states, they are way of relating (to the self, the other and the world) which can become activated throughout life.

The important parts of Klein's theory for our exploration of white minds are as follows:

- when we split we oscillate between idealisation or love and feelings of persecution or intense hatred;
- hated and repudiated parts of the self are projected outwards to protect the ego from becoming overwhelmed by terror, this is why splitting is a defence heavily relied upon following trauma;
- moving from the paranoid-schizoid to the depressive position is required to help the subject to come to terms 'with the reality of the world and its place in it';

- when in the throes of the paranoid–schizoid position, the 'good parts' of the object cannot be tolerated, which often leads to envy, aggression and concomitant envious attacks on the object;
- crucially, splitting functions as a defence to apprehending reality.

We can see at this point how Bion's theorisation of 'attack on linking' finds its foundation in Klein's ideas and, more importantly, how fundamentally whiteness would impair thinking.

The richness of Klein's theorisation could help illuminate much of the contents of *White minds*. From the projective positioning of the black other as the 'bad parts' of the white self and the centrality of envy in the genesis of racialised sadistic violence and attacks on the black object, to the operation of paranoid persecutory beliefs in the white subject [2, 4].

Dissociation is closely related to splitting [5]. This defence is operational when we cannot confront what is unacceptable, what overwhelms us and what brings about feelings of dread, horror or terror. As a result, dissociation is closely related to repression. The concept of dissociation is attributed to French psychologist Janet who first established a link between fragmentation of the consciousness (dissociation) and what was then thought of as 'hysteria' following trauma, at the beginning of the 20th century. Janet clinically observed that traumatised patients seemed to vacillate between 'hyper-experiencing' the trauma and being completely cut off from it. He posited that dissociation was a strategy to detach one's consciousness from the intense emotional activation created by the reliving of the traumatic experience [6].

Dissociation continues to feature within most trauma conceptualisations as it is fundamentally a way to regulate our emotions and in particular manage overwhelming pain and fear. When we dissociate, we disconnect from aspects of our internal or external worlds. Thought, affect, body and/or the environment we inhabit appear fragmented. They do not communicate. Often this is the result of us attempting to escape or flee some aspects of the world. Dissociation often manifests, I suggest, in four main ways:

- When we can understand something theoretically but cannot connect to the associated feelings, let's call this *affective dissociation*.
- When we experience feelings but cannot link these to particular cognitive phenomena, hence, struggle to derive meaning from them or link them to ideas, perhaps we are feeling anxious or sad but don't understand why, we may say this refers to *cognitive dissociation*.
- When experiences are apprehended corporeally, for example our bodies may be showing signs of autonomous activation, or of physical distress or fear perhaps because we are witnessing or experiencing troubling and threatening experiences but we don't recognise or

even notice in ourselves these responses happening in our body, this sort of dissociation we may refer to as *physiological dissociation*, a form of disembodiment.

• When our emotions, thoughts and body appear appropriately connected but are cut off from the world around us. Here, we are not able to make conscious links between ourselves and the world we inhabit, we are cut off from the experiences of those around us and/or do not notice happenings of significance socially and interpersonally. We may refer to this phenomenon as *social dissociation*.

White ignorance, white dissociation

The proposed multidimensional framework to explore dissociative phenomena reveal how operating within white supremacy creates fragmentation and disconnection at different levels of functioning. In summary, dissociation is a form of disconnection from our internal world, from the external world or the connection that exists between the two – if, once more, we conceptualise these 'entities' as separate, a notion we have repeatedly proposed which is largely illusory – allowing us to perhaps better see how dissociation and splitting share a similar root. Putting dissociation and splitting at the centre of the reproduction of whiteness expounds on the harm and pain caused by white supremacy and why it does not appear to be registered, taken in or confronted. At least consciously and at a collective level.

Eddo-Lodge did not use dissociation or splitting as lenses to make sense of the disconnect she wrote about [7]. Nonetheless, the descriptions of disconnection, sensory inaccessibility, of denial of inequality and the refusal or unwillingness to make psychological contact with the speaker when the subject of race is what is spoken about by the black and brown subject, evoke affective, cognitive, social and dissociation. Possibly physical dissociation too, if the white subject is not connected – and often they are not – to their own embodied responses.

Similarly, Akala has suggested that what he sees as an inability to reflexively examine oneself, one's history, as well as one's investment in white supremacy leads the white subject to silence conversations on racism [8]. Typically, the author continues, a person raising the matter of race will be confronted with irrational, and we may in fact say dissociative, responses, including them being derailed by what has been termed 'whataboutery', questions such as 'what about [insert random injustice here]?' The white subject will not engage on the content, instead will attack or disparage the speaker. Atrocities will be minimised or denied, and the black or brown subject will be (in)famously asked to 'move on'. The racial components of a particular situation, experience or event will not be seen.

The common responses Akala highlights mainly illustrate cognitive dissociation and are evocative of the intellectual 'deficits' we covered in the Introduction and our formulation of the epistemic shiftiness of whiteness. Here, however, we are also able to link them to 'paranoid-schizoid' functioning. The white subject is cut off from their actions affectively, cognitively and corporeally. In part, because of this socially sanctioned unreflecting, their actions cannot be integrated. This failure of integration means the white subject cannot locate themselves in the world since the links that exist between themselves and the world are ruptured. So, not only does dissociation create white ignorance, white ignorance sustains in turn the need for dissociation.

Splitting as a cultural or group defence mechanism is an equally serious problem when it comes to racialised power relations. Not only does it reduce the white subject's self-awareness, including awareness of their own racialised functioning, but it, of course, makes connecting to the harm they cause collectively virtually impossible. The structural function of these defences are in the service of the white racial equilibrium [9].

Everyday performance

Boarding school was kind of earth-shattering experience for me. For the first time, I had to learn to cook my own food (my boarding school offered just dinner, nothing else). I learnt how to sleep alone (all my life, I slept with my mom as she would never leave me alone). I learnt how to reply back to asshats. The number of times I got into trouble for fighting at boarding school exceeds the number of US states. I stayed there for two years. My parents could only call me on the weekend as the school didn't allow me to contact anyone regularly (it was a ferociously strict school). Most importantly, I think the two years in that school changed me for good. I grew really thick skin and learnt not to care about things that don't matter. I used to be very emotional but boy, boarding school changed me. I was mad at my parents for a long time because I wasn't ready for boarding school. As a result, I didn't talk to them for many days and hid somewhere if they ever tried to visit me. Ha-ha, now I don't remember the last time I actually shed tears. (Hasan, 2015 [10])

This account, which Hasan made public on social media, describes his lived experience of boarding school. Although it is set in the US context and may not speak of everyone's experience of boarding, it shares many of the themes which have been clustered under what has come to be called 'Boarding School Syndrome' [11]. Boarding school practices provide evidence of the institutionalisation of dissociation. And a reminder that trauma can coexist with material wealth. Boarding schools, which are seen in many Western nations as the territory of the wealthiest and most powerful classes in society, remain aspirational for many within the middle classes, particularly in England and its former colonies.

Sending children to boarding school entails separating them from their parents and therefore their emotional support system. This significant disruption has traditionally been enacted not only for education purposes but also as a form of 'character building'. One of the deliberate goals of sending children to boarding school was to build what was thought of as mental strength. Other goals included fostering attitudes of endurance under the most extreme circumstances, self-reliance, independence and the tolerance of pain. While people in positions of power, certainly in the UK, were disproportionately sent to boarding schools, we now know that these schools have been linked to a range of emotional or behavioural disturbances. In part, this is due to exposure to normalised interpersonal trauma, including for many routine humiliation, sexual abuse and bullying, compounded by disrupted attachments and expectations of silence and loyalty.

Adults sent to boarding school as children learnt to dissociate from pain and suffering. Furthermore, a fundamental political function of boarding schools was to prepare administrators able to run the British empire, thus further establishing these enduring links between trauma, dissociation, racial violence and colonialism. By socialising those who would run the country and its colonies to dissociate from their body, from their own pain and that of others, it is clear that boarding school culture and its normalised or cultural dissociation has greatly assisted the colonial project. It has disconnected the white subject from colonial atrocities, established dissociation as aspirational and created a hegemony imbued with expectations of a 'stiff upper lip'.

Despite much contestation, including critique from phenomenologists and feminist epistemologists, the mind–body dualism, or mind–body split, which proposes that psychological phenomenon is non-physical, or that the mind and body are distinct entities, remains strong; reducing our apprehension of the embodiment of racism and in effect the embodiment of all socio-historical forces [12]. This cultural splitting goes much further than mind and body. It, for example, is also present in the separation of bodies from social structures, individual from groups and the extraction of the 'past' from the present, those modernist formations we have repeatedly called into question.

These Eurocentric illusions are fundamentally related to the exclusion of the body from human subjectivity and continue to have a strong hold on knowledge production, epistemic practices and social arrangements. Everyday manifestations of the cultural embeddedness of dualist logics in society include the separation between mental health and physical health in the delivery of healthcare. And the usual absence of theoretical and even institutional links between psychology and sociology within higher education institutions and scholarship.

White paranoia

> Paranoia denotes here a pathological form of fear based on an excessively fragile conception of the self as constantly threatened. It is also a tendency to perceive a threat where none exists or, if it exists, to inflate its capacity to harm the self. (Hage, 2002, p 419 [13])

Trauma can cause us to react in ways that seem inappropriate or out of proportion. It can cause us to catastrophise, to look out for and expect the worst in the world. Clinically, paranoia may be described as a disproportionate fear that one is in some way at risk despite evidence to the contrary. Paranoia may involve delusional thoughts. However, paranoia is an affective state while delusions can be the cognitive manifestation of paranoia. Delusions are fixed irrational thoughts and beliefs which continue to be strongly held even when presented with contrary evidence. Delusions usually cluster around key themes such as grandiosity, persecution and surveillance. In the context of whiteness, paranoid delusions have tended to be connected to fear of persecution, of malicious harm centred on a fantasised threat to one's whiteness and/or power or fear of foreign invasion. The 'whip hand' of Powell might have created such visceral responses because it directly and powerfully taps into white paranoia. It hooked onto the fear not only that legislation to tackle racial discrimination would disadvantage white groups and thus cause them to lose their racialised priority, but that it would endanger their very survival and, thus, existence.

White paranoia expresses itself through a constant sense of threat; threat from foreign invaders together with any unknown illnesses that they might bring and the threat of losing one's culture. It may express itself through enduring feelings of persecution, of being gagged, silenced and/or at risk of social ostracisation due to 'political correctness' irrespective of reality. For example, we know that the success rates of race discrimination and race-related complaints hover closer to 0 per cent than they do to the 100 per cent mark. Despite this, angst over this so-called cancel culture has become so widespread so as to be a social phenomenon. This is the context of collective gagging and disciplinary anxieties. White paranoia may too engender conspiracies of so-called 'white genocide', the idea that organised attempts to wipe the white race off the face of the earth are in operation. White genocidal delusions have become prominent over the last decade or so and unsurprisingly appear to have gained much traction within settler colonial states with actual histories of first nation, Indigenous or African genocide and, as illustrated by the case of Dylan Roof, can have tragic and murderous consequences. Thus, in addition to the delusional basis of such conspiracies, they also betray that projective processes are in operation whereby white 'perpetrator' groups misattribute part of their history, 'past' actions and motives onto the groups, who were the objects of their violence; a return, one may argue, of the repressed.

In fact, many have argued that white paranoia is a symptom of the postcolonial mind and, arguably, that it is the root cause of border violence, in-land segregation and racist discrimination that former colonial subjects and their descendants continue to be subjected to [14]. White paranoia therefore sustains whiteness as property and whiteness as property is bound to have created a paranoid psychic organisation as the guilt-laden aftermath of crimes committed against Indigenous and racialised groups, an organisation that has become necessary to protect property and land, usually acquired through illegitimate and violent means.

Returning to the clinical literature, the link to trauma again appears. Studies have recurrently found that trauma is significantly associated with persecutory beliefs and even hallucinations. Having experienced at least one lifetime traumatic event was associated in one study with a 2.5 times greater risk of experiencing persecutory thoughts than not reporting any traumatic event. These findings invite us once more to link current thinking and evidence around paranoia to whiteness as a traumatogenic psychosocial phenomenon.

White psychosis

Paranoia is common to the conceptualisation of various forms of so-called mental health problems although it is the hallmark of psychosis [15]. Psychosis is conceptualised as a psychiatric disorder characterised by a loss of contact with reality. This disconnection from reality may become manifest through delusional thinking and hallucinations. Psychosis as a metaphor or conceptual frame for whiteness has been advanced by Andrews [16]. Andrews proposes that membership to whiteness requires the internalisation of a dysfunctional view of reality, and a distorted view of the self and of others. As manifested through an unwavering sense of benevolence, the creation of mythologies of greatness, and the erasure and omission from the white collective consciousness of the darker side of history and the minimisation of racism in society. Whiteness as psychosis goes some way in explaining the flight from reality that characterises racism. It may also help us understand why, by and large, anti-racism interventions seeking to redress structural racism have been ineffective. We may well be dealing with two sets of realities; reality and reality apprehended by white minds, fantasies collectively formed as reality.

There has been renewed interest in the impact of racial imaginaries on social inequality from both social justice activists and theorists/academics. Rankine, for example, has recently posited that the failure of white people to 'police their imagination' is a reason so many encounters between black social actors and the police are turning deadly, stating:

[W]hen White men are shooting Black people, some of it is malice and some, an out-of-control image of Blackness in their minds. Darren Wilson told the jury that he shot Michael Brown because he looked 'like a demon'. … Blackness in the White imagination has nothing to do with Black people. (Rankine, in Kellaway, 2015 [17])

Many innocent and unarmed men, women and even children racialised as black have in reality been described as dangerous monsters, wild beasts, evil/inhumanly strong beings capable of inflicting injuries or death to those confronting them, even when the latter have been armed with state-sanctioned power, weapons and uniforms. However extreme these depictions of blackness as superhumanness may seem, and despite the fact that the terror described may be difficult to reconcile with the objective circumstances of these killings, for the majority of cases, accounts of overwhelming fear by officers were accepted by jurors and led to non-indictments.

What is at stake here is not only the ways in which the black body is represented as both subject and object of the white gaze but how or why such fantasised representations may come to be activated during police encounters. And, perhaps, the more so-called primitive defences that may be triggered in these moments.

The possibility of regression taking place and thus a 'return' to more 'paranoid-schizoid' ways of relating, when police officers interact with black suspects, often through stereotypes, and the internalisation of anti-black tropes may be hypothesised to trigger fantasies, to create supernatural beings. The blurring of boundaries between the fantasy situation and the actual or real situation would mean experiencing high levels of anxiety and a heightened sense of threat or danger when dealing with people racialised as black and, as a result, would render an escalation in the real or objective situation much more likely. It then becomes relatively easy to formulate how the reality of the interaction, particularly in the most anxiety-prone officers, may quickly become distorted to the point where, in the eyes of the officer, they may be dealing with a devil-like creature. It must be noted that the escalation of such situations would require both anxiety and unacknowledged or disowned racism. The failure to take into account and limit the potential activation of such phantasmagoric anti-black imaginaries within policing and law enforcement remains a choice and is further evidence of structural racism.

White fragility

In the framework within which DiAngelo aims to elucidate white responses to racism, white fragility refers to the range of 'defensive moves' those racialised as white perform to disengage from conversations on race and racism [18]. Accordingly, fragility occurs because of a reduced capacity to tolerate race-based stress or distress (lack of racial stamina). The defensive moves believed to provide evidence of fragility include people racialised as white physically removing themselves from conversations on racism, becoming argumentative, denying or minimising the continuing significance of race or racism, and sometimes even becoming aggressive or threatening. These moves, it is proposed, exist to protect the white psychic equilibrium and again to manage cognitive dissonance or the internal tension that arises when people racialised as white are presented with information which challenges their worldview. White fragility or white resistance in confronting racism is, in fact, not new. Black scholars have for many decades written about the very tension and the sophisticated defences contemplating whiteness triggers in white people. As we have seen, about 75 years ago Fanon had already postulated the existence of defensive responses in colonial and oppressor groups and the mental gymnastics they engage in to avoid essentially facing themselves, proposing cognitive dissonance as the frame.

White fragility is sustained by complex neurobiological systems, so that we may say that whiteness is protected physiologically. Our cerebral threat system is configured to identify threats quickly [19]. And we are designed to focus our attention, memory and thinking towards threat-based information, as a priority and, of course, for survival. Our brain does so by triggering feelings of anxiety, via relevant hormonal events that sustain fear or aversive responses to potentially threatening stimuli. Once triggered, our threat responses motivate us to take associated behavioural action. In essence this activates the fight, flight or freeze response. If we believe, consciously or otherwise, that we can overcome the danger by fighting, our brain will gear our body towards doing so. If we feel at risk but think we cannot overcome the danger by fighting, we will generally run away. In the context of conversations on racism, 'fighting' may look like unnecessarily arguing, defending and becoming hostile or angry while a flight response is likely to be characterised by silence, disconnection or removing oneself from the space. A freeze response may look like difficulty thinking, speaking or even moving.

The contemplation of whiteness is rendered more complex by a failure to attend to the body. Without being mindful of racialised threat-based physiological responses, these cannot be reset to a baseline and the white body is in a state of stress while cut off from the same. Yet we know that it is virtually impossible to take in differing perspectives and to be reflexive when under acute stress. Our brains are simply not equipped to do so. The more acute the stress, the more difficult this task will be. Exposure to high levels of stress impairs our cognitive functioning, including our capacity to think flexibly and use complex reasoning skills [20]. When we are stressed or fearful, our autonomous nervous system get into motion and threat responses are activated. Because whiteness splits the white subject from their body they may not even realise they are feeling threatened and may be acting out that sense of threat relationally or indeed institutionally. Discourses of colourblindness further support that disconnection from the embodied. Empirical evidence suggests that our brain responds to racial differences and skin colour is noticed by our brain within milliseconds. Similarly, when presented with images of people racialised as black, threat responses via increased amygdala activities have been repeatedly observed [21]. Further, we know that racial stereotypes evoke more emotional responses and memories than other kinds of stereotypes [22]. So, in summary, threat responses via physiological and neurobiological processes and events underpin and maintain white fragility, which in turn maintain white power. Or, as Yancy proposes, deeply ingrained and automatic racist emotive responses are implicated in the white 'bodily repertoire' through centuries of simply inhabiting a racist world [23].

White aversion

Aversion refers to the sense of repugnance, disgust or strong dislike of a particular stimuli which triggers in us an almost uncontrollable urge to avoid it, almost at all costs. Aversive behaviours exist to protect us from the possibility of facing something which has the potential to harm us. Post-trauma we tend to avoid or withdraw from situations and feelings that remind us of the original trauma. Avoidance is, thus, a core feature of trauma responses pretty much in most conceptualisations of trauma. And, from an evolutionary perspective, it would be expected that we develop aversive responses to places and people, but also memories, thoughts, feelings and conversations associated with the original trauma. We could, therefore, propose that, when it comes to understanding white fragility, framing defensive responses as evidence of aversion once more provides additional support to the white trauma hypothesis.

Neuroscience is again helpful here. Ground-breaking empirical work is being carried out to better understand the neuropsychology and neurobiological basis of white aversion and the mechanisms which may underscore it. This research suggests that race-loaded material activates the cerebral system of people racialised as white in a way that any aversive stimuli would be expected to. Our cerebral threat system is the part of our brain designed to identify threats quickly and to trigger physiological changes to help ensure our survival.

Dissociation and anti-racism

In my anti-racism work over the years I have met three main presentations in white coachees:

- those who are openly distraught and can connect with their sense of grief and guilt when they confront whiteness;
- those who are distraught but simply choose impression management and appear unfazed;
- those who appear emotionless and are genuinely cut off from any feeling.

In terms of percentage the second group is probably the larger group composed of about 60 per cent of my coaching contacts followed by those in the other two groups who I meet more or less with equal frequency. A minority of those who are distraught openly usually cannot bear being distraught in front of me. Feelings of shame are at a high intensity. I tend to be less concerned over the violence that they are capable of doing since connection to vulnerability, connection to the self and higher levels of compassion are required to be authentic in relationships with the racialised other. It is also important when building anti-racism practice. Their main work is to learn to regulate their emotions and distress, so they do not seek soothing from people of colour.

When it comes to the dissociated group, group three, they are by and large the most difficult to reach and engage. To me they are the most challenging group. This is a group of people who are so dissociated from themselves and have mastered the art of cutting off. The individuals in this group tend to have more difficulties connecting with others, including people racialised as black and brown. They require a lot of support and work to commit to anti-racism work. Their key defence is disconnection. They will display no tears. There will be no evidence of distress, guilt or shame. The case for racial justice may be understood intellectually but, actually, human connection is poor. Their challenge is intimacy or the forming of close relationships human-to-human with the other. Allowing themselves to be touched. To be changed. The core challenge is vulnerability. Finally, in terms of the middle group, they have internalised the idea that emotions are undesirable, a sign of weakness or a lack of rationality. They feel them but they disavow them. They think they are in control. But, in actual fact, they are not in control as much as they believe they are. Their internal world leaks in micro ways. These are the ones most likely to engage in proximity avoidance since they constantly fear being found out.

Summary and resistance

DiAngelo proposes that whiteness provides 'protective pillows' to people racialised as white and that this protection insulates them from experiencing racial stress. As a result, the white subject comes to expect to feel racially comfortable at all times, that is to say, they fail to develop racial stamina, racialised ego strength. As this expectation of comfort is socially sanctioned within white supremacy, it is rarely challenged. Not being exposed to racial stress will naturally translate into a lack of experience in managing the strong emotions and physiological responses which can arise in race-based discussions, leading almost inevitably to a defensive posturing. Behaviourally, we may see this as inefficient stress management or poor distress tolerance.

This lack of adequate behavioural strategy is bound to compound anxiety and fear, which will, in turn, increase the likelihood of dissociation or other problematic distancing responses. We have historicised this dissociation and figured it as a cultural inheritance. We argued that, initially, it fulfilled both social and psychological defence functions and allowed colonialists to distance themselves from the violence they carried out on colonised bodies and lands via their concomitant enactments and sadism. More existentially, we may argue that this fear or avoidance of racialised phenomena sits at the core of the dualistic logics of modernism. Dissociation thus becomes a vehicle to keep the body subjugated. The body of racialised others and the body of the racialising subject. This way of being in the world, bolstered by individualism and, today, neoliberalism carries high costs for the white subject. It leads to a false consciousness of a psychotic-like 'divided self'. White hegemony and adherence to white norms of relating constrains the white subject too. It limits their freedom. Freedom to connect. Freedom to live authentic lives. And freedom to think. Our understanding of dissociation can help better formulate resistance to social change as well as the temporality of racialised violence. Disrupting white dissociation may require what Mbembe refers to as 'thinking with the body'. Centring the body in sense-making and in the apprehension of social phenomena. Understanding the body goes a long way in helping us understand the world and the contents of our thoughts. Even those thoughts we dare not think 'aloud' or say to ourselves. Connecting to and reclaiming the body and, as a result, discarding the enactment of dualistic politics in the domain of the everyday may be an important step in reducing splitting and dissociation and associated racial violence relationally and structurally. This is particularly relevant to more insidious and subtle bodily manifestations of racism. In the next chapter we consider the role shame plays in the psychosociality of whiteness and therefore its implication in racialised violence.

White shame

'There is no such thing as white shame, only white denial. Coloniser confronted with his crime is conflicted and desperate to return to his innocent state. All the bodily responses are of denial, refusal, in worst case fear. Shame? No' (Alex, white Ukrainian man, 40s, England)

'White shame is …
To recoil physically and emotionally;
To resist any notion of complicity or bias;
To retort "Who cares that I have suffered too?"' (Beatrice, Anglo Irish white woman, 50s, England)

In 2014, YouGov carried out a study on attitudes to the British empire in Britain [1]. It found that, generally, among the British public, feelings towards the empire tended to be both positive and nostalgic. Three to one, British people surveyed believed the British empire was something to be proud of rather than ashamed of. The same poll sought to discover whether the empire was viewed as a force for good or a force for bad; 43 per cent saw it as a force for good, only 19 per cent saw it as a source for bad. Twenty-five per cent responded that it was 'neither'. Finally, the research also revealed that a third of participants wished the British empire still existed. The poll came about when then prime minister David Cameron paid a visit to the Punjabi city of Amritsar in India, the site of the 1919 Amritsar Massacre which saw hundreds of Sikh anti-colonialism protesters murdered by troops under British command. Of note, and consistent with the poll, Cameron declined to apologise for this colonial atrocity, instead he proposed: 'there is an enormous amount to be proud of in what the British Empire did and was responsible for – but, of course, there were bad events as well as good. The bad events we should learn from – and the good events we should celebrate'. He never actually explained what 'we' had learnt from the massacre [2].

White narcissism, white shame

It takes a special kind of confidence to address descendants and relatives of the Amritsar Massacre and any other colonial atrocities, look them in the eyes and say, "The British Empire was both good and bad and it is important to celebrate the good." All the while, survivors and their descendants continue to mourn the dead and remember the violence. This is the kind of confidence which is apparently averse to shame. Gilroy noted that Britain's relationship with its history exists as absence through its marginality, that through un-acknowledgement and revisionism that 'past' is ever present as evidenced by white nostalgia and melancholia [3]. This ambivalent relation with the 'past' is symptomatic of a fragile sense of pride and omnipotence.

An internalised sense of superiority once more, the essential ingredient of white supremacy, lies at the heart of the enactment of white atrocities. It is also the reason such atrocities are not accepted as atrocities. But for that overvalued sense of self and its derivative psychological attributes (for example, paternalism, self-assurance, arrogance) white supremacy would not have come into being and its confrontation would not be fiercely resisted today. Whites' grandiose sense of self in relation to the worth of lives racialised as black and brown thus feeds the pathology of whiteness and is a function of narcissistic functioning.

Narcissism as a character trait was first identified by the British essayist and physician Havelock Ellis in 1898. He named it after the Greek mythological figure Narcissus who was so absorbed with his handsomeness that he fell in love with his own image reflected in a pool of water. Narcissism, by extension, came to refer to an inflated self-image, fantasised notions of greatness, the tendency to exploit and manipulate others, and use them to inflate one's sense of self and/or to instrumentalise them for one's own gains. Narcissism is also characterised by an unusual detachment or coolness which can quickly turn to anger and rage, if not violence, when one's ego is threatened [4]. Shame constitutes such a threat.

We may think about shame in a number of ways. Primarily it has been seen as the painful emotions people feel when implicated in actions which we believe transgress their sense of morality and lead to negative self-evaluations. White shame may arise when one recognises that the atrocities and suffering of the world one lives in is awash with racism-related atrocities that implicate the self [5].

Peck links shame to white ignorance. She advances what she refers to as 'active white ignorance', which is:

A form of ignorance that is consciously and unconsciously produced by and for white people, which obscures and excludes race-related knowledge from white people's attention. Cultivated within and maintained by norms, habits, discourses, social imaginaries, and institutions, active white ignorance is the result of what W.E.B. Du Bois called a project of 'emphasis and omission,' and is therefore different from innocent gaps in understanding. [6, pp 3–4]

Peck's conceptualisation employs Mills' epistemology of ignorance, and its deliberate collective will not to know [7]. What she adds to Mills' epistemic frame is the affective dimension of this commitment to misinterpret, which she proposes is underscored by white shame. Therefore, shame is never too far from the surface when racism is denied. This take us back to Alex's words. For him, denial and the refusal to confront the reality of white supremacy is operational too, however he sees them as a masquerade. A sham. How might these two perspectives coexist?

Everyday performance

'My mother's racism. Not a happy topic. Mention it to a white friend, and I get a commiserative eye-roll. We all deal with this, the eye-roll says. It also seems to imply that, once these toxic oldies die off, we liberals will inherit the earth. I used to find that eye-roll comforting, as long as I didn't think about my own colonialist tendencies; I couldn't think about my own racism because I didn't believe it existed. When confronted with her racism, my mother would either remind me that she wasn't anything like as bad as Auntie Margaret, who still spouts wild-eyed vitriol about the brown people who had the misfortune to be her neighbours in 1950s Rochester or complain "I can't say anything right!" That complaint was a specific dig at our relationship, and sought to depict me as dismissive and unloving, when really, I should be humouring the old lady, mindful of her special privilege. I used to think the privilege she claimed in these moments was merely that of the mother vis-à-vis the daughter, but I have come to see that it was also white privilege. I had broken more than one pact in my mother's mind. Not just the narcissistic demand that I soothe and stroke her as a dutiful daughter, but also, the exposure of her shame, and mine, in a private, one-to-one discussion of racism. This is a woman who mostly masked her racism or was unaware of it. A white liberal. And she raised me to be one too. But dementia tore away at those shifting velleities of peace and justice for all; the same velleities that had soothed me in childhood with the knowledge of what was right, without inspiring me to any kind of further action. We were the right sort of people and that was that. My father had a friend from Lesotho. ("He likes black people if they're civilised and play cricket," my mother once sneered behind his back.) But he also wrote to my mother when I married a Chinese man, saying "we must avoid miscegenation at all costs." Did he mean it? I like to think not, as he actually got on very well with that husband. But he had absorbed that language; that thought-pattern. It was his unthinking reaction when shocked by my hasty marriage. By the time my mother was in care in England, with a diagnosis of Alzheimer's, and women of colour all around, the veils were wearing thin. When confronted, she refused shame; bounced it back on me. It worked, because I didn't pick her up on everything. I was too exhausted. But if I was exhausted, what must it be like for people of colour? Why am I so fragile? More shame. No change in my mother's behaviour. My daughter seldom visited the old lady, and then only to support me. She and I were sexually harassed by one of my mother's ancient male friends, in front of my mother, who just laughed. More shame. Why didn't I just go no contact? Because the trauma was shared, and in helping her, I was putting at least some of it back where it belonged and trying not to pass it on. The sense of exhaustion and overwhelm was bound up with my own experience of trauma, both in childhood, and retraumatisation as my mother's behaviour deteriorated in later life. This trauma, caused by growing up with parents with severe mental health problems caused by their own traumas, was linked to my inability as a young woman to experience myself in my body; to feel what I felt, and to know who I was, and what I wanted. My biggest joy is that I did … I became me.' (Helen, white woman, 50s, UK)

Shame and 'location of disturbance'

> I'm sorry I was born white and privileged. It disgusts me. And I feel so much shame. (Arquette, quoted in Evans, 2019 [9])

Helen's contribution presents a multigenerational story of shame. Specifically, the transmission or projection of shame as emotional regulation and as a silencing strategy intergenerationally and concomitant introjection. This transmission endured in time and across spaces in the midst of the expectation that racism, perhaps like shame, will die off when the older generations perish. In Chapter 1 we considered the fundamental tenets of group analysis. One core group-analytic idea we have been using throughout the book without explicitly referencing group analysis is that of disturbance. We have overall used the term interchangeably with problem, dysfunction or pathology. Within group analysis, disturbance and what is referred to as the location of disturbance have particular meanings. Adjacent, but richer.

A disturbance in group analysis always speaks of a group dysfunction. It is accordingly conceptualised as a disturbed group communication which may become expressed within specific individuals, the latter only ever a focal point for more distal phenomena both involving them and involving their group. Thinking of the group as an organism, we may link this conceptualisation of disturbance to what is medically known as 'referred pain' when pain one feels in one part of the body is in reality caused by injury elsewhere [9].

Disturbance is believed to always be distortion, dislocation or displacement of group or social forces. It takes many forms depending of course on contexts including individual psychohistories and social histories, what we presented in Chapter 1 as the group matrix. The task of the group analyst is often to correctly locate and explore disturbances. In other words, it is to ask who or to who else does the problem 'belong'? Who is involved in the 'here and now' and who is involved in the 'there and then'? And what histories, including histories of trauma, are being repeated? Always primarily, unconsciously. Helen's trauma history is complex. In that history whiteness–related shame intersects with gender and, specifically, gendered abuse related shame. The family's history of psychological distress intersects with the impact of dementia in the present, providing a multidimensional picture of what I refer to as the intersections of trauma.

The concept of location of disturbance helps to reveal dysfunctional patterns of communication dominated by displacement, misplacement and repression. Older people become the containers for racism, the site of repressed racial disturbance. When they die then, in the family fantasy, so does the racism. Sexually abused women are the repository of the shame of the abuse which they must keep silent, they become the location for the disavowed sexualised disturbance. Women appear to also be tasked with doing the work of healing the family. The designated bodies to carry the family trauma on behalf of the family group. In the midst of this distress, connections are naturally disrupted. Largely because dementia has breached the defensive walls of 'that old lady'. As she speaks without inhibition she becomes the problem for the family, the location of disturbance. Nonetheless, she is not only speaking for herself. This is what is disavowed. She is not the problem to be solved, contained or neutralised. Racism in the 'liberal' family, is.

We started this section of the chapter with a quote by actress Rosanna Arquette. A tweet. Following this tweet about her sense of white shame, Arquette had to make her Twitter account private. She experienced a barrage of abuse and harassment about her words including accusation of racism and of being self-hating. Arquette reported that the FBI had to be consulted to protect her safety [10]. Helen's story and Arquette's differ in key ways. Not least because Arquette's words were uttered in a public forum while she was cognitively intact and was, we will presume, sharing aspects of 'her' 'internal' world and racial identity, consciously. Although there was no report that the trolling and harassment campaigns she was subjected to were motivated by antisemitism, a viable and even likely hypothesis is that Arquette's Jewishness increased the intensity of the angst, hostility and sense of threat of her words. Possibly because it tapped into the collective yet largely repressed shame related to the Holocaust and the very denial of that shame. Further, it may have activated, unconsciously, the antisemitic trope of 'Jewish disloyalty' and the consequent imagined threat that Judaism and Jews are largely still believed to pose to whiteness. As Frosh reflects, '[a]s soon as there is a trace of what on the political right is seen as "white treachery" – which means critiques of whiteness by white people – the spectre of antisemitism looms large' [11].

Whether antisemitism was activated or not, something important unites the response to Arquette's words and the response to those of Helen's mother. We may propose that the direct confrontation of whiteness in the case of Helen's mother, and its direct confrontation in the case of Arquette, led to the expression or manifestation of a collective shame-based disturbance. This disturbance challenged in both cases witnesses, forcing hearers to connect with the phenomena named, albeit repressed. This shame-based phenomenon was already in existence within these systems but was unnamed. Within the family system or family matrix for Helen, and within the socio-political context or the 'foundation matrix' for Arquette. Attempts at locating associated disturbances in those communicating the presence and the intensity of the responses triggered by the articulation of the disturbance provide some evidence that the disturbance, here shame, related to whiteness, is collective. What location of disturbance may additionally help us explicate, is why some bodies may feel white shame so deeply, as it appears is/was the case for Arquette and Beatrice. In contrast, others in the same system or matrix may, on the surface, be disconnected from it. We may argue that some bodies are designated to carry that shame as disturbance on behalf of others.

A cultural note

In 2019 black British MP David Lammy came under fire for criticising Comic Relief under the frame of white saviourism [12]. His criticism was triggered by a tweet and a photograph of English television presenter and journalist, Stacey Dooley. In the said photograph Dooley is sporting a bright smile and apparently holding a camera with a deprived black child in rural Africa as part of a Comic Relief campaign.

Lammy tweeted in response to the picture: 'The world does not need any white saviours. As I've said before, this just perpetuates tired and unhelpful stereotypes. Let's instead promote voices from across the continent of Africa and have a serious debate.' Dooley responded:

> David, is the issue with me being white? (Genuine question) ... because if that's the case, you could always go over there and try [to] raise awareness? Comic

relief have raised over 1 billion pounds since they started. I saw projects that were saving lives with the money. Kids lives.

The public, by and large, was in support of Dooley. She was widely positioned as the victim in the encounter.

The racialised optics of the conflict were arguably in support of that distorted reality. Constructions of white womanhood, some of which we have covered in our reflections on the white female gaze, mean that it would invariably take a huge amount of violence for a relatively petite white woman to be seen as the aggressor when her interlocutor is a rather large, tall, dark-skinned black man. Our collective imaginaries make thinking beyond the gendered and racialised tropes of innocence and virtuosity difficult at the best of times when it comes to white womanhood. Doing so in the context of a white woman engaged in 'charity' work makes it virtually impossible. And so, naturally, Lammy was heavily criticised, trolled and racially abused on social media for daring to be critical of the apparently generous, compassionate and life-changing work the charity engaged in, especially as the perception was that the need was so dire.

How could he make attempting to feed hungry Africans a race issue when he should be grateful? Although Comic Relief eventually made the decision to stop 'sending white celebrities' to Africa as other celebrities weighed in, Lammy's point was largely missed.

Another cultural note

In January 2021, 23-year-old England and Manchester United striker Marcus Rashford became the centre of a political row when he advocated to extend free school meals to children from low-income families during school holidays in England. This was after the footballer had openly criticised the free lunch state provisions. Even though Rashford's efforts were instrumental in getting the government to change direction, deciding that it was right to feed poor British children after all, Rashford was heavily criticised for interfering in politics, for in essence being uppity and inauthentic. His motivation was recurrently criticised. Nobility of intentions, it appears, was absent on this occasion. His campaign became quickly shadowed by racist (and classist) discourses and, again, mass racist trolling on social media.

Examples of white narcissistic grandiosity are not hard to find. It can be recognised in the unconscious need to control people racialised as black and brown, their minds and experiences when they evoke race. In doing so, they are turned into objects that exist as extensions of the self or as a form of narcissistic supply. One of the most compelling examples of white narcissism is white saviourism. Nigerian-American novelist Teju Cole coined the term 'the white saviour industrial complex', following a thread on Twitter to capture the intersection of narcissism, colonialism and sentimentality in Western charitable work. In the thread, which went viral, the novelist wrote: 'The white saviour supports brutal policies in the morning, founds charities in the afternoon, and receives awards in the evening' [13]. The complex is said to refer to the practices, processes and institutions that reproduce the historical inequalities that sustain whiteness and coloniality while, at the same time, providing 'feel-good' opportunities for people racialised as white to take part in saving or rescuing narratives which reinforce white benevolence and virtuosity. The complex disregards the policies and structures that European nations have put in place and maintain and which create the harm and disaster that they purport to wish to undo. The white saviour complex is a complex because it keeps the psychology of whiteness intact. Not only does it allow for the neocolonial control of exploited nations, it further feed discourses of inferiority.

False generosity

In summary, a white woman was fiercely defended for doing charity work in Africa. David Lammy, a man racialised as black, was heavily criticised and harassed for not supporting and feeding hungry children in Africa. Marcus Rashford, another man racialised as black, was similarly criticised and harassed for seeking to feed hungry children in England. These contradictions indicate that the matter at hand has extraordinarily little to do with ethics or with hunger but much to do with who is feeding whom. Stopping white Westerners from feeding hungry African children was deemed heresy. In the same way, we could say that a man racialised as black – who also happens to be from a working-class background – was transgressing, for many, the boundaries of what is acceptable, expected or 'normal' within our society; proposing to feed children in the UK.

'A psychoanalysis of oppressive action might reveal the "false generosity" of the oppressor as a dimension of the latter's sense of guilt. With this false generosity, he attempts not only to preserve an unjust and necrophilic order, but to "buy" peace for himself' [14, p 146]. This extract is from *Pedagogy of the oppressed* by Brazilian educator and author Paulo Freire, and discusses what he refers to as false generosity. False generosity is a form of charity that:

- maintains those in positions of power in a mirage of benevolence whereby the feeding of their ego becomes more important than the feeding of the hungry;
- manages the guilt associated with the injustices one benefits from;
- keeps the status quo intact as it simply addresses the symptoms rather than the root causes of inequality;

- keep oppressed groups in position of dependency and inferiority (which they internalise) and the socially constructed superiority of dominant groups.

Even though Rashford and Lammy's actions could be charged with only addressing symptoms rather than structural causes, we can better understand why their actions and words deeply transgressed whiteness. They disturbed white saviourism narratives and their associated false sense of generosity. The standard configuration within this script is that it is people racialised as white who feed, and it is children racialised as black, ideally based in Africa, who are hungry. The white saviour industrial complex provides endless narcissistic supply to white social actors. Consider, for example, how France continues to portray itself as a benevolent force of light and good. It was not so long ago that French presidential hopeful François Fillon described colonialism as France 'sharing its culture' with the people of the world. The foreign aid discourses in France and elsewhere similarly maintain the colonial illusion of white benevolence. All the while France is still extracting the so-called colonial debt behind the scenes – a debt sustained, let us remind ourselves, to compensate that country for the loss of its colonies after independence. To this day, 14 former African colonies are required to deposit into French state accounts billions of their capital, year on year. These arrangements, together with essentially imposed trade 'agreements', fatten France to an estimated sum of hundreds of millions of euros a year.

Shame, guilt and white tears

The phenomenon of white tears, which features in the book on three different occasions, illustrates the fragility of that narcissism. The usual script that leads to white tears is as follows. A person of colour attempts to speak of their experience of racism [15]. The white individual tries to explain the racism away, usually centring their benevolent intentions. When or if their interlocutor refuses to centre or sanctify these intentions, a number of counter-accusations are likely to be made as follows: (1) that the racialised other misunderstood the interaction; and/or (2) that by assigning racist motivation in the absence of 'evidence' they are in fact 'the real racist' since it is them who are actually prejudiced against white people; (3) should the black or brown subject make the mistake of being affected emotionally by such manoeuvring, for example, by becoming legitimately angry or more forceful in asserting their experience, it is usually not long before the table is turned. A role reversal occurs via performances of distress and/or outrage by the white subject. It is then that white tears tend to follow. White tears defend against feelings of shame evoked by requests for accountability thus reflection. The person of colour becomes the aggressor that needs to be controlled, reigned in and policed. Accusations of bullying and aggression are standard at this stage, rendering black or brown social actors vulnerable to structural violence. White tears through the centring of white distress in racial exchanges is more than about hurt feelings, although there are often hurt feelings involved for all parties. These tears are, in addition to holding the potential for serious structural consequences for the racialised other, recentring whiteness and, in doing so, contributing to the aggrandisement of white social actors, who are positioned as being above the consequences of their words or actions.

A cultural note

Early in 2022 in the UK, following England's defeat in the Euro football final by Italy and the subsequent racial abuse and harassment of the black England footballers who missed their penalties, we saw a perfect illustration of how whiteness policed the other by shaming them into line. During a debate in the House of Commons on racism, triggered by comments made by the England manager accusing the government of stocking the fire of racism, Labour MP Zarah Sultana was asked to 'lower her tone' and accused of shouting by Home Office minister and Conservative MP Victoria Atkins [16].

Sultana's remark was: 'Isn't it the case that the home secretary and the prime minister were stoking the fire of racism, and only now, when the consequences are clear, are they feigning outrage?' To elaborate on her point Sultana made reference to the prime minister describing people racialised as black as 'piccaninnies' with 'watermelon smiles' and comparing Muslim women to letter boxes and bank robbers. She also elaborated on the failure of the government to support the England team for taking the knee. Atkins, in response, requested that Sultana conduct herself in 'a measured and collected way', demanded that she lower her tone and went on to accuse Sultana of shouting. To top off the interaction, the white MP added:

> I don't genuinely think the honourable lady is accusing either the prime minister of this country or indeed the home secretary of racism. That would be a truly extraordinary allegation to make but ... I hope at some point we will be able to work together to tackle racism. That is what we all want to do. That is what the work of this government is directed towards. (Proctor, 2021 [16])

There is no challenge that follows Atkins' words. Sultana is left without support on the issues she brought to parliament.

An extraordinary but also prototypical response to accusations of racism was publicly exposed. Prototypical because it contains the core elements of whiteness, many of which we have already covered:

- appeal to objectivity and balance;
- outrage at the allegation of racism itself;
- paternalistic tone policing;
- projection of aggression and irrationality;
- performance of calm;
- refusal to engage or dissociation;
- gaslighting and revisioning;
- and, of course, white silence in the midst of it all.

What may be less obvious is how Atkins' discursive moves, which weaponise consciously or otherwise the construction of whiteness as reasonableness, achieve a deflection from the serious issue of race within the high office. This is achieved by the positioning of Sultana, if only symbolically, as the uncivilised, irrational brown body. A body that is out of place and does not know how things work in high places. She does not know her place.

Atkins arguably projected shame onto Sultana for being transgressive. What is heard, although not explicitly expressed, is 'how dare you?' and 'you should be ashamed of yourself'. These implicit utterances follow Sultana making legitimate claims and accusations founded on actual and well-documented facts and events. We can also see how the appearance of detachment and objectivity (the even and calm tone; the invocation of balance) are power moves which function to restate white authority, here politically and epistemically. The paternalism in the exchange is striking. Sultana is shut down. It is clear to all that Atkins sees herself as knowing best the rules of the house. She knows best what allegations are 'proper' to make against those at the highest echelons of power in the state. Racism is not one of them.

White pride, white shame

White grandiosity is fragile. It has long been believed to conceal underlying feelings of inferiority, insecurity and insignificance. In other words, grandiosity is a defence against deep-seated insecurities, negative feelings one may come to hold about the self. It is because of this hypothesised core insecurity or fragility that narcissism is believed to lead to defensive behaviours associated with this disposition. The ultimate defence against shame is excessive pride. In this context, white pride is aggressive or retaliatory. White pride is premised upon the conscious desire to derive positive attributes from white racial identity as a response to the contemplation of the horrors of whiteness. It is therefore an attempt at whitewashing white supremacy. An attempt at revisioning, redefining or recreating it, primarily affectively but also cognitively to make it more palatable to the self.

White pride, there is no doubt, is an attempt at making the self invulnerable to perceived attacks on one's sense of goodness and is activated to defend against feelings of shame. It is for this reason that those who engage in defensive pride are vulnerable to feelings of humiliation when they feel what they seek to hide of themselves is exposed. They may engage in rageful retaliation, in withdrawal or in deep feelings of depression.

When I carried out some research into shame to try and contextualise this chapter theoretically, it was interesting that I uncovered little formal scholarship dealing with white shame, with most theoretical attention focusing on guilt. A couple of hypotheses come to mind that make sense of this unbalance. We may propose that this absence is in fact evidence of shame. Indeed, by its very definition, shame hides in shame and is therefore a feeling state which is often disowned or hidden. Our second hypothesis, which is more analytic, may be that part of the shame that has been so widely theorised to belong to people of colour may actually belong to white people.

Freud saw shame as leading to repression and hysteria. But while shame has long been theorised as a sequel of racial violence for the colonised and postcolonial subject, it has not been as widely applied to groups racialised as white, in the context of white supremacy. I have written elsewhere about the problems with formulating shame from individualistic and purely intrapsychic lenses since if those racialised as other act as white shame receptacles and as shame regulation, then shame is particularly intolerable and distress-inducing for the white subject.

It is because of the structural reality that surrounds white tears that white distress has tended to be viewed with suspicion. Psychosocially, it is nonetheless important that we attend to the affective responses and the emotions triggered by the contemplation of racism, which also both have causal and consequential effects on social configurations [4]. Arguably, treating white shame or distress as illegitimate phenomena further encourages white dissociation and therefore splitting. Defence mechanisms, we have argued, are central to the reproduction of whiteness since these affective and cognitive evasions distance the white subject from pain. Including, problematically, black pain and brown pain. It therefore stops people racialised as white from being authentically and humanely present in their relationships with people of colour.

Shame and the scapegoating of 'racists'

One way to think about our society's tendency to want to find, identify and shame those deemed racist is through the group dynamic of scapegoating. Scapegoating may be defined as the process by which projection is used to locate unwanted material onto an object who is then seen to carry these unwanted parts on behalf of a wider group. In group analysis, the defence of displacement is believed to play an important role in scapegoating. Often uncomfortable or unacceptable feelings, such as anger, envy and shame, are displaced and redirected onto that object, often but not always a more vulnerable person or group. The scapegoat can then be persecuted for possessing what those who project onto them are unable to own as being in existence within themselves, often parts that are heavily shame-loaded.

The idea that those who may carry out racist or discriminatory acts could be used as scapegoats may be difficult for some to accept, after all, they have shown evidence of prejudice, discrimination or racism. They do, some argue, deserve the violence, retaliation and shunning they may experience as a result. The question of scapegoating though is not primarily concerned with the morality of the process but rather with the functions it serves.

The fact that a social actor may have been involved in some immoral action, or in the context of white supremacy, in acts of racial injustice, does not eliminate the possibility of them being used as scapegoat if:

- the larger group, institutional or social context use them as a way to discharge onto them their own prejudice, discrimination or racism;
- it leads to the individual being therefore unfairly singled out for the prejudice, discrimination or racism also present in others within a particular context; and
- if by such singling out – which often results in exclusion from a particular context – the group avoids to look at itself and its own functioning when it comes to race.

This propensity some have to become the repository of others' disowned material from a scapegoat perspective may be explained in different ways. Foulkes proposes that the scapegoat may be selected in the first place because they are 'different' or stand out in some marked ways in their environment [17]. This may be because of identity characteristics or, in the context of race, it may be because they use obsolete language, because they are less inhibited with the expression of their beliefs or because of how they express such beliefs.

Perceived differences are then exploited or weaponised by the group when a need in the victim to be punished may exist, perhaps because the individual transgressor may struggle with feelings of racial ambivalence or be acting out sadomasochistic impulses. There may also be a need in the group to punish, perhaps because this allows members to regulate feelings of shame vis-à-vis their own disowned racism. In any event, displacing a pathology that is fundamentally social onto identified individuals is rarely in service of dismantling white supremacy. It is in fact an act that prevents collective ownership.

Summary and resistance

Shame has long been thought of as a powerful and effective tool of social control that is probably as effective as material deprivation, social dislocation or dispossession in keeping marginalised people in their place psychosocially. It makes the latter hesitate and/or refrain from claiming their rights to dignity, equal treatment and full humanity. Essentially, it makes marginalised people do the 'master's work' by becoming subservient and thus inadvertently complicit in systems of devaluation and degradation. Shame is therefore a weapon which sustains the racialised social (dis)order and protects whiteness. The shame burden which is placed on the shoulders of racialised others is projective and a function of white groups' inability to contain racialised shame. Intersubjectivity invites us to consider all actions and interactions contextually and relationally since the mental life of marginalised groups cannot be considered separately from the mental life of socially dominant groups. Rather, mental events and experiences are co-created and continually mutually influenced by each group's processes. Hence, social shame cannot be formulated as a distinct, separate or isolated experience 'belonging' to the psyche of those who are oppressed/marginalised. White shame differs from white guilt. When the white subject feels guilt, it is related to thoughts of feeling bad about some sense of illegitimacy or unearned social advantages. When it feels shame, on the other hand, there is more global and negative assessment about the self. While guilt says, 'I feel bad about what I did', shame says, 'I am bad because of what I did'. Because shame attacks the self, it becomes exceedingly difficult to use that shame to foster the kind of attitudinal and behavioural changes needed to address whiteness. In fact, using shame in this way can cause the opposite effect by increasing the propensity for scapegoating. The value and utility of shame as an anti-racist tool is contested. Some scholars see it as appropriate, for example Peck suggests that white shame is a necessary part of confronting one's complicity within white supremacy. Others emphasise its destructive nature and fear it leads to defensiveness or withdrawal rather than change. My position is that whether we see white shame as helpful or destructive is immaterial. The reality is that shame is an inherent part of the confrontation of whiteness, which is itself a necessary part of anti-racist practice. As a result, dedicating scholarly resources to support the regulation of white shame is likely to yield significant positive results for anti-racism. In the next chapter we explore white ambivalence, its expressions and mechanisms as well as strategies to resist it [7].

8

White ambivalence

'I am a 57-year-old white cis male group analytic psychotherapist who thinks he is rocking it as an "Ally" [and who] finds himself standing by the wheelie bin one evening with a "Jolly Sambo" money box in his hand and is frozen; torn between the decision to throw away this relic of a racialised, white supremacist Empire-permeated childhood in 1960s working-class Lancashire and the treasured memories of playing with the same object at his Nana's feet in front of the coal fire loading it with old pennies over and over again and laughing as it rolled its eyes and lifted its arm to feed itself more pennies. "How could I throw that experience of my Nana's love in the fucking bin?"' (John, white man, 50s, England)

Anyone racialised as white seeking to commit to anti-racism will at some point need to confront their relationship with whiteness, including their internalisation of white supremacy. Although we may often take this step for granted, the problematics and challenges of facing the reality of white supremacy and one's complicity require some exploration. We know that human beings will go to extraordinary lengths to maintain their psychic equilibrium. We examined earlier in the book some of the physiological, psychic and social processes that help the white body flee the reality of white supremacy. When, a decade or two ago, I first encountered *Black skin, white masks* by Fanon, I had such a strong visceral response to it; I did not finish it [1]. I experienced an intense dislike for the words I was reading. I have not experienced this with any other book. I remember discarding the book, and did not touch it again for years. Such reactions always call for our attention. The reality is I was not ready. My mind refused to engage with the contents. My body put out a block. Perhaps this was to protect me from seeing part of myself or the world I was not prepared to see. Yet, *Black skin, white masks* is now one of my most cited texts. It took several painful encounters with whiteness for me to go back to Fanon's words. My experience of the world drove my needing to understand this text. When I needed to understand, and was thus ready and had overcome my embodied and cognitive resistance, they disappeared as though they had never been there. Thinking about this experience in relation to whiteness and specifically white engagement with whiteness, allows me to hold in mind compassionately the defences white people may put in place to avoid contemplating the violence of white supremacy. *White minds* is arguably an attempt at preparing white minds to take this reality in and build sufficient ego strength to bear it without retracting into fantasy.

Ego strength here is used to refer to our psychological resilience and the strength of our core sense of self. It allows us to bear difficult emotions, challenges to our identity and difficult relationships without losing touch with reality, losing our sense of self or fearing annihilation. As we have seen, culturally whiteness tends to encourage the disowning and disavowing of emotions. It is all too easy to underestimate the importance of tolerating difficult emotional states if one is to sustain looking white supremacy in the eye. I have come to believe that emotions, rather than reason, are the most potent psychological blocker to equality and to engagement in anti-racism. The distress and discomfort that is produced in the white subject who seeks to confront the reality of white supremacy is born, we may argue, out of this limited ego strength which, for our particular purpose, may be used interchangeably with racial stamina.

Conceptualising ambivalence

Ambivalence is another central concept to contemporary psychoanalytic thinking which has a long history. It was Eugen Bleuler who first employed the word ambivalence to explain the existence of contradictory emotional states [2]. In his formulation, he identified three forms of ambivalence: voluntary ambivalence; intellectual ambivalence; and emotional ambivalence. Voluntary ambivalence refers to the conscious conflicts we experience over whether we should or should not be doing something or over whether we should be doing something rather than something else. With intellectual ambivalence, our thinking and reasoning in relation to particular experiences or events is expressed both positively and negatively and may appear contradictory. Finally, emotional ambivalence refers to the feelings of love and hate we may feel towards the same object or person. In Bleuler's writing, emotional ambivalence is the most pathological and creates the most distress.

Freud also made use of ambivalence to formulate psychological distress and intrapsychic conflicts. His definition of ambivalence is consistent with that of Bleuler's emotional ambivalence in that he sees it as the 'simultaneous existence of love and hate – toward the same object' [3, p 157]. In contrast to the former, however, Freud's conceptualisation is restricted to the unconscious feelings we feel towards people. Freud later further developed the frame of ambivalence, adding to it the belief that the defence was the result of insufficient fusion, of the life and death instincts leading to disintegrated emotional states. Finally, Melanie Klein, whose related ideas we already encountered when we explored splitting, also engaged with ambivalence, which she saw as the failure to tolerate the fact that both bad parts and good parts could coexist within the same 'object' [4]. She referred to this psychic dynamic as the 'paranoid-schizoid position'. Ideas around ambivalence have further evolved and developed within different schools of psychoanalysis, not all agreeing and disagreeing with particular emphases. Still, they remain dominant and most analytic thinkers would likely agree that ambivalence is a subset of internal conflicts often leading to approach–avoidance dynamics, affecting attachment to loved objects, which may manifest behaviourally, cognitively and affectively [5].

A cultural note

Throughout *12 Years a Slave*, we bear witness to racial ambivalence as evidenced by the brutalisation of Patsey, a beautiful enslaved African woman who suffers at the hands of Epps, her cruel and violent slave master, in the midst of the regular soulful prayers and sermons of antebellum America. McQueen's triumphant 2013 movie poignantly displays the complexities of love–hate racial dynamics. We watch Epps consumed and so painfully conflicted by the sexual attraction and infatuation he feels towards Patsey. We see him go from admiration to contempt, from 'affection' to hatred, and from 'care' to sadism often instantly. One of the most troubling and distressing scenes in the movie is the night he rapes her. Unable to contain his sexual urges, Epps creeps into Patsey's quarters and forces himself onto her as she lies motionless and expressionless, possibly in a dissociative state. This is a survival posture, likely instinctively adopted because of the grave peril she is in. After Epps climaxes, he stares at Patsey for a short moment and, as he sees himself in her eyes, starts hitting and punching her in the face. Then, he attempts to strangle her. He has succumbed to lust and the appeal of black flesh. He is almost instantly consumed by shame, then later in the movie, by fear. Not shame at the harm he has done to Patsey, as this would entail psychological contact, nor fear for Patsey's welfare, as this would require compassion. Rather, Epps feels shame at what he was no longer able to repress. And fears the wrath of the Christian god he prays to, who will turn against him because he has transgressed and trespassed the colour line. Patsey is left paying the price not only for Epps' repressed then unleashed sexual impulses but also for his damaged Christian and virtuous self-concept. The core of his ambivalence.

Although *12 Years a Slave* portrays an extreme form of white ambivalence, racial dynamics in popular culture and in art have been awash with conflicted or mixed feelings towards black and brown objects. Morrison's seminal text, *Playing in the dark*, has demonstrated how the literary imagination of US-produced literary texts is populated often silently, not only with ideas of irrational fear of the 'primitive' or of the unknown black subject but that these have coexisted with feelings of desire and longing towards the same [6]. This complex and contradictory relationship with the racialised other, she proposed, is bound up with the figuration of whiteness and the collective sense of national identity.

Racial ambivalence

Racial ambivalence is an application of analytic ideas of ambivalence to racism [7]. This framework seeks to explain why people racialised as white's attitudes towards racialised others are composed of extremes and apparently opposite evaluations. The master–slave encounter as illustrated by the rape of Patsey speaks to something of this ambivalence. As we have seen, it depicts racial hatred in the midst of lust. Proximity and avoidance of contact are simultaneously sought. Throughout history, intimacy with bodies racialised as black, and particularly the black female body, has been complex and contradictory. Violent sexual and non-consensual intimacies speak most powerfully of that historical ambivalence and help us see why sexual contact has endured in the midst of segregation thus avoidance. In that sense, on the one hand, European colonialists carried out voyages spanning weeks if not months to get to, or to get closer to, foreign lands and 'savage' beings. On the other hand, once there, othering figurations were elaborated to create a safe psychological distance. And again, on the one hand, one imposed violent geographical thus physical boundaries between those racialised as white and colonial subjects; on the other hand, access to colonised bodies and their consumption were regular imperial practices.

Considering approach-avoidance as a central feature of ambivalence explains why people racialised as white may at different points in time repress or dissociate from one side of the conflict: say, move away from their professed hatred of injustice because of the discomfort or distress produced by contemplating racial injustice. At other times they may take action to tackle racial injustice because of the distress, guilt or shame caused by the contemplation of racism. Although ambivalence-related ideas have been, in the main, restricted to analytic thinking in the clinic, a few sociologists have used the concept to formulate social conflicts and group processes. They have proposed that ambivalence is a natural by-product of social transformation and associated shifting social norms, configurations and power distributions so that, while societies may seek progress and social change they may, at the same time, resist it in covert ways.

Ambivalent white racial consciousness is an extension of racial ambivalence theory. It aims to describe the push people racialised as white might experience as they develop an awareness of racial injustice and privilege. Simultaneously, they retreat from this knowledge to maintain a more comfortable stance; denial. These two elements – the push towards awareness of racism and racial privilege and the retreat from this knowledge into a position of comfort – are what form the ambivalence according to that theory.

Everyday performance

'I am a 57-year-old white cis male group analytic psychotherapist who thinks he is rocking it as an "Ally" [and who] finds himself standing by the wheelie bin one evening with a "Jolly Sambo" money box in his hand and is frozen; torn between the decision to throw away this relic of a racialised, white supremacist Empire-permeated childhood in 1960s working-class Lancashire and the treasured memories of playing with the same object at his Nana's feet in front of the coal fire loading it with old pennies over and over again and laughing as it rolled its eyes and lifted its arm to feed itself more pennies. "How could I throw that experience of my Nana's love in the fucking bin?" was the cry in my head. How can I be ashamed and feel guilty about what was a cherished embodied memory of loving and being loved and cherished? Racialised white supremacy, I realised, is inextricably embodied in my secure attachment system. This is one insight into why it's so tricky to become a good white ally – because along with everything else it threatens my hold on what is good. So I can read Resmaa Menakem's *My grandmother's hands* and Emma Dabiri's *What white people can do next*, and I can intellectually accept why I might not really want to relinquish my privilege but this was the most distressing insight for me, and it's why I found myself standing in the cold by the wheelie bin suspended and conflicted, frozen in the moment and why I felt a tear on my face as I let that object drop into the rubbish.' (John, white male, 50, England)

John's generous offering to *White minds* is rich. Here we have someone who is perhaps better aware than most, more conscious than average, when it comes to social inequality, racial injustice and the harm of white supremacy. Someone who considers himself an 'ally'. He stands at a crossroads symbolically as he must decide whether he is going to relinquish a 'racist' object. A toy. Something dear, something cherished but something nonetheless reminiscent of what appears to be happy childhood days and his much-loved grandmother. He freezes and, upon the contemplation of this dilemma, he is distressed. He is distressed not only by the realisation that he is throwing away something steeped in personal history, but also because of the realisation of the dilemma that challenges his sense of self. Distressed that his cherished personal memories are so intertwined with violent histories and that when pit against one another, doing the right thing – which he eventually finds the courage to do – is not such an easy thing to do.

Whiteness, aversion and the fear of contact

Individualism, in its extreme form, inhibits connection, solid attachments and empathy. We have argued previously that socialisation within white patriarchy leads to difficulties in connecting to the self and others; to the development, as formulated, of a false self. We could go a step further and posit that individualism is a defence against human contact and intimacy. Thus, another form of ego protection, and a tool to facilitate violence against this formulation supports dissociation. In our examination of splitting, we considered the fundamental function it serves in the enactment of violence. We can now consider this defence mechanism as a form of fear of contact and intimacy with the self and the other.

Intimate potentialities differ from person to person, often based on psychohistories and, in particular, on experiences of interpersonal trauma. The capacity for intimacy also varies from place to place and from culture to culture. Corporeal arrangements in space tell us something about intimacy and thus about the psychosocial. If we agree that the fear of the black object, the ultimate other, is necessarily the fear of projected material including existential angst related to one's mortality, then the fear of blackness is necessarily the fear of the self. Possibly, too, the fear of death. Thus, avoiding contact with blackness is avoiding contact with the self or, at least, part of the self, but it is also a form of terror management.

The fear of intimacy has merged into many a fantasy designed to protect whiteness. In particular, it merged into the fear of contamination or another expression of the fear of contact. Foreigners, immigrants, racial 'minorities' have all been constructed as the bearers of diseases and germs with the potential to contaminate whiteness. The generation of fear over health risks is, at times, real but mostly exaggerated if not paranoid. It is still central to immigration discourses and is instrumentalised to legitimise draconian border controls, once more evidencing these recurring associations between death anxiety and the other, and other–self boundaries.

The fear of contamination, in part, reflects eugenicist aspirations and a deep-seated wish to maintain white racial purity without which whiteness, as a political project and structure, becomes precarious. Widespread concerns over racial purity would not exist in a context where sexual contact with, sexual desire for or interest in the black or colonial object were non-existent. Blackness, and in particular black maleness, has been imagined as a constant threat to whiteness because of the heterosexual sexual desire it is seen to evoke in women racialised as white. This is largely a function of colonial sexual myths.

Ambivalence towards proximity and intimacy in the West is perceivable through the use of space. The space between bodies is notably larger than in many places populated by bodies racialised as black and brown, where bodies tend to be closer, as they are often confined to smaller spaces. Bodies, space and psychologies can once more be seen to become enmeshed. Any observant traveller would have noticed variance in corporeal proximity. How much intimate sense, in the literal sense, you can have of the other. How much or how little of the other you can access through your senses, your sense of touch, of smell, sometimes even of taste. Exploring whiteness through the prism of intimacy requires us to return to gender constructions.

Dominant masculine norms have been hypothesised to be in direct conflict with emotional expression, intimacy and vulnerability. Male gender role socialisation leads to difficulties with intimacy. Western individualism has been generally promoting autonomy rather than dependence and interdependence and thus less permeable boundaries, replacing, some have argued, the natural desire for closeness and relatedness with competition and a thirst for power leading to abusive and destructive relational configurations and a culture of abuse [8].

It is no surprise that, in this context, intimacy has been feminised and that emotions have been attached to the allegedly less mature beings such as women, children and people of colour, who have been figured as ruled by the senses, the body, libidinal impulses rather than rational thought, objective detachment and judgement. The femaleness of intimacy and the femaleness of emotions mean that the suppression of emotion and contact has been used as a weapon for the advancement of capitalism, colonialism and patriarchy.

Although intimacy manifests in the domain of the interpersonal, and specifically in how comfortable we are with others, it is arguably primarily an intrapsychic process. Or it is at least based on an intrapsychic blueprint so that our capacity for intimacy with another is necessarily contingent upon our capacity to be intimate with ourselves. Essentially, what is being said, is that our capacity to connect with ourselves, to be at home within ourselves and to tolerate or bear all that we are, is intrinsically linked to our capacity to be in contact with and to tolerate others. In fact, *intimus*, in Latin, is the superlative of inside. The primary meaning of intimacy is, thus, to be in contact with one's own inside, one's interior world. The capacity for intimacy is thus both the capacity for human contact and the capacity for self-contact. The crossing of ego boundaries with another, some have said, requires the willingness to be permeable, thus, vulnerable.

In the previous chapter we encountered aversion, and we explored it primarily in the domain of the cognitive. That is to say, how white groups avoid confronting race-related material. However, there is a link to be made here as ambivalence is also implicated in aversive behaviour. Particularly when it comes to the relational. Many of us may recognise this dynamic. You have staff or students of colour. They are in the numerical minority. Perhaps even the only one. They feel excluded or ill at ease in white spaces. They cannot attribute their embodied experience to any overt conflict. Nothing seems to have happened although they may be genuinely distressed. White social actors in these spaces may struggle to understand what may be taking place too. This dynamic may be greatly illuminated by looking at (interpersonal) white aversion.

The intimate conversations I have with white individuals around race and racism have taught me immensely about whiteness as many have trustfully shared fears, and, at times, fantasies, openly with me. The number one fear I hear is the fear of being called racist. It's a haunting fear that, as we saw, is linked to the fear of self. Since the fear 'of being called racist' is the fear of being racist. Most white people struggle to understand that what they fear already exists in them, hence once more, they simply fear part of themselves, and that these parts will be exposed.

I have seen how debilitating the effects of that fear can be. As we have seen earlier, it can lead to all sorts of projective accusations, often accusations of abuse of power targeted at those with the least social and institutional power. However, outside of these more overt forms of paranoid acting out, this fear can have more covert expressions such as distancing, keeping the racialised subject at arm's length or treating them with suspicion or distrust. It can also operate more subtly than that. For those who find themselves in a group as the only person of colour, being surrounded by people who fear being seen, fear being exposed and by extension may avoid contact or closeness to them, the impact would be felt. Even if these fears are not expressed, they will profoundly impact their experience of particular spaces and their sense of safety.

This distance, however protective, takes us to a form of racism referred to as aversive racism [9]. Aversive racism is a form of covert racism which takes place because groups racialised as white disown overt racism and consciously oppose prejudicial racist beliefs and stereotypes – adherence to which is no longer socially acceptable. However, they shift their behaviour when they engage with people of colour, often out of discomfort or fear of proximity. The ambivalence here lies in the disavowing of racism on the one hand and, on the other, avoiding close contact with people of colour. Aversive racism is all about avoidance and may be sustained by the fear of being called racist.

When people of colour struggle to exist within particular white spaces, and struggle with articulating their experiences of these spaces or make sense of their distress, considering white aversion as a possible silent dynamic may help elucidate the intersubjective context.

White identity development

Racial identity development refers to our shifting racial attitudes towards our in-group and towards the dominant group, in our context, whiteness. It speaks of our awareness of the significance of race within society. Many racial identity models exist [10]. Each proposes specific stages that an individual is expected to go through in order to attain a mature racial identity. When it comes to white identity, these models generally describe the process by which people racialised as white come to confront the reality of racism and commit to the development of an anti-racist practice and identity. This process is believed to be dependent on some racial encounter or 'contact' which challenges the individual to move from acceptance of dominant racialised beliefs, stereotypes and negative attitudes towards people of colour. A resulting shift in worldview ensues which centres an awareness of racialisation.

The contact event or encounter is hypothesised to highlight the salience of racism and brings to cognitive salience white privilege and power relations in the white mind. This encounter with racism allows people racialised as white to essentially emerge from racial obliviousness, a state of racial naivety or denial, to racial consciousness. A place where they might start to understand themselves, their experiences of the world and their perspectives as being a function of whiteness. Most models are premised on the idea that this form of racial conscientisation leads to people racialised as white committing to struggle against racism. Thus, the general formulation is that contact leads to a phase of disintegration whereby one's sense of self, others and the world becomes so deeply challenged that it crumbles. This disintegration is associated with distress, guilt, shame and helplessness but must be worked through so as to lead to a new engagement with the world: reintegration, the final stage.

This typical three-phase model offers us something helpful when considering the shift from denial or repression to confrontation, but it is not without problems. A number of criticisms have been advanced over the years towards the logics of these models. Of particular note, the presumed linear and developmental nature is not supported by evidence of current social configurations. We know, for example, that awareness of racial inequality and even opposition to the same are not sufficient conditions to promote sustained engagement in anti-racism and changes in how people racialised as white engage with the world. Some scholars have therefore proposed that the process of racial consciousness, rather than being developmental, is more attitudinal, with therefore no way of guaranteeing that people racialised as white will move into anti-racism as the final step. Further, even if we accepted that reintegration processes were an integral part of white identity development, it is doubtful that once reintegration is reached, people racialised as white would simply remain at that stage without reverting back. Similarly, these models speak little of the particular defences or resistance people racialised as white might engage in so as to avoid the pain of disintegration. They may remain in racial oblivion. This can occur for many perpetually, for some cyclically.

Everyday performance

'One experience I will have because I've only ever gone to mainly white institutions for my education, I have had up until a couple of years mainly white friends and so I was probably every one of those white friends' only black friend and I'm only realising these past couple of years of how negative that was for me because I was their kind of out, you know, I'm not racist I've got a black friend, also the person that they could try out a lot of their micro-aggressions, their racial discrimination, so I've had those conversations with white people about why they can't say this or the other. I've had people in my house say well you lot and actually say it like that, you lot all say [the n-word] in your music, and you know hip hop videos, you lot are saying it then why can't we. I've had the accusations from actual people that I called friend of having a chip on my shoulder and their experience and a ginger person saying this, their experience being the same because you know you are allowed to be racist to ginger people. And I've also done, in those relationships, I realised that I was being a lot of my behaviour was performative. I even said things like I'm going to have to get black on your ass because when people were, which was my code for I'm going to have to insult you, or cuss you out essentially and since falling out with those friends for different reasons, an actual incident that happened between us which has nothing to do with this but also because I realised those aggressions were adding up, stacking up and starting to make me feel like you are not actually my friend, I am here for a purpose other than friendship. I mean it was the fact that we had known each other for years but there is also the fact that I allowed them, I gave them a kind of pass to say a lot of the stuff that they were saying and I also felt like for me they have met a kind of friends of the person of that self-hatred that I sort of talked about and yeah kind of sort of made me feel like I was completing that role of the acceptable black girl, I was kind of led to be.' (Julia, mixed race woman, 30s, UK)

Connection and interpersonal contact are important tools of resistance when it comes to dismantling whiteness, as we have argued in the previous chapter.

Territoriality, border logics and imperialism have made true contact between white, black and brown subjects virtually impossible. Today, normalised segregation keeps that distance going. In this socio-historical context, how may we maintain cross-racial friendships? How possible is it to make psychological contact and sustain intimacy with people who often appear set on ignoring the harm and hurt they cause you? I know plenty of people of colour who avoid friendships with people racialised as white because of repeated acts of complicity often sustained by white amnesia. Julia's testimony demonstrates how the racialised other can become engaged in sadomasochistic or self-harming conduct to maintain cross-racial friendships. The work required to make these friendships work is often taken for granted. The costs are exposed here, and they are significant. Self-alienation. Heartache. Shame. Self-blame. Recurrent assaults on one's sense of self-respect.

White amnesia as ambivalence

Dressner and Brown have contended that in order for social justice to occur, there needs to be a critical consciousness on the part of all people regardless of power and privilege [11]. The scholars also speak of amnesia as a blocker to such conscientisation. This amnesia is not only selective, naturally erasing those parts of the social world which cannot be confronted or contained, it is also functional since it serves to protect whiteness. Therefore, addressing what is referred to in their article as 'white-privileged amnesia' is the way to both ensure consciousness-raising and that people racialised as white make a commitment to social transformation. Their position is as follows: 'Selective White-privilege amnesia refers to a selective loss of memory that (a) denies validation of oppression, (b) prevents accountability by the oppressor and bystanders' witnessing to the oppression, and (c) shields the White community from confronting the devastation and pain that racism inflicts on communities and individuals of color.' Dresser and Brown conclude: 'White people need to experience and acknowledge this pain in order to be mobilised toward action for social justice'. A conclusion we ourselves reached when it came to proposing resistance strategies to white dissociation. Racial consciousness is a necessary ingredient, but it is by no means sufficient to address white amnesia. Amnesia is not an innocent, passive or easily remediable by-product of 'white privilege', rather, here, it is an active process of forgetting and unknowing which is again socially functional.

An autoethnographic note

I was in the developing stage of a friendship with a white woman I got into contact with professionally. This woman had many qualities I value in close relationships.

But racial micro-aggressions or, we might say, subtle racialised slights recurrently presented in our burgeoning relationship. Seeking to attempt to resolve them, I spoke to her about her recurrently covertly contesting my Frenchness. I explained the racism which was laid bare as the basis of her contestation and how it betrayed a worldview that blackness was essentially incompatible with Frenchness. I did what we're taught to do to influence well. I was candid. I made a pathos case, and I made an ethos case. I explained what this meant for me, and the impact of such displacement given my history. I found it hard. I did this because I wanted to give our relationship a chance. She was initially defensive. Denying her actions. Then she cried those same tears we have encountered before. I did not. I consoled her, compassionately. She apologised. She clearly understood. She ordered some books on race. We made up. We met outside of this exchange. Not even a month after my costly emotional engagement, she went on to do the very same thing that she had learnt was oppressive. Not once, but repeatedly, seemingly oblivious to her own regression. Quite a painful thing to witness. Sordid in equal measure. I decided then this relationship was not one I would want to invest more emotional or cognitive labour in, full stop. I stopped responding to all pathos-laden questions about what was going on. And invitations to meet and be friendly at this point were similarly ignored.

The sustaining of true friendships across the racial divide has received much less theoretical attention than matters related to sexualised dynamics or even 'mixed race' romantic entanglements. Yet their problematics have much to teach us about solidarity, about anti-racism and about the politics of 'allyship'. In an essay entitled 'White friend', Ahmed describes the impact of the labour of sustaining these friendships, which are 'not only about dealing with those who articulate racist views or who respond in a hostile way because you are talking about racism. That labour is often performed in relation to many others, including those around you who you might have expected to be more sympathetic' [12]. What Ahmed highlights is not only the emotional cost or heartache of experiencing racism and struggling against it but also the subsequent labour which is required and the associated wounding which occurs when one is not being heard and understood within those relationships with people racialised as white one holds dear. In particular, she articulates, through the sharing of personal testimonies she has gathered in her research, the enactment of subtle power plays and the interference of white authority in these relationships. Critically to the point here, she similarly exposes apparent difficulties that arise with memory for racist events in those white friends. An apparent incapacity to hold onto what they were seen to appear 'to get' previously, almost as though it was 'deleted' from their consciousness, leaving the women of colour who shared their experiences in a recurrent sense of loss, disorientation and mourning over the lack of support. Particularly when the failure to support comes from self-professed allies and others who 'do the work'.

Ahmed's essay and the autoethnographic note illustrate that even when racial consciousness is raised, it is unlikely to be ever fully achieved, thus it is not simply an event, or a destination to be reached for the overwhelming majority of people racialised as white. I speak of 'moments of racial consciousness' for this reason. Amnesia here, I have previously posited, is both a white event and an ongoing process. White amnesia would be a more appropriate descriptor, as moments or periods of amnesia throughout one's lifetime can and do coexist with moments of consciousness. The implications here are equally significant, relationally. I have observed this process again and again. In professional settings but also in friendships. Where something which was acquired and understood at one point, a foundation one may have taken the time to build, a bridge created, crumbles with such rapidity you hardly have the time to recover from emotional demands. These associated demands relate to education and debate requests or particular needs to understand expressed at the beginning of the friendship. Despairing and dispiriting to observe and experience. So, how do we get white minds ready to face the world we all inhabit? Can we hasten this readiness, particularly when many will be spared or refuse to contemplate the experiences that often force racial consciousness? In my work, many say to me that they would have found my words intolerable or too distressing a few years back. Timing appears once more to be of the essence.

Ambivalence and anti-racism

While timing matters when it comes to encountering whiteness, retaining its ontological implications once more defy temporal linearity. In his discussion of the concealment and insidious nature of whiteness, Yancy proposes that whiteness functions as a form of ambush – ambush being the etymology of insidious [13]. Ambushing bodies who are racially marked as other, as we saw earlier in the ambushing of Krystal and her colleague who we met earlier in the book and who were essentially summarily dismissed and ambushed into joblessness after questioning a 'charitable' institution on its apparent racialised child removal practices. This took place in the midst of smiling faces. But bodies racialised as white get ambushed by whiteness too, we may say more ontologically. Hence, even those who commit themselves to anti-racism, or strive to dismantle whiteness, will again and again find themselves caught in its enactment, even as they study and theorise whiteness.

Like Ahmed, Yancy links such ambushes to the embeddedness of whiteness in the habitual ways the white subject engages with the world, and, in particular, their way of relating to bodies racialised as black and brown. That distance, or the gap within which the white subject operates from due to experiencing the violence of whiteness (albeit not overtly), is mirrored in the distance between anti-racist theory and anti-racist practice. The reality is that self-professed anti-racist beliefs do coexist with racist ways of being in the world. Indeed, theorising on whiteness for the white subject as black and brown bodies suffocate is a form of narcissism. It keeps away the white subject from the real-world operation of whiteness as these subjects are, in fact, liable to being 'ambushed' in their efforts to dismantle whiteness, Yancy goes on to propose.

I have observed additional splits in my encounters with white anti-racists, who often have the most sophisticated understanding of whiteness and may even have produced multiple publications on the phenomenon. However, they still struggle to recognise the everyday operation of whiteness. A failure in application of theory. A problem therefore with praxis. A distance which takes us, we may argue, to the heart of white ambivalence.

The problem with ambivalence is not only that it prevents people from engaging in structural transformation and anti-racism or even that it may lead white anti-racists to fail to live anti-racist lives. We also have some evidence that suggests that those with high levels of racial ambivalence (who, for example, have simultaneously high levels of sympathy and high levels of prejudice) are more likely to engage in retaliatory violence and in the degradation of racialised victims following their engagement with racism. These findings are premised on three assumptions:

- that most people racialised as white tend to have racialised ambivalent attitudes;
- that ambivalence towards a victim increases the arousal of guilt in perpetrators; and that
- as a result, perpetrators are likely to seek to mobilise guilt reduction strategies, which may include victim blaming, derogation and, disturbingly, further violence.

Thus, the widespread victim blaming in situations of racial injustice in society is accounted for, as Dalal suggests, the white subject feeling persecuted by the injured object hence attacks as a result [14].

Ambivalence must be addressed in those racialised as white to support engagement in anti-racism. In a model, I adapted Motivational Interviewing (MI) techniques to tackle white ambivalence. MI is a change-focused therapeutic model attributed to psychologists William Miller and Stephen Rollnick [15]. It is a non-directive approach aimed at those contemplating change in their life but who may be hampered by ambivalence. The starting point of the model is that ambivalence is a normal part of the change process. It is a form of self-protection against the anxiety of giving up familiar ways of experiencing and being in the world. It is part of a defence strategy against the losses that giving up harmful habits invariably involves. In the context of whiteness, ambivalence may serve to resist race-related innocence.

MI, at its core, aims to deal with and acknowledge this cycle of ambivalence and encourages behavioural change mostly in people with addictions or in those who are for different reasons struggling with change [15]. The model is underpinned by several principles centred on safeness, collaboration, autonomy and the utilisation of the clients' intrinsic motivation and resources for/towards the change they want to enact in the world to reduce their resistance to it. The model comprises six stages, discussed in the following.

Pre-contemplation

At this stage change has not been considered and individuals may not even be aware that a particular problem with, for example, substance use exists, that help is needed or that they need to make changes to their lifestyle for their own sake and/or that of others. Alternatively, they may feel overwhelmed by the possibility of change. In the context of white supremacy, we may envision this stage as obliviousness to whiteness or as white denial in relation to the harm of racism including the racism one engages in.

Contemplation

In the contemplation stage individuals become increasingly aware of the problem and of the case for change. They are still split between the pros and cons of change and the pros and cons of staying the same. Individuals in this stage, staying with our example, continue to use substances but are curious about living a drug-free life. In the case of whiteness, people racialised as white may continue to act out in racially oppressive ways and/or continue to enjoy their racialised power although they may start to feel conflicted, guilty and/or seek relevant learning or engage in conversations on racism. Still, they will vacillate between wanting and not wanting to change.

Preparation

When the advantages of change outweigh the disadvantages in the mind of the change seeker, the need to alter the status quo takes hold. Specific action planning is instigated. Thus, the preparation stage also entails an examination of one's strengths and weaknesses and an assessment of one's self-efficacy. Individuals in the preparation stage are typically still using substances but intend to stop using them imminently. They begin to set goals for themselves and make commitments. Whiteness wise, individuals gain the courage to confront racism in themselves and others, are making pledges to do better and are gearing themselves for a new engagement with the world.

Action

Individuals in the action stage are now ready for change and begin to actively engage in it. This involves modifying their habits, changing their environment and putting into practice their action plan. When the reality of the task ahead hits home, a grief process may be activated, and it is not unusual at this stage for people to re-evaluate their decision as the honeymoon period ends. When it comes to drug use, relapse may ensue. In terms of whiteness, individuals start to internalise shifts in their worldview, self-image and relationships with people of colour. Here too we may expect that some may question their decision in light of the challenges of embodying anti-racism.

Maintenance

During this stage efforts focus on maintaining the gains achieved in terms of change in the action stage. It is at this stage that old habits and relational patterns are most likely to resurface and test the motivation and will of the now change maker. The temptation to start using substances again recurs frequently. Relapses are common. At this stage, data about challenges, obstacles and barriers is being accumulated and learning from this information will be central in allowing individuals to bounce back and thus sustain changes in the longer term. This trajectory maps onto anti-racism too and leads to a higher level of awareness of the self as an agent of whiteness.

Termination

In the termination stage, the person is expected to have made all of the changes that are required for them to live a drug-free life. If they face new issues, they will continue to resolve them. For some, this is the end of the road. It is of course rarely ever that simple and for many sustaining change is a lifelong journey. For whiteness termination is completely unrealistic. Challenges will continue to arise. In the context of white supremacy, the pressure to revert to older ways of relating, or to regress, will forever loom.

The Whiteness Readiness Model

This section, and Figure 8.1, summarise the Whiteness Readiness Model (WRM) [16]. It describes the main stages for the WRM, which is underpinned by MI principles. The stages of the WRM are pre-contemplation, contemplation, engagement, internalisation and regression, having thus only been slightly amended from the original model. The

Figure 8.1: The Whiteness Readiness Model

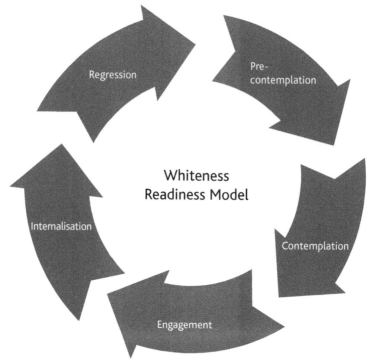

Source: Kinouani (2019)

MI principles have been applied to our anti-racist purposes and highlight associated stages and actions as follows.

Pre-contemplation

Here the aim is to raise doubts about the status quo. To increase awareness of the risks, losses and harm of whiteness and to connect the person racialised as white to alternative ways to act on and be in the world. Statistics on racial injustice and inequality may be helpful as would exposure to their impact and lived experience.

Contemplation

Contemplation is all about addressing the ambivalence. This can be aided by helping the person racialised as white identify the gains they sustain from whiteness. Some strategies may include weighing the pros and cons of whiteness at personal, collective and social level. Assessing personal motivation for wanting to change but also resistance to the same. And increasing the sense of personal agency and hope.

Engagement

This stage is simply about the pragmatics of change making. We concentrate here on action planning and goal setting. In order to maximise the chances of success, any action plan must include some realistic goals, reflection on resources as well as monitoring and accountability mechanisms.

Internalisation

In this stage, change starts to become internalised. New ways of being and relating have been successfully tested. Individuals racialised as white should be supported in identifying challenges to come and to stick to their action plan. Strategies/tools to meet their goals and keep on track despite challenges will be helpful.

Regression

As the change maker processes and integrates new ways of being and relating they will experience pulls towards their older ways of being. Learning reflexively from challenges and 'failings' is critical to build a tolerance for setbacks without becoming completely demoralised. The more prepared for barriers and obstacles the person is, the shorter lived and the less significant the setbacks will be.

Readiness as a repeated event

When it comes to whiteness and anti-racism, we can assume obliviousness rather than consciousness to be the status quo. Hence regression when engaged in change is not only likely, but also the default. That is to say, we can safely assume that the white subject will regress or revert to baseline. Everything in society forces whiteness to go undercover and forces the white subject to disconnect from its violence. So, in this model, regression is expected to recur cyclically. That regression may lead to the change maker or seeker proceeding straight to the internalisation stage in those who are more practised in anti-racism. This stage may lead to contemplation, if not pre-contemplation, in those earlier in their journey who have more ambivalence to work through.

Moments of readiness are really all that we can realistically hope for, followed by longer periods of obliviousness. Internalisation will always be challenged by the cultural ambivalence that we all swim in. Wanting to see, then not tolerating seeing, thus, 'forgetting'. Remembering then becoming oblivious again and again. This is what we all do to differing degrees. Except, of course, in the context of white supremacy, where one is less likely to see or be exposed to critical events or incidents of racism, periods of obliviousness are likely to be much longer and more frequent for those racialised as white.

Proximal ambivalence

> The 'race' idea is powerful precisely because it supplies a foundational understanding of natural hierarchy on which a host of other supplementary social and political conflicts have come to rely. (Gilroy, 2005, p 19 [17])

A controversial consideration for our reflections on ambivalence concerns the impact of racial stratification or hierachisation and the role they play between black and brown subjects, which we started to explore in the opening chapter. Because of the naturalisation of racialised hierarchies, whenever individuals are positioned midway between power and marginalisation in that stratification system, dynamics related to proximity to power are bound to be in operation. To attempt to capture and formulate stratification or hierarchisation related racialised conflicts, I have proposed elsewhere the concept of 'proximal ambivalence'. Proximal ambivalence refers to the conflicts which may be set in motion in those who occupy a middle position within a hierarchical system and are therefore positioned midway between power and marginalisation on significant axes of oppression.

Ambivalence here, I propose, comes about because individuals who are located midway between power and marginalisation within white supremacy – although the thinking could apply to other axes of oppression – are likely to both feel connected to the plight of those who are oppressed since they have and do experience oppression, while simultaneously wishing consciously or otherwise to maintain structures of domination which afford them conditional benefits. Benefits they are rarely willing to relinquish. Benefits which mean they are albeit only conditionally, shielded from the worst brutality, exploitation and extraction whiteness can dish up. Benefits that allow them to aggrandise themselves on the back of those lower down that fantasised hierarchy. A location where maintaining a semblance of psychic integrity is possible because of the existence of the lowest of the low, here those racialised as black.

Because white supremacy rewards anti-blackness and, in fact, access or proximity to its fortress, requires the acceptance of it, proximal groups who have themselves some experience of racialised violence may pose, I suggest, in many contexts, a higher risk to those who are more marginalised than those at the top of the hierarchy, people racialised as white. Not only because they have some experience of oppression, which they want to minimise, and they have also had some taste of power, which they may want to increase. However, because of their experience of violence, parts of them also feel genuine motivation to dismantle injustice. And because they have received benefits associated with their proximity to white power, their interests are served by ensuring the status quo remains the status quo. It is this tension these alternative and apparently mutually exclusive positions produce that we may call proximal (racial) ambivalence.

In other words, proximal ambivalence is the key defence for folks positioned in the middle. Being not quite the master and not quite the most oppressed means that, first, due to identification with the master, full racial consciousness will always be compromised by amnesia, self-deception and denial to protect the master's system. This is, in part, due to the benefits they receive. Second, as a result of identification with the oppressed, the risk or fantasy of falling down that hierarchy and thus experiencing more violence remains central. Like in groups racialised as white, proximal ambivalence may lead to avoidance, repression or dissociation from issues related to inequality and injustice in some situations or particular contexts. Similarly to the most oppressed, proximal groups may experience the pain and distress of oppression, if they allow themselves to connect to their marginalised parts. This dance or tension may lead to inconsistencies, contradictions, sudden changes in position, guilt and shame.

Summary and resistance

In this chapter we have considered a key limitation of racial identity development tools. Specifically, few take into account white ambivalence and propose ways of dealing with it. Yet, ambivalence is central to race dynamics and is grounded in historical push–pull dynamics of the colonial encounter. We have seen that white ambivalence not only maintains the social (dis)order, but it may also, in fact, increase racial violence. MI, a framework that deals specifically with ambivalence, has been introduced. Using its key principles, a model has been proposed to support individuals racialised as white to connect to their ambivalence and to the challenges of doing anti-racism work. This is what the WRM seeks to support. There is an enduring taboo around expressing enjoyment of the benefits of whiteness for those racialised as white. Today, this has become synonymous with white nationalism and white extremism, since consciously connecting to the gratification that whiteness brings is no longer socially acceptable. Nonetheless, this gratification is real, and it exists in varying degrees in all people racialised as white, and it can coexist with a desire for racial justice. Disavowing racial ambivalence means associated conflicts remain inexorably unaddressed. It is these same ambivalence-related conflicts that lead to the social sanctioning of scapegoating or the locating of racial disturbance in those who are more consciously connected to the 'loving whiteness' parts of themselves. Dissociation from white ambivalence maintains whiteness. It stops the contemplation of white complicity. The proposed WRM model allows for an exploration of loving and hateful feelings, and approach-avoidance behaviours and attitudes towards white supremacy, which feed that internal conflict, so as to help reduce the chances of it being acted out relationally and structurally. The final chapter reflects on complicity. It consider some of the mechanisms which enables society and white social actors to support white supremacy passively.

White complicity

Over the past few years, I have been gravely disappointed with the white moderate. I have almost reached the regrettable conclusion that the Negro's great stumbling block in his stride toward freedom is not the White Citizen's Counciler or the Ku Klux Klanner, but the white moderate, who is more devoted to 'order' than to justice; who prefers a negative peace which is the absence of tension to a positive peace which is the presence of justice; who constantly says: 'I agree with you in the goal you seek, but I cannot agree with your methods of direct action'; who paternalistically believes he can set the timetable for another man's freedom; who lives by a mythical concept of time and who constantly advises the Negro to wait for a 'more convenient' season. (Martin Luther King, 1963)[1]

This extract is from 'Letter from Birmingham Jail', an open letter written by Dr King on 16 April 1963 as a response to criticisms by clergymen calling for unity and condemning King's involvement in direct action. The call for unity was based on the notion that racial injustices were best fought through legal means, in court rather than in the streets. That is to say, through civility and respectable means. King's response, which became central to the civil rights struggle, defended his position on both religious and moral grounds. He stood by his actions and saw direct action as a legitimate means of achieving justice when diplomacy and dialogue fail, and when justice is not available through other means. The debate around which methods of protest for racial injustice may best suit white society and which timing will accord with its timetable is evergreen. The disapproval of black liberation methods is too often simply the disapproval of black liberation. This message from King at the height of the civil rights movement acts as a powerful reminder that white comfort has always been a significant blocker to justice and equality.

Today, this same preoccupation with (dis)order and 'negative peace' can be seen in the way Black Lives Matter protests and anti-racism actions such as 'taking the knee' continue to be ridiculed, maligned and fiercely opposed in the press and within most political parties. Hostility and opposition towards Black Lives Matter protests triggered by the murder of George Floyd have been widespread and explicitly expressed by those in high office. In the UK, Home Secretary Priti Patel, on behalf of the state, not only vocalised strong criticisms against both Black Lives Matter and 'taking the knee', but also used racist tropes and stereotypes when describing the protestors as troublemakers, thugs and criminals [1].

A cultural note

It is in this context that the televised performance of dance crew 'Diversity' in September 2020 occurred. The latter, which put on display a choreography about police brutality in support of Black Lives Matter, created mass outrage, a deluge of complaints to the regulator as well and sustained campaigns of racist trolling online towards the dancers. It is perhaps no surprise that when research was carried out into the police handling of the Black Lives Matter protests, significant areas of concern were documented. These included an excessive use of police force, the failure to offer protection to Black Lives Matter protesters targeted by far-right counter-demonstrators, and the enclosure of large numbers of protesters in closed spaces for extended period of times.

The bulk of the opposition to the Diversity performance or the Black Lives Matter movement more generally seems to revolve around three main lines of argument. First, that they are 'too political' or 'too radical'. Second, that they are 'too disruptive' or 'too loud'. And finally, they are often decried for being 'too divisive'. An extension of this is the allegation that they seek to start a 'race war'. In a nutshell, protesting again anti-black state violence in countries, who in theory uphold the sanctity of protest, race equality and free speech, at least for some, is rarely supported. I am still to come across a single method of protest that is deemed legitimate, necessary and well exercised when it comes to racism, particularly anti-black racism. We saw, when we considered the politics of envy and resentment, drawing largely from Hall and Gilroy's scholarship, that the 'whitelash' which occurs as a result of threatened race-related social change tends to trigger imperial anxieties and nostalgia and, with that, attempts to reassert the status quo and the white psychic equilibrium. These racialised manoeuvres always rationalise race away so they appear to have on the surface little to do with white supremacy. Instead, sovereignty, safety, identity, economic anxiety and social disruption become vectors for its coded expression.

An autoethnographic note

The day after the referendum, I woke up not quite knowing what to think or do. Vaguely worried about the future but, in truth, still in a state of disbelief. Perhaps I was even in a daze. But I needed milk. So, I headed to my local Tesco store. Perhaps, too, this was an attempt to bury myself in the mundanity of everyday life, amidst the xenophobic and racist triumph that was how I understood Brexit. Once there, I got the milk and waited at the self-checkout. Someone was checking their items out. I positioned myself right behind them and a queue rapidly formed behind me. Once my turn came, I took one step or two towards the machine. A man racialised as white jumped in front of me. He placed his items on the holding area and proceeded to check out. Uncharacteristically, I said nothing, and I watched him, puzzled. I felt something violent had taken place. The sense of stupefaction and 'out-of-placeness' was amplified. I turned and looked around for a friendly face to connect with. Everyone in the store was racialised as white, averting my gaze and eye contact. Without a word or glance at me, the white man left. I had been disappeared. Twice. First by the white shopper, then by the white crowd. And I left the store alone, even more distraught than when I had left my house. I had never before been cut across in the queue in that way. When I now think of Brexit, I think of that white man.

The above supermarket anecdote takes us back to this recurrent theme of whiteness as territoriality and its deep-seated entitlement to land, space and time as we explored in our examination of temporal phenomena, of the white gaze. In the store, I was exposed to a quotidian enactment of white superiority within a white crowd. Because no customer or staff member said a word during the incident or after, I was left to have to carry the weight of that humiliating and disconcerting interaction alone, in silence. I took my turn after he left and exited the store in silence. Moreover, the exchange acted as a symbolic precursor for racial tensions and conflicts, soon to be expressed in society at large within hours of the results of the referendum and, as such, this story acutely describes the political situation.

The richness of the autoethnographic note lies in the multiple 'levels' of meaning it provides and the socio-political stories it tells, establishing once again these links or parallels between the different levels of the matrix, as we encountered in Chapter 1. Here, what we first have is a representation, if not embodiment, of Brexit by that white man. What was Brexit, if not whiteness seeking to reassert its priority in the UK, at least for a significant proportion of those who voted leave. This collective sense of frustrated entitlement in the foundation, or we may say political matrix, took the form, in the supermarket, of this man reclaiming service before me, hence, asserting his right to priority in the dynamic matrix of the supermarket. The entitlement to service, we may further argue, is a re-enactment of the entitlement to space and bodies, a colonial script or a collective archetype, evocative, we may argue, of the social unconscious.

A basket full of bad apples?

When discriminatory acts are committed by individuals, society tends to be quick to regard the perpetrator as an individual loose cannon. An aberration, rather than as a manifestation of a collective will and a group dynamic they are implicated in. In other words, socially we cannot wait, it seems, to locate that disturbance or pathology in such individual bodies, thus to individualise racist phenomena. This is the logic of the bad apple axiom which serves to distance groups racialised as white from those violent systems they, once more, are all a part of. Locating the problem or disturbance of race or in specific individuals is unhelpful. It takes us away from collective mechanisms and consequent group acquiescence. It is much more troubling to consider that the white shopper who displaced and invisibilised me was acting on behalf of many others, we may even say, on behalf of society.

The bad apple doctrine is frequently put forth to explain away state murder and police brutality. But here too it only gets us so far since such acts of violence are relatively rarely reported, challenged or collectively opposed by the presumed 'good apples'. The good and bad apple binary, we could argue, is another manifestation of splitting. Thus, our focus on social actors deemed racist continues to enable groups racialised as white to split off from 'their' own racism or complicity in racist systems. Many will argue that systemic pressures and the fear of retaliation reduce personal agency and moral choice. This may well be so. Nonetheless, complicity does not require ill motivation. Nor does it necessitate the wilful and conscious involvement of white social actors in structural harm. The idea of the location of disturbance we considered in Chapter 5 encourages us to see the group as the entity enacting racism with particular individuals selected by the group to become the site for its expression, an expression of what is disowned or unutterable in the larger social context. In other words, if, as group analysts posit, every individual behaviour serves a function for their larger context, then the actions of social actors designated to be 'the racists' cannot be interpreted outside of collective wishes, impulses or fantasies.

Put yet another way, for whiteness to survive, the collective 'pathologies' of groups of social actors, nations and society need to be engaged. It is these entities, we may say, that designate those who will do the dirty work on behalf of entire collectives. This group-analytic line of thought has far-reaching consequences. If racist acts are in fact carried out, not by a minority, but vicariously by the majority of people racialised as white, through the hands of a 'minority', white liberals and those who hold progressive political beliefs are therefore equally supportive of white supremacy. At collective and unconscious level. It also means that covert compliance and allegiance encapsulate the essence of white liberals and progressives' participation in racist systems. This includes those more brutal expressions of racist violence inflicted upon racialised others.

Extending on Hannah Arendt's thinking on 'the banality of evil', Applebaum similarly explores white complicity [2, 3]. She proposes that while individuals racialised as white may not be personally responsible for racism as a structure, since they benefit from being racialised as white within white supremacy, there is a moral and ethical requirement to commit to anti-racism action beyond the theoretical so as to see and disrupt the everyday, banalised acts of race-based violence. Violence which necessarily evades those positioned as its primary beneficiaries. Since racism is the ordinary state of affairs, the crux of white complicity here is centred on inaction. Inaction is usually rationalised as neutrality. Neutrality as complicity is thus sustained by denial: the refusal to accept one's implication in the structure and the refusal to be challenged on one's complicity. The fallacy of neutrality is, according to Applebaum, one of the key mechanisms by which whiteness endures.

Unsurprisingly, there continues to be fierce resistance to this conceptualisation of white complicity. Largely because it challenges notions of innocence, benevolence and 'reasonableness'. Partly too because modern thought has framed aggression and destruction in terms of what is actively done, overt and obviously forceful. Conceptualisations of harm which do not fit these constructions tend to be opposed. It is these same constructions of violence which mean we also have a hard time generally accepting that complicity in violence is violence. This is also why strong social forces seeking to locate racism and social pathology more broadly, within the white working class, according to formulations of racism which sees it as crass, overt and unhinged, are in existence. The location of racism within poor whites is also white supremacy in action. Those lower down the stratified hierarchy, which is classed as much as it is racialised, remain the most sacrificeable, the most usable in service of whiteness, and the most disposable to maintain the structure.

Everyday performance

'I'm trying to train myself out of apathetic reactions, which have a large element of shame in them. I have been trained by society not to put my head up, not to step out of line, and I can fall back on a feeling of social punishment if I do the socially wrong thing, so it's easy to support the status quo by staying silent. Learning to push that weight aside uses muscles I have never been asked to use. It was hard to train myself to step in where a crowd does not, but when there is no instant trigger, I don't know how to bring myself to move. If someone is being harassed I know how to judge what is right by ignoring what is deemed popular. The constant prejudicial treatment of people of colour is much harder to see. The shame makes me hide in the crowd, so I do not have to face it. It's related to the horrible feeling you have when you see someone being bullied, but it's wider and more diffuse. I was always taught to walk towards trouble, but I don't know how to face something so wide, so I wait for other people to lead. I deal with this by donating money to black organisations and those [organisations] that more consistently work in areas of poverty and blackness, because that is more efficient than I know how to be. This is not about that, though, I think. But it's a way of finding people who are leading them. I feel that I cannot lift the whole problem at once, and sometimes that leads me to put the whole problem down and flee it, instead of trying to lift one part.' (Laura, white woman, 40s, England)

Laura's candour and self-awareness are frankly commendable. We see in her words the courage to see. The courage to confront her own apathy. And the courage to name and own her cowardice when it comes to challenging whiteness. We also recognise one of the potential root causes of that 'false generosity'; shame. We observe how giving money to charitable causes can be a form of undoing. Therefore, as a defence. But there are other ways to interpret Laura's overwhelm. Group analysis brings an interesting perspective to Laura's silence, 'apathy' and the weight she appears to feel on her shoulders which lead her to hide in the crowd in situations of racial injustice. Stobo proposes that the silence that comes into being once race appears in particular spaces serves to regulate that intersubjective space between the black subject and the white subject [4]. This is a space that contains the unnameable and unspeakable. It contains the terror of what cannot be put into words and spoken; specifically, shared histories of imperialism, colonialism and enslavement. Atrocities which defy our capacity to speak and, sometimes, to act. The feeling of being overwhelmed indicates something of the heaviness of that invisible and nameless disturbance.

A cultural note

On 29 July 2022, Alika Ogorchukwu, a 39-year-old disabled Nigerian street vendor from Civitanova Marche, in northeast Italy, was murdered in broad daylight by 32-year-old Filippo Ferlazzo, an Italian man racialised as white. Ferlazzo was reported to have used Ogorchukwu's own crutch to assault him. He is alleged to have struck the black man repeatedly with it, then, as he lay helpless on the floor, to have strangled him with his bare hands. Ogorchukwu died, it is reported, of suffocation. Images of the killing show Ferlazzo sitting on Ogorchukwu's chest for several minutes with his hands around the black man's neck. The attack and subsequent killing were witnessed. All was captured on mobile phones. No onlooker or passer-by made any attempt to help the disabled black man away from the grip of his white assailant. The killing of Ogorchukwu was, it is reported, triggered by him selling paper handkerchiefs against Ferlazzo's commands or wishes.

The heartbreakingly public murder of Ogorchukwu has sadistic undertones and echoes the murder of George Floyd in the US. It is evocative of the Fanonian conceptualisation of racism as suffocation, an idea we encountered earlier in the book when I recounted experiences of institutional gagging. Furthermore, it again alerts us to the reality that material and capitalist interests and illusory competition are rarely extractible from racial hostility. Much could be said about the symbolism and the sexualised dimensions of the murder too, particularly the use of the crutch and the act of strangulation in and of itself. Much more could also be said about the role Ogorchukwu's disability played in the violence, a phenomenon I have elsewhere referred to as 'negrableism' in an attempt to apply intersectional thinking to the meeting of ableism and anti-blackness. I have proposed that negrableism 'is the specific hatred, fear, distrust, and prejudice directed toward those Black bodies who are disabled and the patterns of structural disadvantage they face because of the intersection of anti-black racism and ableism' [5].

White supremacy and ableism are inseparable. Although colonial logics did not give birth to ableism since ableism precedes colonial and imperial formations of race, modernist constructions of the body and its instrumentalisation in relation to capital acquisition shaped ableist violence and vice versa. Ableist tropes (for example, laziness, social deviancy, evilness) significantly overlap with anti-black formations. Critically, people have been subjected to genocidal and eugenic practices on the grounds of both blackness and disability. Negrableism complicates the formulation of bystanderism in Ogorchukwu's murder. Would a more socially valued black body have activated help-providing behaviours in the white bystanders, or at least increased the chances of intervention? Likely. Would onlookers have experienced higher levels of compassion had the object of Ferlazzo's fury been white or even a white disabled man? There is no doubt.

White silence, white silencing

Regardless of these intersectional interrogations, the inescapable tragic reality is that Ogorchukwu's brutal and tortuous last breaths fell into the abyss that is white silence even though his ordeal was filmed, presumably by many seeking to collect evidence of the violence. Let us assume, rather generously, that this was the case rather than focusing on the possible necrophilic spectacularisation of Ogorchukwu's death. In the supermarket anecdote, I experienced a more mundane expression of the same dynamic. I have no doubt that many saw my treatment and disapproved of it. Perhaps even a few raged silently. Yet, the oppressive behaviour was not challenged. That it was not challenged normalised the violent entitlement and some of the implicit notions the white man expressed through his movement through space. The lack of challenge meant no penalty. This silence is a move to avert looking at whiteness in the eyes which is why my eyes were averted. DiAngelo proposes that keeping silent is an act of allegiance to whiteness which maintains white power [6].

In his conceptualisation of the racial contract Mills describes it as 'a set of formal or informal agreements or meta-agreements', primarily in existence to privilege those racialised as white, as a group, and which tacitly legitimises 'the exploitation of their bodies, land, resources, and the denial of equal socioeconomic opportunities' for racial others [7, p 11]. In other words, the racial contract is a collective agreement which includes, as its central clause, the subordination of people of colour. The racial contract sheds a particular light on white silence and white complicity. Can we in truth speak of complicity if what is described is adherence to a contract? If this contract the upholding of the racialised social (dis)order? If this a contract that guarantees those racialised as white higher status, increased welfare, preferential treatment and prioritised access to material resources?

Within Critical Race Theory, we saw that 'interest divergence' refers to the idea that the racialised interests of white groups and the racialised interests of people of colour diverge when it come to the material and the psychological, thus for white groups to be motivated to change the social (dis)order, these interests must converge [8]. Thus, interest divergence, Mills may argue, finds its genesis in the racial contract or the collective yet implicit agreement that society must be organised to protect the interests and power of white groups. This would necessarily entail the upholding of silences, when silences serve collective interests, even when they clash with particular white individuals' sense of values, ethics or belief system. Collectively, what is not wanted is opposed, challenged and resisted, the status quo therefore cannot but speak something of the collective mind or conscience or motivation. We could say from a slightly different angle the overly entitled and prejudiced man and the murderous white man acted with the tacit support of onlookers, on behalf of the crowds involved, which represent a microcosm of the wider society. Both these crowds and society at large are thus vicariously getting some form of gratification from these white men's actions. Their actions rearticulate, publicly, white supremacy.

When I reflect on my own experiences within social structures at large – my walk alone and in silence, inside and outside the store – post-abuse continues to be much more painful and distressing than the very act that triggered the silence. It is a reminder that professed wishes for equality rarely trump white self-interest, even when that self-interest is only comfort. Stobo reminds us that silence and apathy are the manifestation of the fear of whiteness, which becomes an unexpressed conflict or a disturbance usually located in the black and brown subject via gazes, projection or other forms of attacks, particularly if they break the silence [4]. We may therefore argue that white silence is a mechanism of silencing. It makes it much harder for those who experience racial injustice to speak. That silence consequently leads to silencing. Once more we see, here in relation to white silence, how psychic devices may be mobilised to sustain the status quo. These 'internal' configurations are so powerful that they would trump the white subject's sense of morality and ethics, so that again and again they may hide in a crowd, even when confronted with the public murder of a disabled man.

White proximity, brown complicity

> Any struggle to add a system of oppression, on the bottom of the bottom of the hierarchy have an obvious motivation to resist the system; to remove from your source of oppression. What of those who in some way benefit from the oppression? (Jensen, 2005 [9])

In the summer of 2022, a story of vitriol involving Meghan Markle broke. The story was of two police officers entertaining themselves and their peers using anti-black tropes [10]. Both were sacked by the Metropolitan Police for gross misconduct. One of these officers was a man of South Asian descent. PC Sukhdev Jeer (and his co-convict PC Paul Hefford), worked at the Bethnal Green police station, in London. Jeer was described as the most prolific contributor of the pair in court. According to news reports, among his posts was an image of a golliwog captioned: 'A sneak preview of Meghan's wedding dress'. A picture of a boy racialised as black wearing a hoodie captioned: 'Monkey in the jungle'. And a post stating: 'Everyone is so politically correct these days. You can't even say, Black paint, you have to say, Tyrone, can you please paint that wall?'

Less than two weeks after the videoed beating of Rodney King, on 16 March 1991, Latasha Harlins, an African American schoolgirl, was fatally shot by 49-year-old Korean American, Soon Ja, in her convenience store. The non-custodial sanction on appeal, to the charge of manslaughter, contributed to the 1992 Los Angeles riots. When George Floyd was murdered, Asian America had to once more publicly confront its entanglement with the system of white supremacy [11]. Footage of the last living moments of Floyd showed former police Officer Tou Thao, a Hmong American, standing with his back turned as the man racialised as black lay on the pavement, face down, pleading repeatedly to be allowed to live, while Chauvin's knee was constricting his neck. This was a tragic failure in solidarity. There is no doubt that it was an act of complicity. In the UK we are still, by and large, to come to terms with the same dynamic. When I have experienced anti-black structural violence and serious institutional racism, there was usually a person racialised as brown involved. They were rarely the main protagonist, but they were in positions of power, often in a position to stop the injustice, certainly always in a position to speak. They, too, chose to remain silent.

In the previous chapter we linked proximal ambivalence to the racialised stratification. We proposed that the hierarchisation of racial others creates internal, structural and interpersonal conflicts. And so, since anti-blackness is the glue which keeps the structure of whiteness going, access to whiteness or proximity to the master is premised on the adoption of anti-blackness. In other words, pretty much all racial groups within white supremacy have vested interests in anti-black violence and derive benefits from the same. This investment, often bolstered by divide and conquer strategies, is inscribed within imperial and colonial projects.

In late 19th century, for example, Indians who were indentured servants were moved around British colonies in Africa and the Caribbean in part to make up for the loss of labour resulting from the abolition of slavery; they sustained social hierarchies, believing themselves to be genetically superior to Africans [12].

British rule in East Africa has long sought to enhance the position of diasporic Asians who had come into the region during colonial times and often with British endorsement since they were supporting colonial extraction through the building of infrastructures such as railways [13]. This contributed to the creation of prosperous Asian businesses and senior posts within the colonial administration. During apartheid South Africa in the 20th century, the population was classified into four different groups: native, coloured, Asian or white. The native, the African, was positioned at the very bottom. In fact, efforts by those in the middle of the hierarchy, Asians and people classified as coloured, existed to distance themselves from the natives [14]. A fact that is sometimes illustrated by the words of Gandhi and his – complicated to say the least – race politics.

Gandhi, writing to the Natal parliament in 1893, summarised the climate in South Africa as follows: '[T]he general belief seems to prevail in the Colony that the Indians are a little better, if at all, than savages or the Natives of Africa.' In 1904, he wrote to a health officer in Johannesburg requiring that he 'withdraw Kaffirs' from an unsanitary slum called the 'Coolie Location' where a large number of Africans lived alongside Indians. 'About the mixing of the Kaffirs with the Indians, I must confess I feel most strongly.' Other examples are not hard to find. Quijano argues that in the context of Latin America, the coloniality of power created a caste system with Spaniards at the top of the hierarchy and Indigenous and black people at the bottom. This was a hierarchy that led to varying forms of socially sanctioned discrimination, varying in violence reflecting social and economic colonial realities [15].

These stratified structures, which place the brown subject above the black one, are still in existence within postcolonial societies. In our context, it would not take us long to see the logics of white supremacy and their associated hierarchisation in operation within social structures. Overall, groups racialised as black tend to have worse social outcomes than those racialised as brown who tend to have worse social outcomes than groups racialised as white. These inequalities are evident in the domain of health, mental health, earnings or access to structures of power. In the US there is ample evidence that proximal groups including Asian Americans tend to have easier access to structures of power and enjoy a higher level of state protection due to racialisation alone.

Institutional complicity

Institutions are 'structures through which men fulfil their social tasks' [16, pp 43–44]. Racist psychology is a prerequisite of racist institutions and racist institutions create racist psychology. This speaks to reciprocal relationships embedded in racism and makes the case for the psychosocial framing of whiteness, as explored throughout this book. It is once more proposed that if institutions are extensions of the psychology of those who built and sustained them, then those institutions reproduce whiteness not only because of the way they were configured in the 'past', but because social actors and institutions actively work to ensure that they continue to generate the same kinds of outcomes in the present, working in unison to reproduce and protect these unjust social arrangements.

There is no more perverse illustration of institutional complicity than the protection of inequality and injustice within systems and social provisions allegedly designed to foster justice and equality. When those systems designed to foster justice and equality act as tools to rebirth racial inequality, injustice and whiteness, what we have is a powerful demonstration of systemic complicity, which then sets the tone and legitimises inequality within every single institution on the land. Unconscious bias training, the favourite child of the diversity and inclusion industrial complex, is a good illustration.

There is little doubt that we all have some form of 'unconscious' prejudice and bias. And that our socialisation within white supremacy has an influence on our behaviours, intellectual and affective life which lies outside of our conscious awareness. That micro-phenomena are involved in the creation and recreation of macro structures is not under question. Nearly all our thoughts and behaviours are influenced, at least in part, by us attempting to save cognitive energy. These shortcuts and the associations they rely on will lead to bias. Nonetheless, the dominance of unconscious bias training as the preferred or default approach to tackle inequality in society is attracting mounting criticism, particularly from those with lived experience of discrimination including communities of colour. Anti-racist and socially and/or structurally orientated scholars have been vocal about the problems with unconscious bias training for years.

In 2018, the Equality and Human Rights Commission published an assessment of the evidence for the effectiveness of unconscious bias training. This was carried out in the UK by Atewologun et al [17]. Findings were mixed and, overall, poor. Their report highlighted a number of concerns including that the evidence for the ability of unconscious bias training to effectively to change behaviour remains limited, and that the perspectives of those these training provisions purport to protect, are worryingly missing from the evidence base – why burden ourselves with the experience, after all, of those we say we want to protect from bias and unfairness.

Methodological criticisms around the conceptualisation or operationalisation of unconscious bias are long-standing [18]. Outside of such methodological criticisms, damning sociological critiques have been advanced. They include concerns that unconscious bias training individualises racism and inequality. It fails to pay due attention to social structures. In doing so, it takes away the focus from power and material resources while prioritising the psychological in the framing of inequality [19, 20]. As such, it feeds into white fragility and defensiveness, thereby centring the white racial equilibrium by ensuring discussions on racial discrimination within organisations are palatable, centre whiteness and protect white ignorance [19].

Despite the lack of solid evidence linking unconscious bias training to equality, every year millions, if not billions, globally are invested in it to allegedly make institutions fairer, more 'representative' and hospitable. As a society, would we tolerate the widespread use of an intervention that yielded, at best, mixed results, and, at worst, no results or even worse outcomes, if the matter we sought to remedy was outside of the realm of race equality and justice? It's an interesting question to reflect on, one which calls into question the institutional thus social functions of unconscious bias training. There appears to be a collective and unconscious motivation to retain it as the method of choice to combat race discrimination. The machinery of unconscious bias training, we may argue, has become so successful because it gives the illusion of tackling inequality and injustice while really reproducing the same issues which sustain inequality and injustice.

Summary and resistance

In this final chapter we have considered some of the ways white social actors and institutions become implicated in racial injustice, primarily through absence and omission at collective level. This collective inaction or passive action provides evidence of an agreement, if only unconscious, which takes us back to the racial contract. The association between 'primitivity' and colonial formations of 'savagery' has contributed to many banalised and invisibilised manifestations of violence which are necessarily quieter. This legacy also means we are generally more at peace with racism by omission than racism by commission. We know, empirically, that when people can maintain their self-interests, the threshold for them to take action in situations they morally object to is much higher. But action and inaction, commission and omission, activity and passivity are all engaged in the production and the reproduction of whiteness. However, complicity in the system of white supremacy is not limited to those racialised as white. Because proximity to whiteness carries with it fantasies of access to whiteness – however illusory for some – those able to claim those proximal roles, positions and functions have vested interests in maintaining the structure that essentially keeps them out too. At least partially. Since, failing full access to the master's house, proximity to the master is 'the next best thing', not only in terms of material security but also because of psychic security. Dynamics of complicity in the racially othered, which are essentially dynamics of collaboration, are consequently bound to exist. Although proximal dynamics could be considered in relation to class, gender and their intersection with other axes of oppression, we have confronted them in relation to the racialised hierarchy of white supremacy as an illustration, focusing on black–brown relating and on Asian and black subjects specifically. We have established that as long as white supremacy exists as a stratified caste system, as long as adjacent groups continue to aspire to claim proximity to whiteness and those aspirations are rewarded structurally, we will continue to have anti-blackness in groups racialised as brown. As such, proximal dynamics in our racialised context are necessarily anti-black dynamics. These dynamics have been widely documented within all non-black communities of colour, including Latin, Arab and Indigenous groups. Resisting complicity is fundamentally about accepting that passivity and inaction are more potent in sustaining whiteness than naked brutality and aggression. It is also reconnecting to personal and collective values, in light of the ongoing harm of whiteness. And being prepared to accept our place in that structure as agents of harm. Harm, as we have previously argued, does not limit itself to bodies racialised as black and brown. The white subject has a choice even if a racialised collective agreement exists. They can challenge their complicity and commit to the struggle against the racial contract [7].

Note

[1] Reprinted by arrangement with The Heirs to the Estate of Martin Luther King Jr., c/o Writers House as agent for the proprietor New York, NY. Copyright © 1963 by Dr Martin Luther King, Jr. Renewed © 1991 by Coretta Scott King.

Whiteness and resistance: by way of conclusion

We have a tendency to separate structures from individuals, the 'past' from the present, the individual from their group, relationships and environment in ways that can be deeply unhelpful, arbitrary and consistent with Western individualism and modernist formations. *White minds* has sought to argue that psychological, social, spatial and temporal realities are co-constitutive, inseparable and arguably part of the same phenomena or communicational field.

Although this proposition challenges much of our worldview, being prepared to confront the disorientation it may produce is central to recognising patterns of harm and interrupting processes of repetition, continuation and maintenance that sustain whiteness across time and space.

I have attempted to present a psychosocial analysis of the same. That is to say, an analysis of whiteness grounded in these intersections. An analysis which sought to demonstrate that the internal–external binary, when it comes to race, and any other social phenomena for that matter, is hardly tenable.

My analysis has placed groups racialised as white under the microscope, in doing so subverting the white gaze and transgressing the direction of power. This oppositional gaze has invited us to explore the quotidian workings of whiteness and its everyday performances through personal reflections, stories and anecdotes, thus, through cultural, autoethnographic and historical material. A historicised approach which has provided, I have argued, 'evidence' of the production and reproduction, articulation and rearticulation of racialised violence.

'Evidence' that sameness and continuation can coexist with change, fragmentation and disruption has established the complex temporality of whiteness. A temporality which is embodied for the postcolonial subject and can be viscerally apprehended through recognisable patterns leading to a sense of knowing without knowing.

We have explored particular dysfunctions and disturbances in white minds resulting from the mobilisation of defences, fantasies and impulses which keep that white bubble intact in the midst of professed concerns for reason, justice and fairness in the white subject. We have sought to confront the psychosocial pathology of whiteness head on.

For the reader racialised as white, such a confrontation is likely to have given rise to difficult feelings, perhaps even some confusion. That disturbance, though, if felt, was already there. It exists within every single part of our society thus in the white body. Black and brown backs have been repeatedly designated to carry it silently and rummage through it, often alone, and in the cold. Those racialised as black and brown have had to attempt to make some meaning of it, simply to survive. For white bodies, making contact with the disturbance, feeling it, I would say even feeling it in their bones, is central to starting to grasp the fortress of white supremacy kept at bay by various forms of dissociation and splits, not least the dualist separation of body and mind.

Studying white minds and the mechanics of racialised power cannot be done without making links between entities and phenomena and requires us to fundamentally reject separatism. To reject, too, neoliberal ideals, which are, we may argue, an extension of colonial logics. We have used conceptual tools across disciplines to help us make connections across time, space and bodies.

Principally, we have drawn from psychology, analytic thinking, sociology and history. However, our project has been more than a theoretical exercise. The ultimate aim of *White minds* has always been resistance. The ultimate aim of resistance is social transformation, thus liberation, which calls for both the imagining of new world orders and the reinterpretation of the world as it is currently (dis)ordered. We have seen that disinvesting from white supremacy has profound implications for the white subject, their identity, their place within and their being in the world. These ontological and existential investments sustain the psychic and psychosocial dysfunctions which have been under interrogation.

In truth, I am not convinced that white groups at collective level would ever want to transform the psychological configurations that continue to uphold structures of power that benefit them out of care, compassion or ethical concern. This is a naive proposition with absolutely little to no precedent in history. However, increasingly I am convinced that white collective action from a place of care, compassion or ethical concern is not required for white structures to be dismantled.

Self-awareness and an understanding of the harm that white supremacy causes white minds and bodies, beyond the material, is more likely to trigger involvement in anti-racism in white groups and lead us to that critical point of 'interest convergence'. If, of course, white eyes accept the invitation to see the world and to see themselves. We may say I have more faith in white self-interest as a motivational force for social transformation than I have faith in compassion towards the brutalisation of bodies racialised as black and brown.

Whiteness seeks to strip those it harms of dignity. But, as we have seen, having one's dignity contingent upon the harm and humiliation of others is a precarious place to be. Although this may well be a way to defend against the vulnerability that being connected to one's humanity may bring, the costs of such ways of being in the world are significant. I happen to believe the white subject knows that. At least, on some level. White ambivalence exists, after all, for a reason. And so white groups are harmed. This harm is ongoing. This harm will continue until society reconfigures white psyches.

It may be easy to be seduced by the colonial glamour of saviourism or to seek to undertake grand actions, which are witnessed and praised, to allegedly effect social change. Such omnipotent and narcissistic positioning is harmful and keeps white dissociation and, by implication, whiteness going. Many who have made whiteness their field of study are still to do the tough and painful self-reflective work of looking in the mirror, to do the introspective work of unlearning whiteness and repeatedly dismantling its structure within themselves, the structure that permeates their very subjectivity.

Locating the need for change and transformation outside of the self averts that dreaded gaze. This avoidance inevitably sabotages liberatory work and keeps the system we claim we wish to dismantle, intact. It is therefore a strategy to retain white power while expressing anti-racist and decolonial wishes. Further evidence, we may argue, of white ambivalence. In summary, approaches to liberatory work that excludes the self from the work keep internalised social configurations out of awareness, thus out of transformation. They leave the many dysfunctions we have covered in the book unaddressed, free to do harm and to continue to edify the structure of whiteness. They become the postcolonial subject's problem to name, to navigate, to survive and to resist. Distracting us in the process from our fundamental right to exist as human beings. For those of us doing the work that might allow more of us to be free from enduring racialised brutality, this takes us back to square one again and again since the change we attempt to create crumbles under the weight of white amnesia.

White liberals love to support performance-based action such as the sporting of safety pins, black squares and other so-called 'virtue signalling' empty gestures as they 'check their white privilege' or engage in confessional practices. I have little time for such self-deceptive performances. They create the appearance of solidarity while camouflaging complicity and resistance to change. They help the white subject keep the Fanonian mask on.

As I said at the start of the book, there is no revolutionary claim in *White minds*. I have no grand call to action and this book will not end with a bang. I put forth instead the humble proposition of sustained, targeted action. Targeted anti-racism action in the domain of the everyday. Not some grandiose (delusional) claim to decolonisation or dismantlement when one cannot even stand one's own reflection. That targeted action must first and foremost start with one's mind and with one's body. As we said at the start of the book, looking consciously into the 'darkness' of whiteness is really the only way of not becoming absorbed and disappeared by it. And, as part of that, looking consciously into the 'darkness' of the self is where I invite us to start. Collectively, alone and together.

Here, beyond declarations of solidarity, you are invited to explore the key psychic and psychosocial processes we have examined; white envy, white sadism, white dissociation, white trauma, white shame, white ambivalence and white complicity. Not as an abstract project but as a reflective, affectively engaged and embodied undertaking. You are invited to seek out evidence of times, if only moments, of their re-enactments and repetitions in your relationships with black or brown humans, within the institutions you inhabit and the histories you are embedded in. It is these repetitions that collectively sustain the temporality of whiteness.

Reiterations through scripts, habituation, group processes, or simply convenience and comfort. Confronting the silent gratification they may have brought about, letting go of their libidinal charge may mean connecting to the despair, terror and meaninglessness that whiteness keeps at bay. This is hard work. Possibly the hardest work a human being socialised into notions of beneficence and virtuosity can be asked to do.

I do not expect atonement. I do not even care much for white apologies. This will not bring back the millions of bodies murdered because of individual greed and societal hoarding. It will not provide oxygen to their descendants who every day are still drowning at sea seeking a share of what was pilloried and stolen from their lands, what is essentially theirs. It will not quieten the screams and cries of the mutilated and torn bodies of the ancestors some of us continue to carry and even hear. But repair, connection and growth have the potential to stop the intergenerational cycle of white violence and to save the white subject from themselves. Repair, connection and growth cannot happen if the white subject refuses to accept reality.

There is no other way, if other ways to exist are to emerge. The aim is to be more connected to the self, thus to the other and to the world. Reclaiming the humanity of others is reclaiming it for the self. This is the liberatory invitation for white minds, for those who wish to transgress the social (dis)order. This project is for those who are sane or perhaps mad enough to see the brutal madness we are all forced to exist under. It is for those who are prepared to think of harm beyond what is currently formed as harm. Once more, looking consciously into the 'darkness' of whiteness is really the only way of not becoming absorbed and disappeared by it. I hope we all find the courage to see the white structures that exist within ourselves and outside. I hope we can find it in us to confront the 'darkness' of whiteness.

References

Preface

1. hooks, b. (1994) *Teaching to transgress: Education as the practice of freedom.* London: Routledge.
2. Kinouani, G. (2021) *Living while black: The essential guide to overcoming racial trauma.* London: Ebury.
3. Mbembe, A. (2005) Variations on the beautiful in the Congolese world of sounds. *Politique africaine,* 100(4), 69–91.
4. Fricker, M. (2017) *Epistemic injustice: Power and the ethics of knowing.* Oxford: Oxford University Press.
5. Frosh, S. (2010) *Psychoanalysis outside the clinic.* London: Palgrave.
6. Lorde, A. (2018) *The master's tools will never dismantle the master's house.* London: Penguin Books.
7. Hill Collins, P. (2002) *Black feminist thought.* New York: Routledge.
8. Gilroy, P. (1995) *The black Atlantic: Modernity and double-consciousness.* Cambridge, MA: Harvard University Press.
9. Montenegro, M., Pujol, J. and Posocco, S. (2017) Bordering, exclusions and necropolitics. *Qualitative Research Journal,* 17(3), 142–154.
10. Fanon, F. (1952) *Black skin, white masks.* New York: Grove Press.
11. Fanon, F. (1964) *Towards an African revolution.* New York: Grove Press.
12. Fanon, F. (1968) *The wretched of the earth.* New York: Grove Press.

Introduction

1. Dyer, R. (1997) *White.* London: Routledge.
2. Gilroy, P. (1995) *The black Atlantic: Modernity and double-consciousness.* Cambridge, MA: Harvard University Press.
3. Foucault, M. (1977) *Discipline and punish: The birth of the prison.* New York: Pantheon Books.
4. Yancy, G. (2017) *Black bodies white gazes: The continuing significance of race.* Lanham, MD: Rowman & Littlefield.
5. Mills, C.W. (1997) *The racial contract.* Ithaca, NY: Cornell University Press.
6. APS (Association for Psychosocial Studies) (2013) *What is psychosocial studies?* Association for Psychosocial Studies. Available at: www.psychosocial-studies-association.org/about/
7. Foulkes, S.H. (1990) *Selected papers: Psychoanalysis and group analysis.* London: Karnac.
8. Harrell, S.P. (2000) A multidimensional conceptualization of racism-related stress: Implications for the well-being of people of color. *American Journal of Orthopsychiatry,* 70(1), 42–57.
9. Bryant-Davis, T. and Ocampo, C. (2005) Racist incident based trauma. *The Counselling Psychologist,* 33(4), 479–500.

10. Carter, R.T. (2006) Race-based traumaticstress. *Psychiatric Times*, 23(14), 1–93.

11. Carter, R.T. (2007) Racism and psychological and emotional injury: Recognizing and assessing race-based traumatic stress. *The Counselling Psychologist*, 35(1), 13–105.

12. Mbembe, A. (2016) Frantz Fanon and the politics of viscerality. A talk given to Duke University's Franklin Humanities Institute. Available at: https://youtu.be/lg_BEodNaEA

13. Morrison, T. (1992) *Playing in the dark: Whiteness and the literary imagination*. Cambridge, MA: Harvard University Press.

14. Fanon, F. (1967) *The wretched of the earth*. Harmondsworth: Penguin.

15. Aiyegbusi, A. (2021) The white mirror: Face to face with racism in group analysis part 2 – mainly practice. *Group Analysis*, 54(3), 421–436.

16. DiAngelo, R. (2018) *White fragility: Why it's so hard for white people to talk about racism*. Boston, MA: Beacon Press.

17. Baldwin, J. (1963) *The fire next time*. New York: Dial Books.

18. Yancy, G. (2017) *Black bodies white gazes: The continuing significance of race*. Lanham, MD: Rowman & Littlefield.

19. Gordon, L. (2021) Storming the Capitol building is not a privilege. APA blog. Available at: https://blog.apaonline.org/2021/01/12/storming-the-capitol-building-is-not-a-privilege/

20. Gilroy, P. (2008) *Postcolonial melancholia*. New York: Columbia University Press.

21. Fanon, F. (1952) *Black skin, white masks*. New York: Grove Press.

22. Fricker, M. (2009) *Epistemic injustice: Power and the ethics of knowing*. Oxford: Oxford University Press.

23. Dalal, F. (2002) *Race colour and the process of racialization: New perspectives from group analysis psychoanalysis and sociology*. London: Routledge.

24. Bion, W.R. (1959) Attacks on linking. *International Journal of Psychoanalysis*, 40, 308–315.

25. Said, E.W. (1978) *Orientalism*. New York: Pantheon Books.

26. Tuhiwai-Smith, L. (1999) *Decolonizing methodologies: Research and indigenous peoples*. London: Zed Books.

27. Hall, S. (2001) Constituting an archive. *Third Text*, 15(54), 89–92.

28. Goldberg, D.T. (1993) *Racist culture*. Oxford: Blackwell.

Chapter 1

1. Wilderson III, F.B. (2008) *Incognegro: A memoir of exile and apartheid*, edited by J. Burrell. Cambridge, MA: South End Press.

2. Hsiung, H.-J. and Chen, C.-J. (2019) Time passing is relative motion: Conceptualization of time in Chinese. *Concentric*, 45(2), 246–270.

3. Simeon, D., Guralnik, O., Schmeidler, J., Sirof, B. and Knutelska, M. (2001) The role of childhood interpersonal trauma in depersonalization disorder. *American Journal of Psychiatry*, 158(7), 1027–1033.

4. Salami, A., Andreu-Perez, J. and Gillmeister, H. (2020) Symptoms of depersonalisation/derealisation disorder as measured by brain electrical activity: A systematic review. *Neuroscience and Behavioural Reviews*, 118, 524–537.
5. Baraitser, L. (2017) *Enduring time*. London: Bloomsbury.
6. Imani, N.O. (2012) The implications of Africa-centered conceptions of time and space for quantitative theorizing: Limitations of paradigmatically-bound philosophical meta-assumptions. *Journal of Pan-African Studies*, 5(4), 101–111.
7. Sharpe, C.E. (2016) *In the wake: On blackness and being*. Durham, NC: Duke University Press.
8. Hartman, S. (2007) *Lose your mother: A journey along the Atlantic slave route*. New York: Farrar, Straus and Giroux.
9. Frosh, S. (2013) Psychoanalysis, colonialism, racism. *Journal of Theoretical and Philosophical Psychology*, 33(3), 141–154.
10. Frosh, S. (2021) Psychoanalysis in the wake. *Psychoanalysis, Culture & Society*, 26, 414–432.
11. Bollas, C. (2018) *The shadow of the object: Psychoanalysis of the unthought known*, 30th anniversary edition. London: Routledge.
12. Conrad, J. and Goonetilleke, D.C.R.A. (1999) *Heart of darkness*, 2nd edition. Turpin: Broadview.
13. Baldwin, J. (1962) Letter from a region in my mind. *The New Yorker*. Available at: www.newyorker.com/magazine/1962/11/17/letter-from-a-region-in-my-mind
14. Fanon, F. (1952) *Black skin, white masks*. New York: Grove Press.
15. Kinouani, G. (2021) *Living while black: The ultimate guide to overcoming racial trauma*. London: Ebury.
16. Rustin, M. (1994) *The good society and the inner world*. London: Verso.
17. Hall, S. (2018) *Essential essays: Foundations of cultural studies and identity and diaspora*. Durham, NC: Duke University Press.
18. Moreton-Robinson, A. (2004) Whiteness, epistemology and Indigenous representation. In A. Moreton-Robinson (ed) *Whitening race: Essays in social and cultural criticism*. Canberra: Aboriginal Studies Press, pp 75–88.
19. Quijano, A. (2000) Coloniality of power, Eurocentrism, and Latin America. *Nepantla: Views from the South*, 1(3), 533–580.
20. Harris, C.I. (1993) Whiteness as property. *Harvard Law Review*, 106(8), 1709–1791.
21. Trafford, J. (2021) *The empire at home internal colonies and the end of Britain*. London: Pluto Press.
22. Garner, S. (2007) *Whiteness: An introduction*. London: Routledge.
23. Green, M, Sonn C. and Matsebula, J. (2007) Reviewing whiteness: Theory, research and possibilities. *South African Journal of Psychology*, 37(3), 389–419.

24. Neely, B. and Samura, M. (2011) Social geographies of race: Connecting race and space. *Ethnic and Racial Studies*, 34(11), 1933–1952.

25. Dyer, R. (1997) *White: Essays on race and culture*. London: Routledge.

26. Verdugo, R. (2008) Racial stratification, social consciousness, and the education of Mexican Americans in Fabens, Texas: A socio-historical case study. *Spaces for Difference: An Interdisciplinary Journal*, 1(2), 69–95.

27. Gilroy, P. (1993) *The black Atlantic*. Cambridge, MA: Harvard University Press.

28. Akala (2018) Natives: *Race and class in the ruins of empire*. London: TwoRoads.

29. Brown, K. (2000) Coloured and black relations in South Africa: The burden of racialized hierarchy. *Macalester International*, 9, Article 13. Available at: http://digitalcommons.macalester.edu/macintl/vol9/iss1/13

30. Lentin, A. (2017) Racism, class and the racialized outsider: A response. Available at: www.alanalentin.net/2017/04/12/racism-class-and-the-racialized-outsider-a-response/

31. Alam, O. (2012) 'Islam is a blackfella religion, whatchya trying to prove?': Race in the lives of white Muslim converts in Australia. *La Trobe Journal*, 89, 124–139.

32. Frosh, S. (2023) *Antisemitism and racism: Ethical encounters through psychoanalysis*. London: Bloomsbury.

33. Fields, K.E. and Fields, B.J. (2012) *Racecraft: The soul of inequality in American life*. New York: Verso.

34. Choudhury, C.A. (2022) Racecraft and identity in the emergence of Islam as a race. *University of Cincinnati Law Review*, 91(1).

35. Rollock, N. (2018) The heart of whiteness: Racial gesture politics, equity and higher education. In J. Arday and H.S. Mirza (eds) *Dismantling race in higher education: Racism, whiteness and decolonising the academy*. Basingstoke: Palgrave Macmillan, pp 313–330.

36. Baderoon, G. (2017) Animal likenesses: Dogs and the boundary of the human in South Africa. *Journal of African Cultural Studies*, 29(3), 345–361.

37. Foulkes, S.H. (1990) *Selected papers: Psychoanalysis and group analysis*. London: Karnac Books.

38. Hopper, E. and Weinberg, H. (2017) *The social unconscious in persons, groups, and societies, Volume 3: The foundation matrix extended and reconfigured*. London: Karnac Books.

39. Kinouani, G. (2020) Difference, whiteness and the group analytic matrix: An integrated formulation. *Group Analysis*, 53(1), 60–74.

40. Hopper, E. (2001) The social unconscious: Theoretical considerations. *Group Analysis*, 34, 9–27.

41. Durkheim, É. ([1898] 1965) Individual and collective representations. In *Sociology and philosophy*, translated by D.F. Pocock. London: Cohen & West, pp 1–34. [Originally published in Revue de Métaphysique et de Morale, 6, 273–302.]

42. Freud, S. ([1914] 1955) *Beyond the pleasure principle*. New York: Liveright.

43. Hopper, E. (1996) The social unconscious in clinical work. *Group*, 20(1), 7–42.

Chapter 2

1. Fanon, F. (1952) *Black skin, white masks*. New York: Grove Press.

2. Sartre, J.P. (1946) *Being and nothingness: An essay on phenomenological ontology*. New York: Washington Square Press.

3. Joseph, F. (2008) Becoming a woman: Simone de Beauvoir on female embodiment. *Philosophy Now*. Available at: https://philosophynow.org/issues/69/Becoming_A_Woman_Simone_de_Beauvoir_on_Female_Embodiment

4. Hook, D. (2022) *The mirror stage: A guide to reading Lacan's seminal essay*. Seminar aid, Birkbeck College, University of London.

5. Lacan, J. (1949) The mirror stage. Paper delivered on 17 July 1949 at the Sixteenth International Congress of Psychoanalysis, Zurich.

6. De Beauvoir, S. (1949) *The second sex*. Harmondsworth: Penguin Books.

7. Yancy, G. (2017) *Black bodies white gazes: The continuing significance of race*. Lanham, MD: Rowman & Littlefield.

8. Ngo, H. (2019) 'Get over it'? Racialised temporalities and bodily orientations in time. *Journal of Intercultural Studies*, 40(2), 239–253.

9. Kinouani, G. (2015) Brexit, the body and the politics of splitting. *Race Reflections*. Available at: https://racereflections.co.uk/brexit-the-body-politics-of-splitting/

10. Ahmed, S. (2007) A phenomenology of whiteness. *A Feminist Theory*, 8(2), 149–167.

11. Goldberg, T. (2017) Between trauma and perpetration: Psychoanalytical and social psychological perspectives on complicated histories in the Israeli context. *Theory & Research in Social Education*, 45(3), 349–377.

12. Deggans, E. (2022) Racist 'Star Wars' fans aren't new: Why doesn't Disney do more to protect its actors? NPR. Available at: www.npr.org/2022/06/02/1102509719/star-wars-obi-wan-kenobi-moses-ingram-racist-messages-disney

13. Shapiro, S. (2013) Richard the great. *The New York Post*. Available at: https://nypost.com/2013/05/28/richard-the-great/

14. Césaire, A. (1955) *Discours sur le Colonialisme*. Paris: Présence Africaine.

15. Dyer, R. (1997) *White: Essays on race and culture*. London: Routledge.

16. Dalal, F. (2002) *Race colour and the process of racialization: New perspectives from group analysis psychoanalysis and sociology*. London: Routledge.

17. Collier, H. (2019) Jon Snow says 'he has never seen so many white people in one place' during report of pro-Brexit rally. *The Evening Standard*. Available at: www.standard.co.uk/news/politics/jon-snow-says-i-ve-never-seen-so-many-white-people-in-one-place-during-report-on-probrexit-rally-a4105051.html

18. Waterson, J. (2019) Jon Snow cleared by Ofcom over 'white people' comment. *The Guardian*. Available at: www.theguardian.com/media/2019/aug/05/jon-snow-channel-4-news-cleared-by-ofcom-for-white-people-comment

19. Lorde, A. (1987) The uses of anger: Women responding to racism. *Women and Language*, 11(1), 4–4.

20. Drustrup, D., Liu, W.M., Rigg, T. and Davis, K. (2022) Investigating the white racial equilibrium and the power-maintenance of whiteness. *Analyses of Social Issues and Public Policy*, 22(3), 961–988.

21. Berenson, E. (2017) The politics of atrocities: The scandal in the French Congo [1905]. Available at: https://revistas.ucm.es/index.php/HPOL/article/view/60054/4564456547071

22. Kinouani, G. (2021) The invisible gaze of white women. *Race Reflections*. Available at: https://racereflections.co.uk/the-invisible-gaze-of-white-women/

23. MYMU (2022) What is the 'rape culture?' Marshall University. Available at: www.marshall.edu/wcenter/sexual-assault/rape-culture/

24. Hill Collins, P. (2002) *Black feminist thought*. New York: Routledge.

Chapter 3

1. Morrison, T. (1993) White people have a very very serious problem: Toni Morrison on Charlie Rose. Available at: https://youtu.be/n2txzMkT5Pc

2. Mitchell, D. (2018) The people's grocery lynching, Memphis, Tennessee. *JSTOR Daily*. Available at: https://daily.jstor.org/peoples-grocery-lynching/

3. Phillips, C.D. (1987) Exploring relations among forms of social control: The lynching and execution of blacks in North Carolina, 1889–1918. *Law & Society Review*, 21(3), 361–374.

4. Wells-Barnett, I.B. (1997) *Southern horrors and other writings: The anti-lynching campaign of Ida B. Wells, 1892–1900*. Boston, MA: Bedford Books.

5. Ore, E. and Houdek, M. (2020) Lynching in times of suffocation: Toward a spatiotemporal politics of breathing. *Women's Studies in Communication*, 43(4), 443–458.

6. Blackwell, D. (1994) The emergence of racism in group analysis. *Group Analysis: International Journal of Group-Analytic Psychotherapy*, 27(2), 197–210.

7. Yancy, G. (2017) *Black bodies white gazes: The continuing significance of race*. Lanham, MD: Rowman & Littlefield.

8. Schlapobersky, J. (2016) *From the couch to the circle group: Analytic psychotherapy in practice*. London: Routledge.

9. Piela, A. (2018) Wearing the niqab in the UK: What is British culture, anyway? LSE blog. Available at: https://blogs.lse.ac.uk/religionglobalsociety/2018/09/wearing-the-niqab-in-the-uk-what-is-british-culture-anyway/

10. François, M. (2021) 'I felt violated by the demand toundress': Three Muslim women on France's hostility to the hijab. *The Guardian*. Available at: www.theguardian.com/world/2021/jul/27/i-felt-violated-by-the-demand-to-undress-three-muslim-women-on-frances-hostility-to-the-hijab

11. Klein, M. ([1957] 1975) Envy and gratitude. In *The writings of Melanie Klein, Volume 3: Envy and gratitude and other works*. New York: The Free Press, pp 176–235.

12. Fanon, F. (1952) *Black skin, white masks*. New York: Grove Press.

13. Kates, S. and Tucker, J. (2019) We never change, do we? Economic anxiety and far-right identification in a postcrisis Europe. *Social Science Quarterly*, 100(4), 494–523.

14. Ryan, J. (2016) 'This was a whitelash': VanJones' take on the election results. CNN. Available at: www.cnn.com/2016/11/09/politics/van-jones-resu lts-disappointment-cnntv/index.html

15. Danewild, I. (2021) Policing the (migrant) crisis: Stuart Hall and the defence of whiteness. *Security Dialogue*, 53(1), 21–37.

16. Hall, S., Critcher, C., Jefferson, T., Clarke, J. and Robert, B. (2013) *Policing the crisis: Mugging, the state and law and order*. London: Springer.

Chapter 4

1. Kinouani, G. (2021) *Living while black: The essential guide to overcoming racial trauma*. London: Ebury.

2. Marcus, J. (2021) Derek Chauvin trail: George Floyd told police I can't breathe 27 times as defendant accused of betraying badge. *The Independent*. Available at: www.independent.co.uk/news/world/americas/derek-chau vin-trial-george-floyd-video-b1824023.html

3. Schwartz, G.L. and Jahn, J.L. (2020) Mapping fatal police violence across US metropolitan areas: Overall rates and racial/ethnic inequities, 2013–2017. *PLoS ONE*, 15(6), e0229686.

4. Inquest (2023) I can't breathe: Race, death and British policing. Available at: www.inquest.org.uk/i-cant-breathe-race-death-british-policing

5. Rabe-Hemp, C. (2008) Female officers and the ethic of care: Does officer gender impact police behaviors? *Journal of Criminal Justice*, 36(5), 426–434.

6. Phillips, J. (2005) *The Marquis de Sade: A very short introduction*. Oxford: Oxford University Press.

7. Grimwade, R. (2011) Between the quills: Schopenhauer and Freud on sadism and masochism. *International Journal of Psychoanalysis*, 92(1), 149–169.

8. Buckels, E.E. (2018) The psychology of everyday sadism. Doctoral dissertation, University of British Columbia.

9. Baumeister, R.F. and Campbell, W.K. (1999) The intrinsic appeal of evil: Sadism, sensational thrills, and threatened egotism. *Personality and Social Psychology Review*, 3(3), 210–221.

10. Bulut, T. (2017) The concept of sadism in the current empirical literature. *UDK*, 343.

11. Fromm, E. (1973) *The anatomy of human destructiveness*. New York: Holt, Rinehart, and Winston.

12. Berenson, E. (2018) The politics of atrocity: The scandal in the French Congo (1905). Available at: https://recyt.fecyt.es/index.php/Hyp/article/view/58497/38993

13. Yancy, G. (2008) Colonial gazing: The production of the body as 'other'. *Western Journal of Black Studies*, 32(1), 1–15.

14. Thomas, G. (2007) On psycho-sexual racism and pan-African revolt: Fanon & Chester Himes. *Human Architecture: Journal of the Sociology of Self-Knowledge*, 5(3), 20.

15. Mbembe, A. (2017) *Critique of black reason*. Johannesburg: Wits University Press.

16. Wilson, C.A. (1996) *Racism: From slavery to advanced capitalism*. Thousand Oaks, CA: SAGE.

17. Stinchcombe, A.L. (1994) Freedom and oppression of slaves in the eighteenth-century Caribbean. *American Sociological Review*, 59(6), 911–929.

18. Scully, P. (1995) Rape, race, and colonial culture: The sexual politics of identity in the nineteenth-century Cape Colony. *South Africa. American Historical Review*, 100(2), 335–359.

19. Donovan, K. (2014) Female slaves as sexual victims in Île Royale. *Acadiensis*, 43(1), 147–156.

20. Aidoo, L. (2018) *Slavery unseen*. Durham, NC: Duke University Press.

21. Mangan, L. (2021) The Underground Railroad review: Harrowing, magical, masterful TV. *The Guardian*, 14 May. Available at: www.theguardian.com/tv-and-radio/2021/may/14/the-underground-railroad-review-barry-jenkins

22. Graham, M. (2021) How racism in animal advocacy and effective altruism hinders our mission. Available at: www.wildanimalinitiative.org/blog/antiracism-in-animal-advocacy

23. Borry (2020) Why immigration detention is not the answer: Borry's story. Freedom from Torture. Available at: www.freedomfromtorture.org/real-voices/why-immigration-detention-is-not-the-answer

24. Mbembe, A. (2019) *Necropolitics*. Durham, NC: Duke University Press.

25. Kinouani, G. and Asani, F. (2021) Migration, homelessness and internalised displacement. *Health and Social Science*, 19(2).

26. Stein, T. (2020) Racism and violence are not new and won't change until we do. *Psychology Today*. Available at: www.psychologytoday. com/us/blog/the-integrationist/202005/racism-and-violence-are-not-new-and-wont-change-until-we-do

27. Foulkes, S.H. (1990) *Selected papers: Psychoanalysis and group analysis.* London: Karnac Books.

28. Frosh, S. (2023) *Antisemitism and racism: Ethical encounters through psychoanalysis.* London: Bloomsbury.

29. Reed, A. (2016) The whiter the bread, the quicker you're dead: Spectacular absence and the post-racialised blackness in black queer theory. In P. Johnson (ed) *No tea, no shade: New writing in black queer theory.* Durham, NC: Duke University Press.

Chapter 5

1. Powell, E. (1968) 'Rivers of blood' speech, Conservative Political Centre, Birmingham, 20 April.

2. Hirsch, S. (2020) *In the shadow of Enoch Powell.* Manchester: Manchester University Press.

3. Ross, J. (2015) Dylann Roof reportedly wanted a race war: How many Americans sympathize? Washington Post. Available at: www.washingtonp ost.com/news/the-fix/wp/2015/06/19/dylann-roof-reportedly-wan ted- a-race-war-how-many-americans-feel-like-he-supposedly-does/

4. Mogobe, B.R. (2002) The philosophy of ubuntu and ubuntu as a philosophy. In P.H. Coetzee and A.P.J. Roux (eds) *Philosophy from Africa: A text with readings.* Oxford: Oxford University Press, pp 230–237.

5. hooks, b. (2000) *All about love: New visions.* New York: William Morrow.

6. Arendt, H. (1958) *The origins of totalitarianism*, 2nd enlarged edition. New York: Meridian Books.

7. Césaire, A. (2001) *Discourse on colonialism.* New York: New York University Press.

8. Bion, W.R. (1961) *Experiences in groups and other papers.* London: Tavistock Publications.

9. Fassin, D. and Rechtman, R. (2009) *The empire of trauma: An inquiry into the condition of victimhood.* Translated by R. Gomme. Princeton, NJ: Princeton University Press.

10. Peoples, K. (2019) *Why the self is, and is not, empty: Trauma and transcendence in the postmodern psyche.* London: Routledge.

11. Garland, C. (ed) (1998) *Understanding trauma: A psychoanalytical approach.* London: Routledge.

12. Freud, S. ([1856–1939]1961) *Beyond the pleasure principle.* New York: Liveright.

13. Bion, W.R. (2013) Attacks on linking. *The Psychoanalytic Quarterly*, 82(2), 285–300.

14. Szykierski, D. (2010) The traumatic roots of containment: The evolution of Bion's metapsychology. *The Psychoanalytic Quarterly*, 79(4), 935–968.

15. Moore, E., Gaskin, C. and Indig, D. (2013) Childhood maltreatment and post-traumatic stress disorder among incarcerated young offenders. *Child Abuse & Neglect*, 37(10), 861–870.

16. Muldoon, O.T., Haslam, S.A., Haslam, C., Cruwys, T., Kearns, M. and Jetten, J. (2019) The social psychology of responses to trauma: Social identity pathways associated with divergent traumatic responses. *European Review of Social Psychology*, 30(1), 311–348.

17. Hirschberger, G. (2018) Collective trauma and the social construction of meaning. *Frontiers in Psychology*, 9, 1441.

18. Volkan, V. (2001) Transgenerational transmissions and chosen traumas: An aspect of large group identity. *Group Analysis*, 34(1), 79–97.

19. Benjamin, J. (1988) *Shadow of the other: Intersubjectivity and gender in psychoanalysis*. New York: Routledge.

Chapter 6

1. DiAngelo, R. (2017) White fragility lecture at the General Commission on Religion and Race, City of Oakland. Available at: https://youtu.be/DwIx3KQer54

2. Dennis, E. (2022) The paranoid-schizoid position and envious attacks on the black other. *Psychoanalysis, Self and Context*, 17(2), 141–153.

3. Klein, M. ([1946] 1975) Notes on some schizoid mechanisms. In *The writings of Melanie Klein*, Volume 3. London: Hogarth Press, pp 99–110.

4. Dalal, F. (2002) *Race colour and the process of racialization: New perspectives from group analysis psychoanalysis and sociology*. London: Routledge.

5. Lynn, S.J., Maxwell, R., Merckelbach, H., Lilienfeld, S.O., van Heugten-van der Kloet, D. and Miskovic, V. (2019) Dissociation and its disorders: Competing models, future directions, and a way forward. *Clinical Psychology Review*, 73, 101755.

6. Howell, E.F. (2005) *The dissociative mind*. London: The Analytic Press/ Taylor & Francis.

7. Eddo-Lodge, R. (2017) *Why I'm no longer talking to white people about race*. London: Bloomsbury Circus.

8. Akala (2018) *Natives: Race and class in the ruins of empire*. London: Two Roads.

9. Drustrup, D., Liu, W.M., Rigg, T. and Davis, K. (2022) Investigating the white racial equilibrium and the power-maintenance of whiteness. *Analyses of Social Issues and Public Policy*, 22(3), 961–988.

10. Hasan, S. (2015) Cora. Answer to What was/is your boarding school experience? Quora. Available at: www.quora.com/What-was-is-your-boarding-school-experience

11. Patterson, B.A. (2020) Boarding school syndrome: A phenomenological study giving single-gender military boarding school alumni a voice to tell their stories of life after graduation. Thesis, Liberty University, Lynchburg, Virginia.

12. Purser, A. (2018) 'Getting it into the body': Understanding skill acquisition through Merleau-Ponty and the embodied practice of dance. *Qualitative Research in Sport, Exercise and Health*, 10(3), 318–332.

13. Hage, G. (2002) Multiculturalism and white paranoia in Australia. *International Migration & Integration*, 3, 417–437.

14. Sharma, A. (2009) *Racism postcolonialism Europe*. Liverpool: Liverpool University Press.

15. Tiernan, B., Tracey, B. and Shannon, C. (2014) Paranoia and self-concepts in psychosis: A systematic review of the literature. *Psychiatry Research*, 216(3), 303–313.

16. Andrews, K. (2016) The psychosis of whiteness: The celluloid hallucinations of 'amazing grace' and 'belle'. *Journal of Black Studies*, 47(5), 435–453.

17. Kellaway, K. (2015) Claudia Rankine: Blackness in the white imagination has nothing to do with black people. *The Guardian*. Available at: www.theguardian.com/books/2015/dec/27/claudia-rankine-poet-citizen-ameri can-lyric-feature

18. DiAngelo, R. (2018) *White fragility*. Boston, MA: Beacon Press.

19. Gilbert, P. (2009) Introducing compassion-focused therapy. *Advances in Psychiatric Treatment*, 15, 199–208.

20. Sousa, N. (2016) The dynamics of the stress neuromatrix. *Molecular Psychiatry*, 21, 302–312.

21. Ronquillo, J., Denson, T.F., Lickel, B., Lu, Z.L., Nandy, A. and Maddox, K.B. (2007) The effects of skin tone on race-related anygdala activity: An fMRI investigation. *Social Cognitive and Affective Neuroscience*, 2(1), 39–44.

22. Stevens, F.L. and Abernethy, A.D. (2018) Neuroscience and racism: The power of groups for overcoming implicit bias. *International Journal of Group Psychotherapy*, 68(4), 561–584.

23. Yancy, G. (2017) *Black bodies white gazes: The continuing significance of race*. Lanham, MD: Rowman & Littlefield.

Chapter 7

1. Dahlgreen, W. (2014) The British Empire is 'something to be proud of'. YouGov. Available at: https://yougov.co.uk/topics/politics/artic les-reports/2014/07/26/britain-proud-its-empire

2. Watt, N. (2013) David Cameron defends lack of apology for British massacre at Amritsar. *The Guardian*. Available at: www.theguardian. com/politics/2013/feb/20/david-cameron-amritsar-massacre-india

3. Gilroy, P. (2008) *Postcolonial melancholia.* NewYork: Columbia UniversityPress.
4. Grenyer, B.F.S. (2013) Historical overview of pathological narcissism. In J.S. Ogrodniczuk (ed) *Understanding and treating pathological narcissism.* Washington, DC: American Psychological Association, pp 15–26.
5. Morgan, M.L. (2008) *On shame.* New York: Routledge.
6. Peck, E. (2021) Active ignorance, antiracism, and the psychology of white shame. *Critical Philosophy of Race,* 9(2), 342–368.
7. Mills, C.W. (1997) *The racial contract.* Ithaca, NY: Cornell University Press.
8. Evans, M. (2019) Rosanna Arquette apologises for being born 'white and privileged' as she says it 'disgusts' her. *Metro,* 8 August. Available at: https://metro.co.uk/2019/08/08/rosanna-arquette-apologises-born-white-privile ged-says-disgusts-10542880/Refered pain Watson, 2018
9. Watson, K. (2018) How does referred pain work? Healthline. Available at: www.healthline.com/health/pain-relief/referred-pain#causes
10. Ritschel, C. (2019) Rosanna Arquette says FBI told her to make Twitter private after controversial 'white privilege' tweet. *The Independent.* Available at: www.independent.co.uk/life-style/rosanna-arquette-twit ter-white-privilege-trump-harvey-weinstein-a9047071.html
11. Frosh, S. (2023) *Antisemitism and racism: Ethical encounters through psychoanalysis.* London: Bloomsbury.
12. Badshah, N. (2019) 'White saviour' row: David Lammy denies snubbing Comic Relief. *The Guardian.* Available at: www.theguardian.com/tv-and-radio/2019/feb/28/david-lammy-stacey-dooley-comic-relief-white-savi our-row-uganda-red-nose-day
13. Cole, T. (2012) The white-savior industrial complex. *The Atlantic.* Available at: www.theatlantic.com/international/archive/2012/03/the-white-savior-industrial-complex/254843/
14. Freire, P. (1968) *Pedagogy of the oppressed.* New York: Seabury Press.
15. Hamad, R. (2019) *White tears.* Melbourne: Melbourne University Publishing.
16. Proctor, K. (2021) Zarah Sultana was told to 'lower her tone' by minister during racism debate. Politics Home. Available at: www.politicshome.com/news/article/victoria-atkins-zarah-sultana-race-debate-comm ons-shouting
17. Foulkes, S.H. (1990) *Selected papers: Psychoanalysis and group analysis.* London: Karnac Books.

Chapter 8
1. Fanon, F. (1952) *Black skin, white masks.* New York: Grove Press.
2. Falzeder, E. (2007) The story of an ambivalent relationship: Sigmund Freud and Eugen Bleuler. *Journal of Analytic Psychology,* 52(3), 343–368.

3. Freud, S. ([1856–1939] 1961) *Beyond the pleasure principle*. New York: Liveright.
4. Klein, M. ([1946] 1975) Notes on some schizoid mechanisms. In *The writings of Melanie Klein*, Volume 3. London: Hogarth Press, pp 99–110.
5. Dollard, J. and Miller, N.E. (1950) *Personality and psychotherapy: An analysis in terms of learning, thinking, and culture*. New York: McGraw-Hill.
6. Morrison, T. (1992) *Playing in the dark: Whiteness and the literary imagination*. Cambridge, MA: Harvard University Press.
7. Glen Has, R., Katz, I. and Moore, L. (2016) When racial ambivalence evokes negative affect, using a disguised measure of mood. *Personality and Social Psychology Bulletin*, 18(6), 786–797.
8. Jordan, J., Kaplan, A., Miller, J.B., Stiver, I. and Surrey, J. (1991) *Women's growth in connection: Writings from the Stone Center*. Cambridge, MA: Harvard University Press.
9. Kovel, J. (1970) *White racism: A psychohistory*. New York: Pantheon.
10. Wijeyesinghe, C.L. and Jackson, B.W. (eds) *New perspectives on racial identity development: Integrating emerging frameworks*. New York: New York University Press, pp 1–10.
11. Dressner, L. and Brown, A.L. (2007) Unveiling white privilege: A case of selective amnesia resulting from white privilege. AAMFT Newsletter
12. Ahmed, S. (2016) White friend. *Feminist Killjoys*. Available at: https://feministkilljoys.com/2019/05/31/white-friend/
13. Yancy, G. (2008) *Black bodies white gazes: The continuing significance of race*. New York: Rowman & Littlefield.
14. Dalal, F. (2002) *Race colour and the process of racialization: New perspectives from group analysis psychoanalysis and sociology*. London: Routledge.
15. Miller, W.R. and Rollnick, S. (2013) *Motivational Interviewing: Helping people to change*, 3rd edition. New York: Guilford Press.
16. Kinouani, G. (2019) Readiness for whiteness: A model. *Race Reflections*.
17. Gilroy, P. (2005) *The black Atlantic: Modernity and double-consciousness*. Cambridge, MA: Harvard University Press.

Chapter 9
1. Sparrow, A. (2020) Priti Patel condemns minority at Black Lives Matter protests as 'thugs and criminals' – as it happened. *The Guardian*. Available at: www.theguardian.com/politics/live/2020/jun/08/uk-coronavirus-johnson-says-anti-racist-protests-were-subverted-by-thuggery-live-news-covi d19-updates
2. Arendt, H. ([1906–1975] 1994). *Eichmann in Jerusalem: A report on the banality of evil*. New York: Penguin.
3. Applebaum B. (2010) *Being white being good: White complicity white moral responsibility and social justice pedagogy*. Washington, DC: Lexington Books.

4. Stobo, B. (2005) *Location of disturbance with a focus on race, difference and culture*. Master's dissertation, Birkbeck College.

5. Kinouani, G. (2021) Intersectionality, ableism and colonial logics. *Race Reflections*.

6. DiAngelo, R. (2012) Nothing to add: A challenge to white silence in racial discussions. *Understanding & Dismantling Privilege*, 2(1), 1–17.

7. Mills, C.W. (1997) *The racial contract*. London: Cornell University Press.

8. Bell, D.A. (1980). Brown v. Board of Education and the interest-convergence dilemma. *Harvard Law Review*, 93(3), 518–533.

9. Jensen, R. (2005) *The heart of whiteness: Confronting race, racism and white privilege*. San Francisco, CA: City Lights.

10. PA Media (2022) Met police officers fired after sharing racist joke about Meghan. *The Guardian*. Available at: www.theguardian.com/uk-news/2022/jul/01/met-police-officers-fired-after-sharing-racist-joke-about- meghan

11. Yam, k (2020). Officer who stood by as George Floyd died highlights complex Asian American, black relations. NBC News. Available from: www.nbcnews.com/news/asian-america/officer-who-stood-george-floyd-died-asian-american-we-need-n1221311

12. Alibhai-Brown, Y. (2018) Foreword. In K. Bhopal (ed) *White privilege: The myth of a post-racial society*. Bristol: Policy Press, pp xiii–xiv.

13. Mangat, J.S. (1969) *A history of the Asians in East Africa: c. 1886 to 1945*. Oxford: Clarendon Press.

14. Brown, K. (2000) Coloured and black relations in South Africa: The burden of racialized hierarchy. *Macalester International*, 9, Article 13. Available at: http://digitalcommons.macalester.edu/macintl/vol9/iss1/1

15. Biswas, S. (2015) Was Mahatma Gandhi a racist? BBC. Available at: www.bbc.com/news/world-asia-india-34265882

16. Kovel, J. (1970) *White racism: A psychohistory*. New York: Pantheon Books.

17. Atewologun, D., Cornish, T. and Tresh, F. (2018) Unconscious bias training: An assessment for the evidence of effectiveness. Available at: www.equality humanrights.com/sites/default/files/research-report-113-unconscious-bias-training-an-assessment-of-the-evidence-for-effectiveness.pdf

18. Lai, C.K., Skinner, A.L., Cooley, E., Murrar, S., Brauer, M., Devos, T. et al (2016) Reducing implicit racial preferences: II. Intervention effectiveness across time. *Journal of Experimental Psychology: General*, 145(8), 1001–1016.

19. Tate, S.A. and Page, D. (2018) Whiteness and institutional racism: Hiding behind (un)conscious bias. *Ethics and Education*, 13(1), 141–155.

20. Bourne, J. (2019) Unravelling the concept of unconscious bias. *Race & Class*, 60, 70–75.

Index

References to endnotes show both the page number
and the note number (15n1).

A

ableism and white supremacy, relationship
    between 155
active white ignorance 115
affective dissociation 103
Afropessimism 17
Ahmed, S. 39
Akala 104, 105
All about love (hooks) 88
ambivalence, white 99, 126, 128–129
    and anti-racism 140–143
    conceptualisation of 129–131
    everyday performance of 132–133,
        137–138
    racial 131–132
    and readiness as repeated event 145–147
    and resistance 147–148
    white amnesia as 138–140
    and white identity development 136–137
    and whiteness, aversion, and fear of
        contact 133–136
    and Whiteness Readiness Model
        (WRM) 143–145
amnesia, white 138–140, 147, 164
Andrews, K. 108
anti-blackness 7, 14, 109, 146
    and black sexuality 82
    and complicity 150, 155, 157–158, 161
    and emptiness 82
    and envy 55, 56, 65
    and sadism 71, 78
    and white gaze 44, 47
    and whiteness, time and space 35n3, 19,
        21, 27, 28
    see also blackness
anti-racism 2, 27, 53, 89, 108
    and ambivalence 128, 129, 136, 139,
        140–145, 147
    and dissociation 112
    resistance to 8, 163, 164
    and white complicity 150, 159
antisemitism 26, 27, 28, 118–119
Applebaum, B. 153
approach-avoidance dynamics 130, 131,
    147–148
archives, importance of 13–14, 98
Arendt, H. 89, 153
Arquette, R. 117, 118, 119
Atewologun, D. 160

Atkins, V. 123, 124
attacks on linking, theory of 35n1, 96,
    97, 103
authoritarian populism 65
autism 29–30
autoethnographic notes 13, 14, 17–18
    on white ambivalence 138–139
    on white complicity 151
    on white envy 57
    on white gaze 43–44, 45, 46
aversion, white 111, 135–136

B

bad apple axiom 152–153
Baldwin, J. 8, 21, 82
basic assumptions group 92, 93
Being and Nothingness (Sartre) 36
Berenson, E. 75
Beyond the pleasure principle (Freud) 34
Bion, W.R. 12, 35n1, 92, 96, 97, 103
black gaze, whiteness' fear of 44
black jealousy 59–63
black joy 52, 59, 66
Black Lives Matter 4, 150
black neurosis 60
Black Panther (film) 52, 59
Black skin, white masks (Fanon) 37, 128
blackness 6, 22, 86, 109, 155
    and ambivalence 134, 139
    fear of 133
    objectification of 47
    and sadism 81, 82
    and white gaze 38–39, 41, 44
    see also anti-blackness
Blackwell, D. 57
Bleuler, E. 129
Boarding School Syndrome 105–106
bodies
    and ableism 155
    ad white gaze 39–40
    colonised 75, 78, 113, 131
    and enslavement 23, 45, 75, 78, 83
    policing of 40, 80
    racialisation of 22, 24, 26, 37, 39, 41,
        59, 66
    sexual power of 64, 131
    space between 134
    and time and space 39, 163
    valuing of 14
    of women 37–38, 45, 59

Bollas, C. 20
Brexit campaign 18, 43, 64–65, 94, 151
Brown, A.L. 138
brown complicity 157–159

C

Cameron, D. 114
cancel culture 107
Carter, R.T. 20
cerebral threat system 110, 111
Césaire, A. 89–90
Chauvin, D. 68, 69, 71–72
Child Protective Services 74
chosen glory 98–99
chosen trauma 98–99
Choudhury, C.A. 26
cisheteronormativity 49
cisheteropatriarchy 88
cognitive dissociation 103, 105
cognitive dissonance 90, 110
cognitive manoeuvring 11
Cole, T. 121
collective anxiety 43
collective conscience 5, 32, 88, 108
collective fantasy 43
collective gagging 107
collective gaze 41
collective trauma 97–99
collective white self-concept 90
coloniality of power, notion of 23
complicity, white 149–155
  and bad apples axiom 152–153
  and brown complicity 157–159
  everyday performance of 153–155
  and institutional complicity 159–160
  and resistance 160–161
  and white silence and white
    silencing 155–157
Conrad, J. 21
conscientisation 57, 58, 136, 138
containment, concept of 96
Critical Race Theory 3–4, 156
cultural archives 13, 98
cultural notes 13
  on white ambivalence 130
  on white complicity 150, 154–155
  on white envy 52–53
  on white gaze 39, 43, 45
  on white sadism 77
  on white shame 119–120, 123
  on white trauma 85–86

D

Dalal, F. 11–12, 141
De Beauvoir, S. 37–38
De Sade, M. 72
delusions 107
Dennis, E. 101
detention centres 78–79

DiAngelo, R. 101, 109, 112, 156
dissociation 19, 22, 76, 90, 101
  and anti-racism 112
  everyday performance of 105–107
  and resistance 112–113
  and splitting 101–104
  and white aversion 111
  and white fragility 109–111
  and white ignorance 104–105
  and white paranoia 107–108
  and white psychosis 108–109
distress 2, 8, 122, 123, 125, 156
  and ambivalence 130, 131, 133, 135–136,
    140, 147
  and dissociation 110, 112, 113
  and envy 54, 60
  psychological 88, 95, 118, 129
  and sadism 68, 69, 74
  tolerating 66–67
  and trauma 91–93, 92, 97
disturbance, and group analysis 117–118
Dooley, S. 119–120
Dressner, L. 138
Durkheim, É. 32
dynamic matrix 31, 33, 151
dysfunctional modes, and whiteness 3

E

Eddo-Lodge, R. 101, 104
ego strength 113, 129
Einstein, A. 16
Ellis, H. 115
embodied self-consciousness 41
emotional ambivalence 129
emptiness, and anti-blackness 82
envy, white 52–59
  and black jealousy 59–63
  everyday performance of 53–54
  politics of 63–66
  and resistance 66–67
epistemic shiftiness, of whiteness 10, 22, 105
epistemology of ignorance 11, 116
Equalities Act 48
Equality and Human Rights
    Commission 160
equivalence, concept of 34
estrangement, and masculinity 89
ethnographic notes 13, 19
  on white ambivalence 138–139
  on white complicity 151
  on white envy 57
  on white gazes 43–44, 46
  on white trauma 86–87
  on whiteness, time and space 17
Eurocentrism 29, 33, 97, 106

F

false consciousness 89, 90, 113
false generosity 121–122, 154

Fanon, F. 37–40, 47, 60, 62, 78, 90, 110, 128
fantasy
  collective 43
  competitive 72
  of exceptionalism 29
  and fear of intimacy 133
  of homogeneity 26
  paranoid 44
  of past 35
  of power struggle 71
  of primitivism 62
  and proximity to whiteness 161
  racialised 22, 29, 31
  of racialised sexual phantasm 47
  and reality 109
  significance of 8, 11, 21, 24, 32, 37, 42, 81, 99, 107–109, 118, 162
  and trauma activation 87
  Western 22
female gaze, white 47–50, 120
feminised gaze 46
Ferlazzo, F. 154
Fillon, F. 122
Floyd, G., murder of 16, 68, 69–70, 80, 150
forgiveness, expectation of 45
Foucault, P. 5, 10
Foulkes, S.H. 82, 126
foundation matrix 31, 33, 119
fragility 160
  and dissociation 109–111
  and shame 115, 122, 124
  and trauma 88, 93, 94
France, extracting colonial debt 122
Freedom from Torture campaign 78
Freire, P. 121
Freud, S. 33–34, 95, 125, 129–130
Fromm, E. 73
Frosh, S. 27, 28, 119

G

Garner, S. 23
gaslighting, notion of 1, 10
gaze, white
  and blackness 38–39
  and bodies 39–40
  and everyday performance 40–41, 48–49
  female 47–50
  and subjectivity sand identity 36–37
  as white shield 41–46
Gilroy, P. 11, 65, 115, 146
Goldberg, D.T. 13
Goonetilleke, D.C.R.A. 21
Gordon, L. 11
grandiosity 94, 107, 120, 124
gratitude, and envy 67
group analysis
  concept of 5
  and disturbance 117–118

and scapegoating 125–126
and white complicity 154
and white envy 57–59
group matrix 31, 33, 81–82
group processes 31–33
guilt, and white tears 122–123

H

Hage, G. 107
Hall, S. 13, 22, 65
harassment, meaning of 48
Harris, C.I. 23
hierarchisation 25, 28, 79, 146, 158, 159
Hill Collins, P. 92
historical notes 13, 55
hooks, b. 44, 50, 88
Hopper, E. 32
humiliation, and white sadism 76, 80

I

I can't breathe 72
ignorance, white 104–105, 115
imperial and colonial past, significance of 4, 13–14
imperialism 9, 13, 89, 93, 114, 131, 138
  boomerang effect of 89
  colonial 34, 45, 94, 95, 154, 158
  and complicity 150, 155
  and nostalgia 4, 64
  and sadism 71, 76, 79
In the wake (Sharpe) 19
individualism, significance of 133
innocence, white 91–93
institutional complicity 159–160
intellectual ambivalence 129
interest-convergence 4, 163
interest divergence 156
intergenerational socialisation 30
internalised racism 60
intersubjectivity, importance of 127, 154
intersuffering 88
intimacy, notion of 133–134
intrusion, concept of 96
invisibility, of whiteness 24

J

jealousy and envy, distinction between 61
  see also black jealousy; envy, white
Jensen, R. 157–159
Jewishness 27, 28
Jones, A.K. "Van" 64

K

Kellaway, K. 109
King, M.L. 149
Klein, M. 102, 130

L

Lacan, J. 36–37
Lammy, D. 119, 120, 121
Leave campaign 64–65
Lentin, A. 27–28
'Letter from Birmingham Jail'
   (King) 149
liability, whiteness as 23–24
Living while black (Kinouani) 68, 74
location of disturbance 117–119
Logan's Run (film) 39–40
lynching 54, 55–56, 62, 66, 101

M

male gaze 37–38, 48, 49, 58
masculine identity, and trauma 88–89
Mbembe, A. 7, 35n2, 75, 113
Miller, W. 141
Mills, C.W. 11, 156
mind–body dualism 106
moral superiority 79, 89
Morrison, T. 7, 52, 82, 131
Moss, T. 55, 61, 62, 66
Motivational Interviewing (MI)
   techniques 141–143
Muslims 27, 57–59

N

narcissism 9, 47, 73, 74, 94, 141, 164
   and shame 114–116, 120–122, 124
   and vulnerability 92
   and whiteness 89
natural (dis)order 63
necropolitical (dis)order 25, 29
necropolitics 7, 35n2, 25, 29, 48, 79
necropower 71, 79
negrableism, notion of 155
neutrality, fallacy of 9, 44, 118, 153
Ngo, H. 38–39
nostalgia, imperial 4, 64
notes, importance of 13, 55
   see also autoethnographic notes;
   cultural notes

O

Obama, B. 64
object relations theory 102–103
Ogorchukwu, A., murder of 154–155
ontological pain, and whiteness 82–83
oppositional gaze 44
oppression 88, 138, 146–147, 157, 161
   class 63
   gaze 40, 47
   and power 12, 146
   racial 24, 27, 94
   as sexualised project 47
other, racialised 30–31, 60, 138
otherness 26, 27, 41, 42

P

paranoia 107–108
   and delusion, compared 107
   and psychosis 108
   racial 62, 86–87
paranoid-schizoid position 102, 105,
   109, 130
Pass-Whites 26
past
   and disturbances 20
   preverbal collective understanding of 21
   significance of 19
Patel, P. 150
patriarchy 54, 133, 134
   and white gaze 48, 49, 50
   and white trauma 88, 89, 92
Peck, E. 115–116, 127
Pedagogy of the oppressed (Freire) 121
penal and punitive border discourses,
   significance of 65
People's Grocery Store tragedy 55, 56, 59
personal matrix 31, 33, 81
phenotypes 25–26
physiological dissociation 103–104
Playing in the dark (Morrison) 131
police brutality 16, 68, 69–72, 80, 150
Policing the crisis (Hall et al.) 65
positivism 9, 10
Powell, E. 85
power struggle 71
pride, white 124–125
Proctor, K. 123
projective violence 67
property, whiteness as 23
proximal ambivalence 146–147
proximal dynamics, significance of 161
Pryor, R. 39–40
psychoanalysis 20, 121, 130
psychological triggers, significance of 68
psychology, field of 6
psychosis, white 96–97, 108–109
psychosocial thinking 5
public spaces, and bodies 39

Q

Quijano, A. 23

R

racecraft 26, 27
racial ambivalence 131–132
racial conscientisation 136
racial consciousness 140
racial contract, conceptualisation of 156
racial equilibrium, white 45
racial identity development 136
racial inequality, racialisation of 42
racial stratification, and whiteness 24–29
racial violence, as sexual violence 47–48

racialised body schema 22, 24, 26, 37, 39, 41, 59, 66
racialised other *see* other, racialised
racialised sexual phantasm 46, 47
racism without racists 5
racist psychology and racist institutions, relationship between 159
racist violence 20, 22, 54, 56, 153
Rankine, C. 108–109
rape 48, 49, 62
Rashford, M. 120, 121
rational irrationality 11
readiness as repeated event 145–147
Reed, A. 82
referred pain 117–118
repetition compulsion 33–34, 87
repression, concept of 95
'Rivers of Blood, The' speech 85, 95
Rollnick, S. 141
Roof, D. 85–86, 107

S

sadism 68
  cultural, and colonial discipline 75–78
  defining 72–73
  everyday performance of 73–74, 78–79
  institutionalised 80–81
  and police brutality 68–72
  and resistance 83–84
  and social unconscious and group matrix 79–82
  structural 80
  types of 73
  and whiteness and ontological pain 82–83
sadomasochism 77
Sartre, J.P. 36
saviourism, white 121, 122
scapegoating 91–92, 125–126
scientific racism 25
Second Sex, The (De Beauvoir) 37
self-alienation 89
self-compassion 67
self-consciousness, embodied 41
self-hate 21, 50
self-inflicted pain 77
self-representation, white 63
sensation seeking, notion of 73
sexual harassment, and white gaze 48, 49–50
sexualised envy, idea of 54
sexualised fears 62
shadow group 92
shame, white 92, 114
  everyday performance of 116–117
  and false generosity 121–122
  and guilt and white tears 122–123
  and location of disturbance 117–119
  and resistance 127

and scapegoating of racists 125–126
and white narcissism 114–116, 120–121
and white pride 124–125
Sharpe, C.E. 19–20
silence and silencing, white 155–157
slave ship, as literary device 19–20
Snow, J. 43
social dissociation 14, 104
social (dis)order 11, 55, 62, 76, 79
social reality 11, 45
social scripts 98
  and group processes 31–33
  importance of 29–31
  and repetition compulsion 33–34
social unconscious 31–33, 59, 81, 152
socio-political anxieties 65
space
  between bodies 134
  policing of 40
  public spaces 39
  and time *see* time and space
  white spaces 21–24
Stobo, B. 154, 156
structural harm 74, 92, 152
subjective realities 12, 94
subjectivity, and identity 36–37
suffocation, racism as 7, 29, 56, 141, 155
Sultana, Z. 123, 124

T

technologies of power 5, 26–27
terror, notion of 95
threatened egotism, notion of 73
time and space 16–18
  and body 39–40
  and knowing and remembering 18–19
  and reproduction mechanisms 29
  and resistance 35
  and social scripts 29–34
  and whiteness 19–29
toxic masculinity 88
Trafford, J. 23
trauma 85–90
  analytic concepts of 95–97
  chosen 98–99
  collective 97–99
  everyday performance of 90–91
  intersections of 118
  and paranoia 86–87
  and resistance 99–100
  and victimhood and resistance 93–95
  and white innocence, violence, and basic assumptions 91–93
triggers, importance of 68
Trump, D. 64
12 Years a Slave (film) 130
Two Distant Strangers (short film) 16, 17, 18

U

Ubuntu 88
unconscious bias training 6, 159–160
Underground Railroad series 77
United Kingdom Independence Party
  campaign 64
unthought known 20–21

V

values, norms, and cultural capital,
  whiteness as 23
victimhood, trauma, and resistance 93–95
voluntary ambivalence 129
vulnerability 28, 41, 73, 112,
  134, 163
  and shame 123, 125, 126
  and trauma 88, 89, 92–94, 97, 99

W

Wells-Barnett, I.B. 56
West, notion of 22
whataboutery questions, significance
  of 104
'White friend' (Ahmed) 139
white genocide, idea of 107
white spaces and whiteness 21–24
white superiority 42, 60, 151
white supremacy 11–12, 161
  and ableism 155
  disinvestment in 82–83
  and dissociation and splitting 104

and internalisation of racism 60–61
reproduction of 28
significance of 22
and trauma 87–88
and white gaze 47
and white shame 115
white traumatisation within 97
white tears 122–123
whitelash 64, 65, 150
whiteness
  as ambush 140
  and aversion and fear of contact 133–136
  and dysfunctional modes 3
  epistemic shiftiness of 10, 22
  fear of black gaze 44
  harm of 89
  and ontological pain 82–83
  as property 108
  as psychosis 108
  as territoriality 14, 18, 57, 58, 65, 75,
    89–90, 138, 151
  and time and space 19–29
Whiteness Readiness Model
  (WRM) 143–145
*Why I'm no longer talking to white people
  about race* (Eddo-Lodge) 101
Wilderson III, F.B. 35n3
work group, notion of 92
working class 63, 65

Y

Yancy, G. 5, 38, 39, 58, 111, 140, 141